Graffiti Alphabet

A	B	C	D	E	F	G	H	I
Λ	BB	C	DD	E	ΓΓ	G6	h	I

J	K	L	M	N	O	P	Q
J	⋉	L	MM	N	OO	PP	O

R	S	T	U	V	W	X
RR	S7	U	VV	W	XX	∞

Y	Z	Space	Carriage Return	Back Space	Period
ɤ	Z	—	/	—	tap twice

Graffiti Numbers

0	1	2	3	4
OO	I	2	3	L

5	6	7	8	9
5b	6	7	88	9

Graffiti Punctuation

.	,	'	?	!	–	()	/	$	@	#		
·	/	'	?				–	C)	/	S	O	N

%	^	&	*	<	>	–	+	=	\|	\	{
∞	Λ	8	∞	<	>	⌐	⋉	Z	1	\	3

}	[]	~	`	;	:	"	tab
3	E	3	N	⌐	/	1	N	Γ

que®

cut here

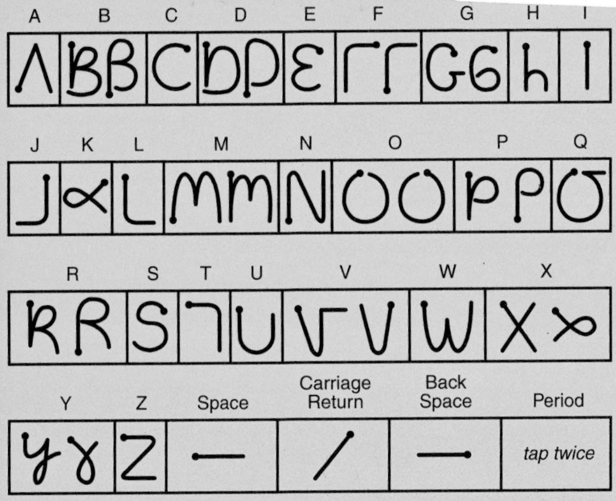

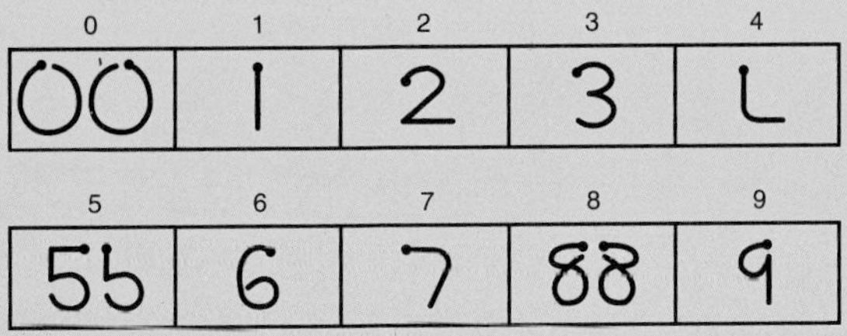

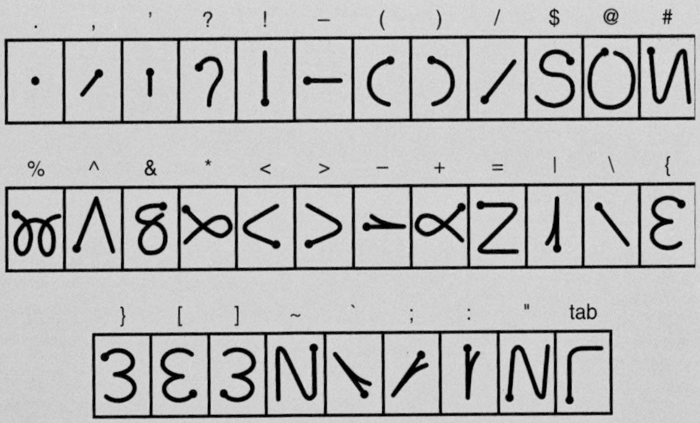

Writing Symbols and Extended Characters

All writing symbols and extended characters begin with the Shift stroke in the Graffiti writing area of your Palm III:

Shift

Symbols and Extended Characters

When the Symbol Shift is active, a slanted Shift symbol appears in the lower-right corner of the screen. The next stroke that you make creates the symbols or extended characters shown in the following table:

•	™	®	©	‘	’	“	”	§	·	+	–

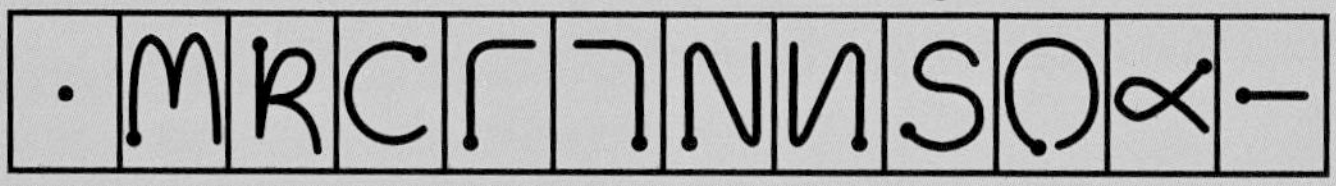

X	÷	=	¢	¥	£	¿	¡	ß	µ	ƒ	ø

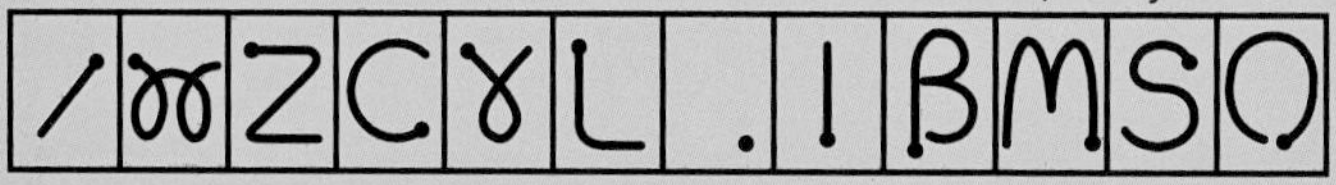

Graffiti Navigation Strokes

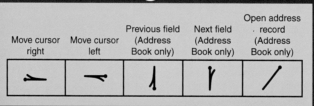

Move cursor right	Move cursor left	Previous field (Address Book only)	Next field (Address Book only)	Open address record (Address Book only)

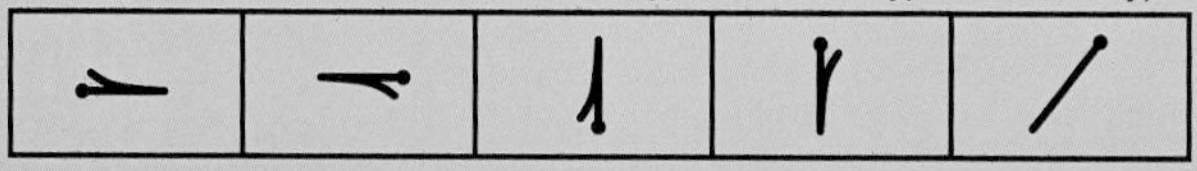

201 W. 103rd Street, Indianapolis, Indiana 46290 (317) 581-3500

THE COMPLETE IDIOT'S GUIDE® TO

PalmPilot™ and Palm III™

by Preston Gralla

que®

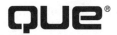

A Division of Macmillan Computer Publishing
201 W. 103rd Street, Indianapolis, IN 46290

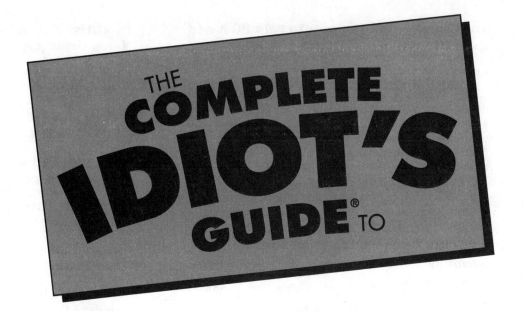

The Complete Idiot's Guide to PalmPilot and Palm III

International Standard Book Number: 0-7897-1967-3

Library of Congress Catalog Card Number: 99-60353

Printed in the United States of America

First Printing: *March 1999*

01 00 99 4 3 2

Trademarks

Warning and Disclaimer

Executive Editor
Angela Wethington

Acquisitions Editor
Jamie Milazzo

Development Editor
Faithe Wempen

Managing Editor
Thomas F. Hayes

Project Editor
Lori A. Lyons

Copy Editor
Chuck Hutchinson

Technical Editor
Graham Rogers

Illustrator
Judd Winick

Indexer
Chris Barrick

Proofreader
Debra Neel

Layout Technician
Lisa England

Contents at a Glance

Contents

About the Author

Preston Gralla *is Executive Editor at ZDNet; he founded and is in charge of its* `PalmPilotSoftware.com` *site, where he writes a monthly column on PalmPilot software titled "Preston's PalmPilot Picks." He is the author of ten books, including the* The Complete Idiot's Guide to Online Shopping *and the best-selling* How the Internet Works. *He was the founding managing editor of* PC Week *and a founding editor of* PC/Computing. *Gralla has written about technology for many magazines and newspapers, including the* Los Angeles Times, USA Today, *and* PC Magazine. *He lives in the Boston area with his wife, two children, and a rabbit named Polichinelle. The rabbit is the only member of the family who doesn't clamour for time on his various PalmPilots and Palm IIIs.*

Dedication

To Palmheads everywhere, who form such a tight fraternity and sorority that while I was sitting in a café writing a chapter of this book, a fellow PalmHead strolled by my window seat, saw my Palm III sitting open next to my double-decaf capuccino, pulled his Palm III out of his pocket to flash it at me to show his solidarity, and gave me a big thumbs-up. If the physical distance weren't so great between us, I'm sure we would have beamed our appreciation at each other not just in hand signals, but using our IR ports as well.

Acknowledgments

For this, my tenth book, I'd like to thank everyone who helped it through at Macmillan, including John Pierce, to whom I first floated the idea; Renee Wilmeth, with whom I spoke about it at length; acquisition editor Jamie Milazzo, who fine-tuned it and finalized it; and development editor Faithe Wempen, who always made me sound more coherent than I often felt. Thanks also go to tech editor Graham Rogers, who made sure that all my PalmPilot taps and hints were correct. And thanks go to editors Lori Lyons and Chuck Hutchinson, proofreader Debra Neel, layout tech Lisa England, and indexer Chris Barrick.

And, of course, as always, thanks to my agent Stuart Krichevsky, my wife Lydia, and my children Gabriel and Mia. Kids, time to hand over the PalmPilot now! I need to check my To-Do List!

Tell Us What You Think!

As the reader of this book, *you* are our most important critic and commentator. We value your opinion and want to know what we're doing right, what we could do better, what areas you'd like to see us publish in, and any other words of wisdom you're willing to pass our way.

As Executive Editor for the General Desktop Applications team at Macmillan Computer Publishing, I welcome your comments. You can fax, email, or write me directly to let me know what you did or didn't like about this book—as well as what we can do to make our books stronger.

Please note that I cannot help you with technical problems related to the topic of this book, and that due to the high volume of mail I receive, I might not be able to reply to every message.

When you write, please be sure to include this book's title and author as well as your name and phone or fax number. I will carefully review your comments and share them with the author and editors who worked on the book.

Fax: 317-581-4663

Email: pcs@mcp.com

Mail: Executive Editor
General Desktop Applications
Macmillan Computer Publishing
201 West 103rd Street
Indianapolis, IN 46290 USA

Introduction

If you're like almost anyone these days, your life always seems on the verge of heading out of control: You have too many deadlines, too much to do, too much to keep track of, and too little time to do it all in. You have meetings and appointments, travel conflicting with home life, hundreds and hundreds of people and things to keep track of, and every day you discover more of them. Just thinking about it makes my head spin.

Well, you're not alone. I'm like you. I never have enough time, and I always have too much to do. And at times I've certainly shown it. Put my car keys in the refrigerator and tried to hang a milk carton on a key hook? I've been known to do that. Missed an important meeting with my boss because I mistakenly also scheduled a luncheon with an old friend from high school? Sure. (But don't tell my boss about it, please.... I made up some half-plausible excuse at the time, and it bailed me out of hot water.) Forgotten my parents' anniversary and my brother's birthday? Yes. Sorry, Mom and Dad. Sorry, Jay. I didn't mean to. It's just that I had to drive Gabriel to his soccer game, and those dates just slipped my mind each time. Missed meetings and deadlines, double-scheduled events, misplaced important phone numbers, forgotten to do important things that absolutely had to be done? Yup. Been there, done that, done that and done that, time and time again.

Guess what, though? I don't have these problems any longer. And I don't have these problems any longer for one simple reason: I've started using the PalmPilot. Yes, I know it sounds silly and simplistic, and I know that it sounds too good to be true. After all, how can a tiny little device, which amounts to nothing more than a metal case with some glass on it and some electronics inside, how can this simple little thing help me get my life under control?

Well, it can and it has. Using this little digital companion, I'm now on time and on schedule, I can retrieve a phone number or address with the flick of a button and the tap of a stylus, and I've gotten my life organized, under control, and in neat order. I even remembered my parent's anniversary this time around. (About putting the keys in the refrigerator...I have to admit, that still happens on occasion. Chalk it up to the early onset of Alzheimer's maybe, but losing track of my keys seems to be in my nature.)

This book will teach you how to get your life organized and under control with the PalmPilot. I've done it using the PalmPilot's built-in features such as the Address Book, Date Book, Memo Pad, To-Do List, Expense reporter, and more, so I know that you can, too. Getting started just takes a little bit of reading, a little bit of stylus tapping, and soon you can get your life organized and under control as well.

Sure, I know that you can find other books that teach you how to use the PalmPilot. Well, this one certainly does that—and does it well, better than any of them, if I may say so myself. But it does more than that. Because anyone can teach you what buttons to press—and that's where those books end off. This one teaches you much more; it shows you how to use those buttons to take control of your life. You'll learn how to use the PalmPilot to better schedule your time, to track your expenses, to make the most effective use of travel time. This book will even show you how you can use the PalmPilot to create mailing lists, for example.

So, what are you waiting for? Check out how to use this book; then read on and start tapping away on your little digital friend. Now is the time to get organized.

How to Use This Book

First things first. As you no doubt know, the PalmPilot has gone through several different names in its short life. It started out being called the Pilot. The next generation of devices after the Pilot was called the PalmPilot. Then for the *next* generation and beyond, it was finally called the Palm—as in Palm III. In general, I use the generic term *PalmPilot* to describe them all—Pilots, PalmPilots, and Palms. The screen shots you'll see throughout the book are from the Palm III, and the computer screen shots are from Windows.

Okay, we've gotten that out of the way. Now on to how the book is organized. This book has five parts. It starts by teaching you the basics of how to use the PalmPilot. Then it shows you how each of the major programs and features such as the Address Book and Date Book can help you get your life under control. From there, I'll cover how the PalmPilot can keep you in touch with others via email, infrared beaming, and other kinds of communication. Then I'll clue you in on how to supercharge your life with the PalmPilot—how to make the most out of business travel, for example. Finally, I'll cover how to best maintain and troubleshoot the PalmPilot.

Part 1, "Get Ready to Take Control of Your Life: Getting Started with Your PalmPilot," starts with the basics. You'll start by learning all the reasons that a PalmPilot can help you organize your life, and you'll learn the differences between the different versions of the PalmPilot. You'll learn what to do when you turn on your PalmPilot for the first time and how to set up a HotSync for sending information back and forth between your PalmPilot and computer. You'll also get a guided tour of the PalmPilot's main screen and learn how to use the Palm Desktop software as well.

In Part 2, "Organizing Your Life with Your PalmPilot," you'll get down to brass tacks. In this part, you'll learn how to use all the PalmPilot's main features to get your life under control: the To-Do List, Memo Pad, Address Book, Date Book, and Expense reporter. You'll also learn how to use categories and the find functions to organize information so that you can find anything fast.

Part 3, "Using Email, Internet, and Infrared Communications to Keep You in Touch," shows how you can connect with the world using your PalmPilot. You'll learn how to use email and a modem and even how to browse the World Wide Web. You'll also learn about one of the most amazing features of the PalmPilot—the ability to send and receive information using the infrared beam. Every time I do it, I feel like I'm in the middle of an episode of *Star Trek*.

In Part 4, "Supercharging Your Life with the PalmPilot," you'll see all the different ways that you can use the PalmPilot to power up your life. Whether you're installing new software to fax from the PalmPilot, read documents such as a street map of New York City, make better travel plans, or customize every aspect of the PalmPilot for the way that *you* live and work, you'll find all the information you need here.

Read Part 5, "Troubleshooting and Maintenance for Your Digital Companion," and you'll find out how to handle any problem that may ever come up, from resetting to keeping battery consumption to a minimum.

Appendix A, "Easter Eggs and Stupid Digital Tricks," is for flat-out fun. Want to see a little palm tree waving in the breeze? How about some hidden photos? Or a taxi driving across the screen? You'll be able to do all that and more when you head here.

Appendix B, "Glossary: Speak Like a Geek," defines computer and technical terms that you might be confused about.

Appendix C, "What's on the CD?," lists what you will find on the CD that accompanies this book.

Extras

I've used a few conventions in this book to make it easier for you to follow. For example, things you tap, type, press, click, and select appear in color, like this:

Click **Cancel**

This book also gives you extra secrets, inside tips, and bits of information that provide extra information. You'll find them in these boxes:

Check This Out

This box offers tips, advice, and extra information for helping you organize your life with the PalmPilot.

TechnoTalk

This box defines computer and PalmPilot terms for you.

Part 1

Get Ready to Take Control of Your Life: Getting Started with Your PalmPilot

You took your dog to the skating rink and left your kids at home with a bowl of Kibbles 'N Bits. You showed up at your company's annual budget-planning meeting in your Bozo nose and mask because you thought it was the Halloween party. You gave your spouse a list of five non-negotiable contract demands on the eve of your anniversary, forgetting that you weren't negotiating the new Forster account.

You've got big troubles, buddy. And there's only one thing that can solve them: your nice, new PalmPilot.

In this first section, you learn all the basics of using your PalmPilot, including how to start it for the first time, how to use all its major features, how to HotSync information between your PalmPilot and your computer, and how to use the Palm Desktop software on your PC or Mac. After you get through with this section, you'll know everything there is to know about the basics of running your PalmPilot, and you'll be on your way to taking control of your life.

So come on in and read. Because a poodle on ice skates is not a pretty sight.

Chapter 1

So What Did You Buy a PalmPilot for, Anyway?

In This Chapter

- How the PalmPilot can help organize your life
- How the PalmPilot can help you when you travel
- Descriptions of all the different Pilots, PalmPilots, and Palms—and how to upgrade from one to another
- A look at what future Palms might be like

It's a typical afternoon in your life. You have a sales report due in 30 minutes, you have a strategic planning meeting with your boss in 10 minutes, your expense reports are late, your spouse is angry because you forgot your anniversary yet again, and after work you have to drop your daughter at ballet school and then take your dog to the veterinarian for his annual checkup.

So what do you do? You offer flowers to your boss and kiss him to make up for forgetting about your anniversary, deliver your sales report to your spouse, forget to file your expenses so you're out $273.59, and after work you dutifully drive your dog to ballet school (the tutu doesn't even fit poor Rover properly—and he looks *terrible* in pink) and then take your daughter to the vet for distemper shots.

What's wrong with this picture?

What's wrong is that you don't have a PalmPilot to help you organize your life. If you did, none of this mess would have happened; you would have waltzed through the afternoon and the rest of your hectic life with nary a hitch. (Well, you might experience a hitch or two; the tutu still doesn't fit Rover very well, and he still looks terrible in pink.)

In this chapter, you take a look at all the ways the PalmPilot can help you get your life organized and under control. You also take a brief tour of all the different varieties of the Pilots, PalmPilots, and Palms. So come along. You can start to find out how you can hold the key to a better, more organized life in the palm of your hand.

What Do You Need a PalmPilot For?

Remember those bulky daytime organizers everyone seemed to carry around a few years back? You were supposed to keep your schedule in there, your To Do Lists, your contacts, your assorted notes—and *supposed to* is the key term here. Unfortunately, these organizers never seemed to work. If you were like most people, you mainly just posted a whole lot of yellow sticky notes all over the book until it looked like nothing so much as a yellow blizzard.

Well, your PalmPilot can do everything those old organizers were supposed to do and more—much more, in fact. (The PalmPilot is not great for posting sticky notes, though. After all, it *is* kind of small.) Using the PalmPilot is the easiest way to organize virtually every aspect of your work, play, and home life. You can organize your life with the PalmPilot in these main ways:

- **Keep your schedule with the Date Book.** You can schedule all your meetings, deadlines, events, and anything else you need a calendar for. You also can schedule recurring events, attach notes to events, and use special search functions to find any event fast.
- **Record names, addresses, and contacts with the Address Book.** Phone numbers, addresses, email addresses, fax numbers—you can record all that information for anyone and any place. And the Palm's "find" and "category" features make it simple to find contacts as well.
- **Keep track of everything you need done with the To-Do List.** You can also organize your to-dos into categories, attach notes to them, set dates for when they need to be done; in short, with this list, you can always remember your anniversary, the deadline for finishing your marketing report, and the day and time of your next golf date.
- **Jot down notes with the Memo Pad.** Say good-bye to yellow sticky notes forever. Have a thought, a plan, or a brainstorm? Just jot it down, categorize it, and it's yours forever.
- **Track your expenses with Expense.** Have a wallet stuffed to the gills with credit-card slips, parking receipts, and chits? Do you often forget what you've spent when? Record all your expenses with Expense, and you can make filing expense reports or keeping track of your expenses much easier.
- **Read and respond to email when you're away from your computer.** Make better use of train commutes, airplane flights, and other times when you're away from your computer. You can read email and write email messages without a computer; just use the palm of your hand.
- **Do quick calculations with Calculator.** Don't sweat; a lot of people didn't do well in math in school. And even if you did, the human brain wasn't made for lightning-fast mathematical calculations. When you need to figure out

anything from sales tax to percentages to any similar kind of math function, the built-in calculator can do what you need.

- **Synchronize everything between your PalmPilot and your computer.** If you're sitting at your computer, you can jot down notes, contacts, and to-dos; put together your schedule; and then have all that data sent straight to your PalmPilot by using the HotSync capability. Similarly, you can put the information into your PalmPilot and sync it with your computer. This feature solves one of the biggest drawbacks of using the old daytimers: They were paper-based, so you couldn't get at the information in them when you were at your computer.
- **Make your life on the road easier.** The PalmPilot is great at many things—and is especially useful when you travel. From tracking expenses to writing email, finding contacts, and just about anything else to do with travel, it helps keep you organized and on time when you're away from home. It just can't tuck you into bed at night. But I hear that 3COM, which makes the devices, is working on that feature for its next model.
- **Perform all these tasks while being small enough to fit in your pocket and letting you write by hand instead of having to use a keyboard.** This small tool, which fits in your palm and your pocket, features Graffiti, a handwriting-recognition program for letting you jot down notes, ideas, appointments, addresses, and anything else that you're tracking.

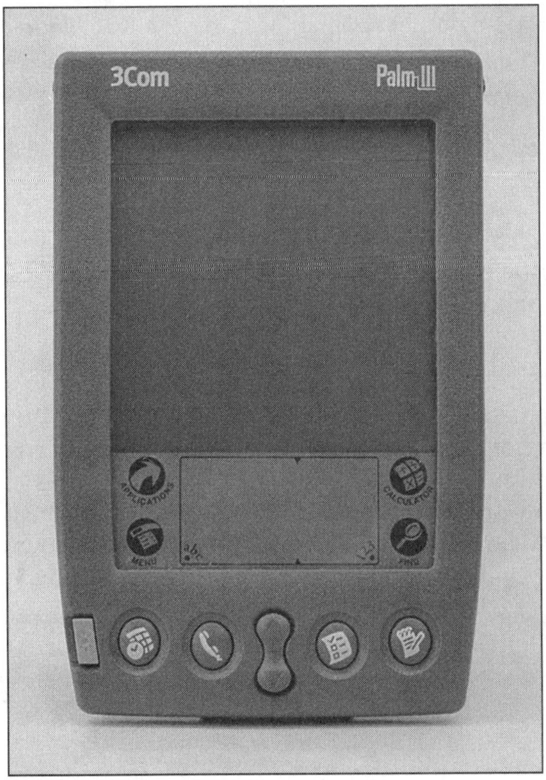

Here, you see the Palm III—and all the ways you're going to use it—will make your life a whole lot easier and more productive.

A Whole Lot of Pilots, PalmPilots, and Palms

Several models of Pilots, PalmPilots, and Palms have been released in the last several years—so much that at times keeping them all straight seems impossible. So, before you go about getting your life organized with the diminutive little companion, taking a quick gander at all of them—and what they can do—is worthwhile. They all have different capabilities and can perform different tasks, depending on the model that you use. Keep in mind, though, that you can upgrade many of them as well, by adding memory or other gizmos and gadgets. So even if you have an older model, you can bring it up to snuff and do all the organizing tricks that the latest model can. In the last part of this chapter, you'll take a look at the different models and ways that they can be upgraded.

What's a Palm PC?

The Palm and PalmPilot aren't the only computers that fit in the palm of your hand. Some Palm PCs are made by other companies to run on the Windows CE operating system. Although they look a whole lot like the Palm and PalmPilot and do similar things, in fact, they run on a completely different operating system.

What Are the Pilot 1000 and Pilot 5000?

The first generation of these little digital helpers was called the Pilot. Two of them were available: the Pilot 1000 and the Pilot 5000. Don't ask me (or anyone else, for that matter) why they have the numbers 1000 and 5000 at the end of them. Makes them sound more impressive, I think.

Although these Pilots don't do nearly as much as today's more powerful Palms, they did set a precedent for every other Palm and PalmPilot that was to come afterward. They were designed for the sole purpose of helping people keep their lives in order. They didn't include full-blown word processors or assorted bells and whistles, nor did they have the capability to wake you up in the morning and make your coffee and toast. They were palm-sized, simple to use, and their batteries lasted a long time.

These early Pilots had a Date Book, an Address Book, a To-Do List, a calculator, and a Memo Pad program—the same way that all PalmPilots and Palms after them have these kinds of programs.

The Pilot 1000 and the Pilot 5000 were identical in every way except that the 1000 had 128KB of memory, and the 5000 had 512KB of memory. The Pilot 1000 could store about 2,500 calendar items, memos, and names and addresses. The Pilot 5000 could store about twice that number, or 5,000 of them. (Could that be where 3COM got the 5000 name for it? If so, why isn't the other Pilot called the 2500? Mysteries abound.)

What does "KB" of memory mean?

Computer memory is measured in bytes. A byte is the amount of memory required to store the equivalent of a single character, such as the letter *l*. A kilobyte is approximately 1,000 bytes—and is generally shortened to the letters *KB*. So 128KB of memory means that the Pilot can store approximately 128,000 bytes.

A megabyte, which is 1,000 kilobytes, is commonly abbreviated as *MB*.

The Palm III and other Palms can do a whole lot more than the original Pilots, in good part because they have more memory. If you own one of these early Pilots, don't despair; help is on the way. You can upgrade it so that it is just like the Palm III, with one small exception: You cannot use the backlight feature on the Palm III, which makes the screen more readable. For about $130, you can upgrade your Pilot to the Palm III. You get a memory card, which you slip into the Pilot. Don't be scared; upgrading is really not much more difficult than changing a battery. For details, head to 3COM's Web site at `www.palm.com`.

What Is the PalmPilot Personal?

After the original Pilots were released, engineers were ordered back into their cubicles (or cages, depending on whether they were allowed to roam free) and told to improve the Pilots. So they did. They came up with the PalmPilot Personal.

The PalmPilot Personal does everything that the Pilot did and added a bunch of new tricks of its own. It added these features:

- **The Expense feature** Engineers, like everyone else, have a hard time keeping track of their expenses. So they added a program to let you track your expenses when traveling (or even when not traveling) that you could then easily turn into an expense report.

- **Palm 2.0 operating system** An operating system lets your little device do all its tricks, from allowing you to write memos to jotting graffiti to syncing with your computer. Version 2.0 of the operating system added all kinds of goodies, such as a month-at-a-glance view to the calendar and scrollbars to let you more easily move through long documents. These features made organizing your life a whole lot easier.
- **512KB of memory** More memory means you can store more items. This, as we all know with our impossibly busy lives, is a good thing.
- **Backlighting** The original Pilots had screens that were tough to read, especially when you didn't have a whole lot of light around. A feature was added to let you light the screen from behind for better viewing—although doing so cuts down on battery life.
- **Games** Okay, let's get real here. What good is a computer—even one that fits right in your hand—unless you can play games on it? So the PalmPilot Personal offers SubHunt, MineHunt, Puzzle, and more.

If you have a PalmPilot Personal, you can easily upgrade to a Palm III, just like those with Pilots can. You do so the same way: Pay about $130 to 3COM to get a memory card to slip into the PalmPilot.

What Is the PalmPilot Professional?

When the PalmPilot Personal was released, so was the PalmPilot Professional. As you can guess by the name, the Professional does more than the Personal. And as you can no doubt guess, it costs more as well. The PalmPilot Professional does everything that the PalmPilot Personal does; plus, it adds these extra tricks as well—most of which are good, indeed, for those wanting to use it to take control over their lives:

- **1MB of memory** That's double the memory on the Personal Edition. That's also enough memory for 10,000 names and addresses, calendar events, memos, and the like. Even you or I, with our busy lives, would be hard pressed to fill up this baby with stuff. If we tried hard enough, though, I bet we could do it.
- **Capability to connect to the Internet** You can hook a modem to your PalmPilot Professional (or buy a neat little modem that slips onto the bottom of the PalmPilot) and then connect to the Internet. You need extra software to browse the Web or send and receive email directly from the PalmPilot—but still, it's the thought that counts. Anyway, the extra software doesn't cost a whole lot, so it's worthwhile.
- **PilotMail** Using this program, you can transfer mail from your desktop computer to the PalmPilot and read mail there. You also can compose mail on your PalmPilot, send it to your desktop computer, and then use your normal email program to send mail from it. What you can't do, though, is send and receive mail directly on the Internet with your PalmPilot (unless you buy extra software). Now, you're probably wondering why a computer would 1) be designed

to connect to the Internet, and 2) be given an email program that wouldn't allow you to send and receive email directly via the Internet. I'm wondering the same thing. Maybe those engineers they locked in the cages are taking their revenge on us.

If you want all the functionality of the Palm III in your PalmPilot Professional, you can spend about $130, and 3COM will send you a memory board you can slip into your Professional to make it do all the Palm III's tricks, as outlined next.

How is the IBM WorkPad different from the PalmPilot?

IBM released a device called the WorkPad that looks and works remarkably like the PalmPilot. And there's good reason for that similarity: It's the same device. IBM licensed the rights from 3COM to release the WorkPad. The IBM engineers, however, worked overtime to differentiate the two devices. So they made the WorkPad black, not gray. And they made the on/off button red, not green. And that's it. Hey, the engineers took a long time to come up with differences that big. Cut them a little slack. Okay, so maybe they did add a few new things. The WorkPad includes some extra software, including a program that allows you to HotSync directly to the IBM ThinkPad by using the infrared port.

What Is the Palm III?

Back in 1998, 3COM decided to rename the device once again and rolled out a new version, called the Palm III. Many people call it by its real name, but several people still refer to it as the PalmPilot. That's generally what I call it in this book. The Palm III added a whole lot of stuff that makes organizing your life even *easier*. These main things were added:

- **The Palm III was given the capability to beam things to other Palms.** As far as I'm concerned, we're talking science fiction here. Using an infrared beam located on the bottom of the Palm, you can beam business cards, memos, and even entire programs to other people who have Palms. Weird but true.
- **The memory was doubled to 2MB.** Now the Palm III can handle 20,000 names and addresses, memos, appointments, and assorted stuff.

- ➤ **A new version of the operating system—OS 3—was introduced.** In many ways, the software was improved. You can change fonts to make text easier to read. You can more easily install software onto it. You can find other stuff there as well.
- ➤ **It was given a plastic flip cover to protect the screen.** The glass screen of previous PalmPilots could be scratched or even shattered. The flip cover now protects it.
- ➤ **The Palm Desktop 3.0 was introduced.** This software runs on your desktop computer, and it mirrors exactly what's on your Palm. As a result, you can track names and addresses, to-dos, and other items when you're running your PC. Anything you do in this software synchronizes with your Palm—and everything you do in your Palm synchronizes with this software. So whether you're using your PC or your Palm, you're working with the same information. Check out the following figure to see what the Palm Desktop looks like.

The Palm Desktop 3.0: Information is shuttled between here and your Palm, so you can easily keep track of your life by using your Palm or your computer.

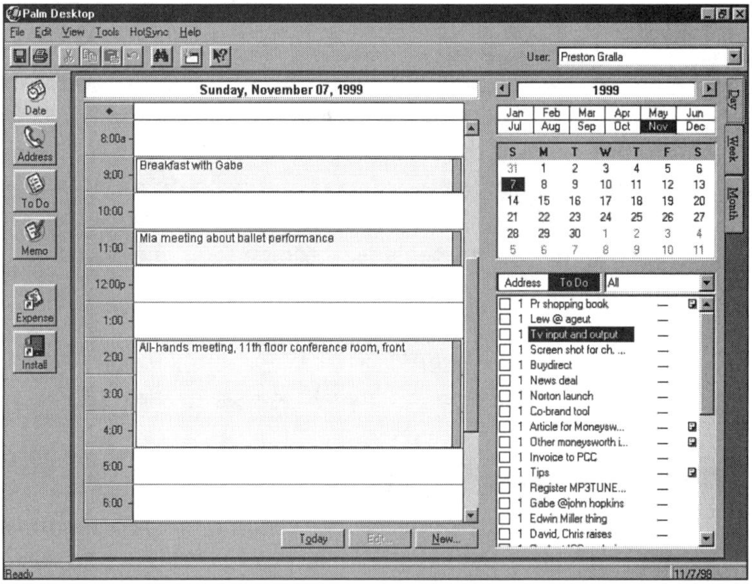

- ➤ **The case itself was redesigned.** It's now tapered, the screen is more readable, and other cosmetic changes have been made as well. The Palm III rates higher on the coolness chart.

What is flash memory?

The PalmPilot comes with *flash memory,* a special kind of memory that enables you to easily upgrade the unit's operating system. The next time a new operating system comes along, you won't need to buy any special memory card; you can install it right into your flash memory.

What's a PDA

Every once in a while you might hear someone refer to a Palm or PalmPilot as a *PDA*. The term *PDA,* which stands for *personal digital assistant,* was first coined by Apple Computer to describe its Newton, a PalmPilot-like device that never quite caught on and was eventually killed by Apple. Rumor has it, by the way, that at some point Apple tried to buy the PalmPilot from 3COM but was rebuffed.

The Palm VII and Beyond

As I write this book, engineers have finished their plans for the next version of the Palm, called the Palm VII. Yes, you read that right, the Palm VII. (And I bet you always thought engineers were good at counting.) 3COM evidently decided that the numbers IV, V, and VI weren't classy enough and so jumped all the way up to VII. The Palm VII costs a good deal more than the Palm III (it should cost a little under $800). The main advance is that it features a super-cool wireless connection to the Internet. Using this feature, wherever you are, you can connect, send and receive messages, and get information from Web sites without having to use a phone line. Just pop up a little antenna, and you're online. You'll also have to pay an access fee of $10 or more per month. I know that $800 is a lot of money, so the Palm VII won't be for everyone. But I want one. I want one now!

The Least You Need to Know

- Each of the PalmPilot's built-in applications can help you organize a different part of your life, such as your schedule, To-Do Lists, and list of contacts.
- You can synchronize information on your PalmPilot and information on your PC by using the HotSync capability.
- The PalmPilot is ideal for taking along on trips because it allows you to keep a schedule and also to keep track of your expenses.
- The earliest of these devices was called the Pilot; the second generation, the PalmPilot; and the current generation is called the Palm.
- You can upgrade from the Pilot or PalmPilot to the Palm by buying a memory card for about $130 and then slipping it into your Pilot or PalmPilot.

NOW, IF YOU'LL STEP THIS WAY.
PILOT TOUR

Chapter 2

Prepare to Get Organized: A Guided Tour of the PalmPilot

In This Chapter

- Learning about the PalmPilot's screen, contrast controls, and backlight buttons
- Understanding what the application and silkscreened buttons do
- Using the Graffiti writing area
- Taking a look at what the controls in the back of the PalmPilot do
- Learning about the battery, infrared port, and serial port

Before you can get your life organized with your little digital companion, you first need to know how the thing works. Before you can do that, though, you need to know what all the little buttons, gizmos, recessed slots, and other neat things are there for. Maybe you can't tell a book by its cover, but you *can* judge the PalmPilot by its outer case.

In this chapter, you take guided tour of the PalmPilot. You're going to look at the PalmPilot's case, screens, cradle, and other assorted features. I don't cover in detail the software that comes with it. For that information, turn to Chapter 4, "Organization 101: Touring the PalmPilot's Main Screen."

Are You Really Sure This Thing Is a Computer?

The first point to realize about the PalmPilot is that, yes, it is in fact a computer. It may not look like one; after all, it has no keyboard, no monitor, no mouse, no disk drives, no incomprehensible error messages, and no inane computer commands that sound as if they were written by someone for whom English is a seventh language, and poorly spoken at that. I mean, can something this small, this approachable, and dare I say it, this cute (uh oh, clearly I've been spending too much time alone with my Palm III...) actually be a computer?

Yes, it can be. Inside the hard case is a little microprocessor, just like a microprocessor is inside your PC or Mac. The PalmPilot also contains memory and built-in software that do all the things I'll talk about later that help you organize your life. In fact, the PalmPilot contains more memory and power inside it than was in many of the original desktop computers back in the dark ages of the 1980s.

What microprocessor is inside the PalmPilot?

For the geeks of the world who care about such things, the Palm III is powered by a Motorola 68328 chip.

The major difference between the PalmPilot and PCs and Macs is that the PalmPilot was designed for one purpose alone: to help you get your life under control. Because of that, you won't find the wide range of software on the PalmPilot that you'll find in a normal computer. And you won't be able to plug all kinds of things into it, such as scanners and printers—although you can hook up your PalmPilot to a modem to get email and browse the Web, as you'll see in Part 3, "Using Email, Internet, and Infrared Communications to Keep You in Touch."

What you will find in the PalmPilot, though, is a little computer that's been designed from the ground up to help you organize your life, and the built-in software helps you do just that. Because you carry it around with you, you get information into the PalmPilot not via a keyboard or mouse, but instead by writing with your stylus in a special area of the PalmPilot. Handwriting-recognition software built into the PalmPilot takes your keystrokes and turns them into letters. You tap on the screen to do a lot of your work as well.

Checking Out the Front Panel and Controls

It's time to start your tour of the PalmPilot. (I know, it's not quite the same as a guided tour of the Loire Valley in France, but on the other hand, the PalmPilot costs only a little over $300—and just try to get a tour of the Loire at *that* price.) What better place to start than the beginning, with the PalmPilot's front panel and controls—basically, the front of the device.

Check out the following figure, which shows you the front of the PalmPilot with all the parts and pieces labeled. You're looking at a Palm III. Other versions of the PalmPilot are similar but not identical.

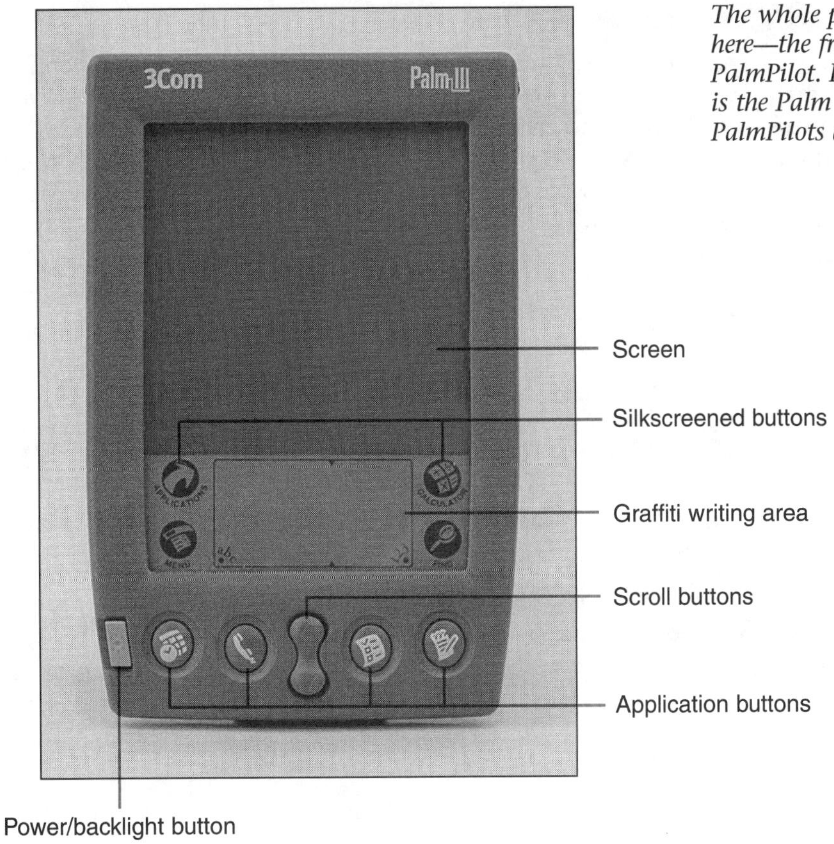

The whole process begins here—the front of the PalmPilot. Pictured here is the Palm III, but other PalmPilots are similar.

As you can see, the front of the PalmPilot has on it the following:

- The screen
- The power and backlight button
- The application buttons
- The scroll buttons
- The silkscreened buttons
- The Graffiti writing area
- The flip case

Next, I describe what you need to know about each of these areas to help you organize your life.

Looking at the Screen

The screen, also called the display area, is the place where all the action happens. Here, all the programs run, and you see all the stuff you're tracking, such as your To-Do List, memos, addresses, and calendar. The screen does more than just display information, though. It's also a touch screen, which means that when you run programs, you touch the screen with the stylus to perform certain tasks, such as scheduling an appointment by touching on the time and date of the week when you want it scheduled.

You can use things other than a stylus on the touch screen.

You use the stylus that comes with the PalmPilot on the touch screen. But nothing special in the stylus makes the touch screen work; you can use other things as well. Some people use their fingertips, and you can buy a variety of stylish styli as well. Be careful not to use a normal pen or pencil on the screen, though, because writing on it with ink or pencil can damage it.

Icons (little pictures) on the screen represent all the programs in your PalmPilot. To run a program, touch the icon with your stylus. The following figure shows the icons on the screen.

It's touch and go: Tap any of the icons on the screen to run a program.

Powering Up with the Power and Backlight Button

You want to turn on your PalmPilot? Press the power and backlight button. You want to turn it off? Press again. Simple, no? Notice that when you turn your PalmPilot on or off, it starts up or shuts off instantly, unlike a computer, which takes about two or three decades to do the same thing, give or take a year or two.

The PalmPilot also comes with a backlight that you can turn on to make the screen more readable. (The Pilot 1000 and Pilot 5000 didn't have this backlight. Pity their poor owners; they're all being fitted for glasses right now.) The backlight has a nice kind of green eerie glow to it—kind of an underwater, aquarium-like light.

To turn on the backlight, press down the power and backlight button for about two or more seconds (if you press down for less time, you'll turn off the PalmPilot). To turn off the backlight, press down again for two or more seconds (and if you press down for less time, you'll turn off the PalmPilot).

I can find only one problem with the backlight feature: It sucks up battery juice big time. Use it a lot, and you'll be changing your batteries several times a month.

WriteRights can diminish screen glare and protect your screen.

Some people feel that the PalmPilot's screen has too much glare on it and therefore is difficult to read. Also, screens sometimes can be scratched. You can reduce the glare and protect your screen by buying WriteRight screen protectors at `www.conceptkitchen.com`. The protectors also make it feel as if you're writing with your stylus on paper instead of on glass. A year's supply of 12 costs about $27.99.

Running Software with the Application Buttons

The application buttons are the four large buttons that run across the bottom of the PalmPilot. You press these buttons when you want to run a particular piece of software, such as the Memo Pad or Address List, to help you organize your life. Why are the buttons called "application buttons" when they, in fact, run software? They have this name because another term for *software* is *application*.

Pictured in the following figure are the four buttons, labeled according to what program they run when you press them.

When you're running your PalmPilot, just press any of these buttons, and you immediately switch to that program. Let me give you a little timesaving tip: If your PalmPilot is turned off and you want to run one of these programs, you don't need to turn it on and then press the application button. Instead, just press the application button. The PalmPilot turns on and jumps you right into that program.

Read this rundown on what each of the buttons does. I'll cover all this information in more detail in Chapter 4, "Organization 101: Touring the PalmPilot's Main Screen."

- **Date Book** The left-most button with the picture of the clock in front of a warped-looking calendar runs the Date Book. This calendar program helps you keep track of your schedule, appointments, and meetings. Use this program, and you'll never again show up at the doctor's office for an appointment that you never scheduled—when you, in fact, are supposed to be in Denver giving a presentation at the annual sales meeting.
- **Address Book** The next left-most button button with a tiny picture of a telephone runs the Address Book. Here, you keep track of names, phone numbers, and addresses, including email addresses.
- **To-Do List** The next-to-last button with the little picture of an odd-looking piece of paper with checks and boxes on it (skipping the scroll button) runs the To-Do List. Here, you—well, yes, you guessed it—keep track of all the things you have to do.
- **Memo Pad** The rightmost button with the picture of a reporter's notebook and pen runs the Memo Pad. Not hard to imagine what the Memo Pad does—it lets you write memos.

These four buttons run the main programs you use to get your life organized: the Date Book, the Address Book, the To-Do List, and the Memo Pad.

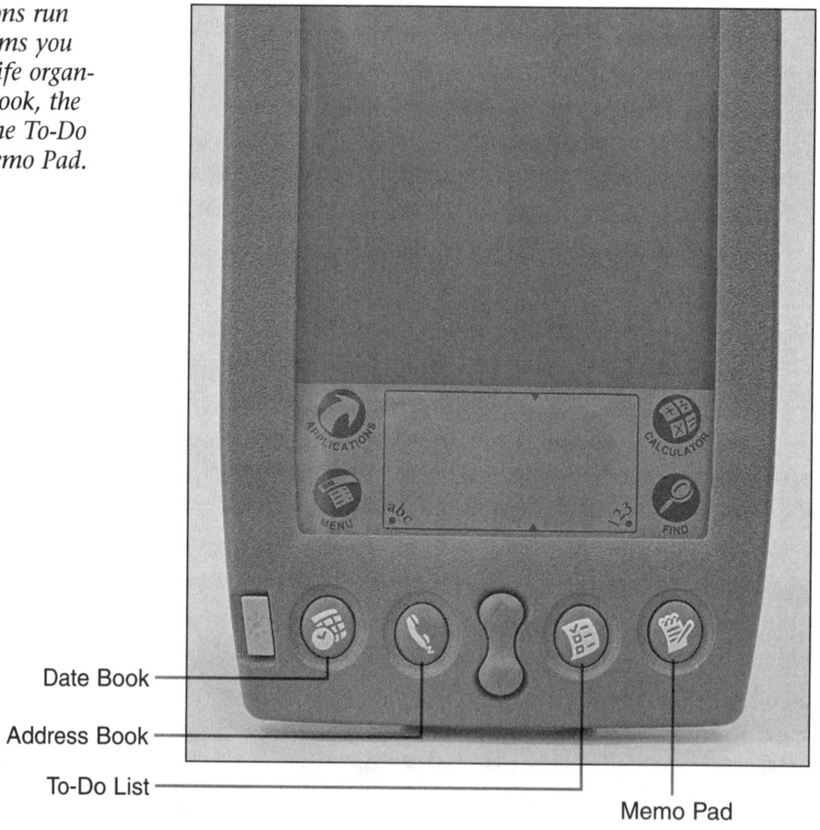

Make your life easier by reassigning the application buttons.

Maybe you find yourself hardly ever using the Memo Pad, but you run the PalmPilot's Expense program all the time to track your expenses. Wouldn't it be nice if you could run Expense by just pressing the Memo Pad button?

Yes, it would be nice, and yes, you can do it. You can reassign any of the application buttons to run any PalmPilot program. Check out Chapter 21, "Customizing Your PalmPilot for the Way You Live and Work," to see how to reassign buttons.

The Scroll Buttons

Right smack dab in the center of the bottom of the PalmPilot are the scroll buttons. On a Palm III, the buttons are combined into one large button in a kind of distended hourglass shape. Earlier models have two separate buttons.

You use these scroll buttons to see what's on the screen above or below what's currently showing. You scroll through a screen by pressing these buttons. Press the **up** button to scroll up, and press the **down** button to scroll down. (See, I told you the PalmPilot was easier to use than a computer. If the PalmPilot were a PC, the buttons would probably be called "Tactile-Sensation Screen Application Positioning Hardware Modules (TSSAPHMs)" and "up" would go down, and "down" would go up. Then Bill Gates would try to make that a standard for the world.)

The Silkscreened Buttons

On the bottom portion of the glass front of the PalmPilot are four "buttons" that, in fact, aren't physical buttons at all; they're button shapes that have been silkscreened onto the glass. Tap them with your stylus, though, and they work just like buttons and run programs or perform functions. With these buttons, unlike the application buttons, you can't tap on them to turn on the PalmPilot.

Pictured in the following figure are the four buttons, labeled according to what program they run when you press them.

Tap and run: Here, you see the four silkscreened buttons and what each of them does when you tap on it with the stylus.

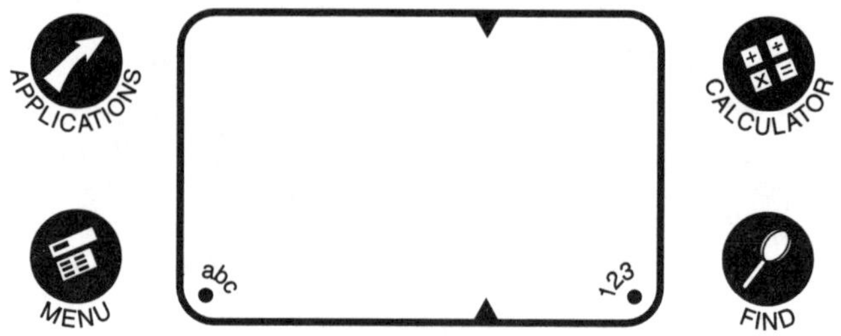

The **Applications** button brings up a list of all the programs on your PalmPilot, as you can see in the following figure. I'll cover all these programs in more detail in Chapter 4, "Organization 101: Touring the PalmPilot's Main Screen."

You see all the programs on your PalmPilot when you tap on the Applications button.

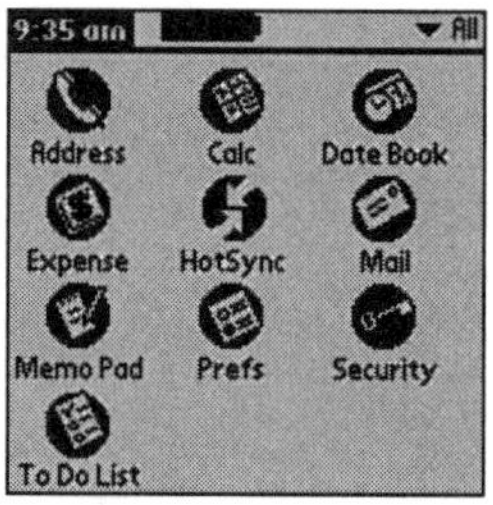

The **Menu** button runs a menu in any program that you're currently running. A menu on the PalmPilot isn't something that you order food from; instead, it lists for you all the tasks you can perform in a program you're currently running, such as cutting and copying text, adding an event to your calendar, and deleting records. The following figure shows the Date Book's menu. Turn to Chapter 8, "Taking Control of the PalmPilot's Applications, Menus, and Records," for more information on how to use the menus. Not only are the menus big time-savers, but they also contain many options that will help you organize your life better. Now if only I could find an option that added two hours to a day, that's one I would use all the time....

When you tap on the Menu silkscreen button when you're in the Date Book, you see this menu.

The **Calculator** button runs a calculator, which does pretty much what you would expect a calculator to do—it calculates. (What a concept!) Tap the numbers and functions on the calculator, and it does math magic, as you can see in the following figure.

Doing math magic is easy on the PalmPilot when you use the Calculator.

The **Find** button helps you find stuff on your PalmPilot. Tap on the button, and you get a screen, as you can see in the following figure, that lets you type in a word to search. Then tap **OK**, and you find every single item on your PalmPilot that includes that word—whether it be a name or address, a To-Do item, or an entry in the Date Book. You name it; the PalmPilot finds it. Now if it could only find those socks that keep vanishing from my dryer.

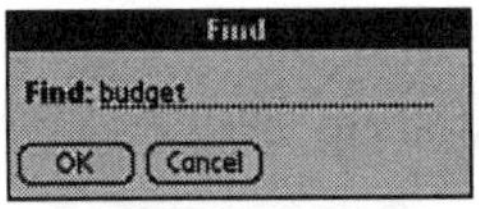

You can search using the PalmPilot's Find feature.

The Graffiti Writing Area

Finally, a way to write graffiti without being arrested for vandalism. To get information and other stuff (*stuff:* a technical term meaning "things") into your PalmPilot, you use a stylus to write in the Graffiti area, shown in the following figure. To write things, you use a special kind of alphabet called *Graffiti*. It's a lot like the regular alphabet, with only a few minor changes. I'll cover more details about Graffiti in Chapter 7, "Digital Magic: Taking Notes with Graffiti.

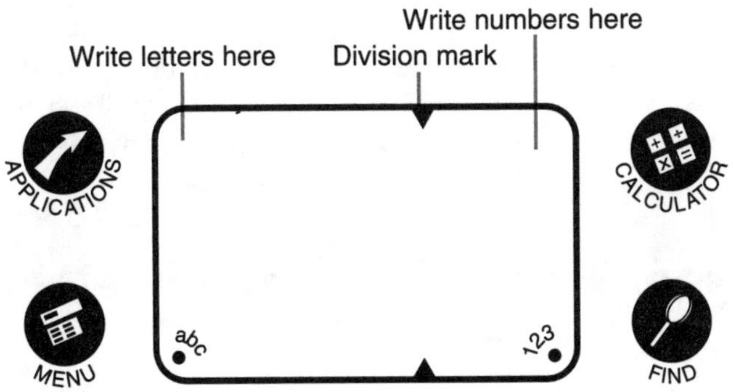

Write Graffiti without getting arrested for vandalism: You enter text and numbers into your PalmPilot here.

The Graffiti area is divided into two sections. On the left section, you write letters. On the right section, you write numbers. Believe it or not, when people start using the PalmPilot, one of the biggest mistakes they make is trying to write numbers in the letter area. Don't do it. It won't work. The first time I tried it, I wanted to write the number *5270836*, and it came out *Sztobyg*, which sounds a lot like the town in Poland where my grandfather grew up.

Notice that the letters *abc* are printed on the lower-left corner of the Graffiti area, and the numbers *123* are printed on the lower-right corner. They're available to help you put in text and numbers. Tap on the button next to *abc,* and a little keyboard pops up with all the letters of the alphabet. Tap a letter on the keyboard, and you input that letter. Tap on the little button near the *123,* and a number keyboard pops up instead. You'll find this feature is a great help for inputting oddball characters (and no, it's not me I'm talking about) such as > or %.

Use Graffiti cheat sheets.

When you buy a PalmPilot, you get a set of Graffiti recognition stickers, which are essentially cheat sheets that show you the Graffiti alphabet, for quick reference. If you have a Palm III or higher, you can make sure they're always at hand by trimming them slightly and pasting them inside the Palm's flip cover. That way, whenever you're unsure of how to write a character, the answer is staring you right in the face.

Flipping About the Flip Case

The flip case is a plastic case that comes with the Palm III and later PalmPilots. When you want to use your PalmPilot, you flip up the case. When you're done, flip it down. The metal case protects the screen and the front of the PalmPilot. If you're fashion-minded, you should know that you can replace your flip case with a different-colored one. Fuchsia, anyone?

Using the Back Panel Doors, Buttons, Ports, and Gizmos

Okay, now it's time to turn your PalmPilot on its back. Don't worry; it won't be upset. It's used to this kind of thing.

Back here, you find a variety of things that you don't use as commonly as all the gizmos, gadgets, and widgets on the front of your PalmPilot. I'm not saying that this stuff isn't important; in fact, without all the things hidden back here, your PalmPilot couldn't run.

Check out the following picture, which shows all the different things on the back of the PalmPilot—in this instance, on a Palm III. As you can see, the back of the PalmPilot has on it the following:

- A stylus
- A reset button
- A contrast wheel
- A battery cover
- An infrared beaming port
- A HotSync connection, also called a serial port (By the way, this serial port looks very different from the one on your computer, so don't look for one like that here.)

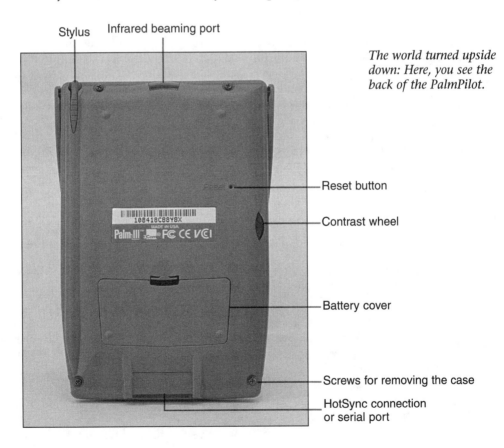

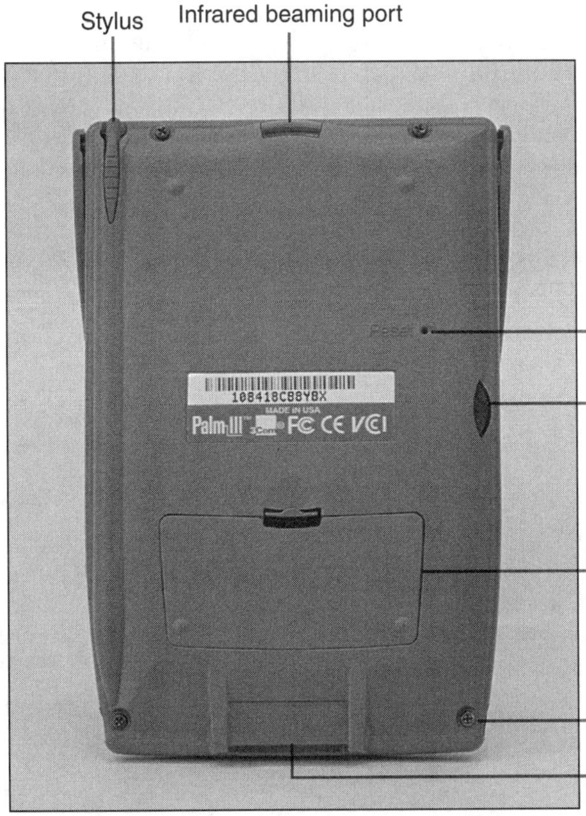

The world turned upside down: Here, you see the back of the PalmPilot.

Next, you learn what you need to know about each of these elements before getting your life organized.

The Stylish Stylus

The stylus slips into a slot in the back of your PalmPilot. You use it to write Graffiti and use the touch screen. The Palm III and higher comes with a stylus with a metal barrel that feels more comfortable and substantial than the all-plastic stylus that came on earlier models. You can also buy a replacement stylus if you want.

The Reset Button

Sometimes bad things happen to good people. Yes, even to you. And to your PalmPilot as well. Your PalmPilot could freeze, lock up, and appear to go kaput. When you try to turn it off by pressing on the **On/off** button, it doesn't even turn off. It just sits there, refusing to move or do anything, like a stubborn child. More often than not, you have this problem because you've installed some kind of software that doesn't get along with your PalmPilot.

So what to do? You need to reset your PalmPilot. At this point, the little reset button comes in. Well, it's not really a button; it's more a tiny little hole, but everyone calls it a button. To reset your PalmPilot, you need to push in that little button inside the hole. If you own a Palm III or higher, screw off the top of your stylus to find a little wire-like thing you can use. If you don't have a Palm III, straighten out a paper clip and use it to push the button. Push only until you hear a click. If you push too hard, you could damage the PalmPilot. By the way, some engineers, who know about such things, worry that using a paper clip could cause damage because it's metal pushing against metal. They recommend instead using a toothpick.

You can perform three kinds of resets with your PalmPilot, depending on how bad a problem you've come across: a soft reset, a warm reset, or a hard reset. You can do each as follows:

- **A soft reset** This type of reset turns off your PalmPilot and unfreezes it. Now you're ready to start work again. No damage done. You perform a soft reset by pushing the wire on top of your stylus or a paper clip inside the reset button.
- **A warm reset** You try this type of reset if, for some reason, the soft reset doesn't solve the problem. Soft resets might not solve some kinds of startup problems. For these problems, you might have to do a warm reset. To do a warm reset, press down on the **Scroll Up** button. While you're pressing it, push the wire on top of your stylus or a paper clip inside the reset button. When you do a warm reset, none of your data is erased; it remains safe. Any add-ons or patches you added to the PalmPilot, however, are erased.
- **A hard reset** This type of reset is more hardcore than a warm reset or a soft reset. Use it only if you have to—in other words, if a soft reset doesn't work. A hard reset erases all the information you've put into your PalmPilot—and I

mean everything, including your name. It basically puts the PalmPilot back to the way it was when you unpacked it from the box. This is not a good thing. To do a hard reset, hold down the **on/off** button and push the wire on top of your stylus or a paper clip inside the reset button. You then get a message asking whether you really, really want to do a hard reset. If you do, press the **up** button. If you don't, press the **down** button.

All is not lost if you do a hard reset.

If you do a hard reset, you probably figure your life is gone; all your appointments, your contacts, your To-Do List, and everything else have vanished. Don't give up hope, though; you can restore all that information in various ways. Turn to Chapter 24, "Cures for the PalmPilot's Most Common Problems," for details on how to restore.

For more information about hard, warm, and soft resets, and troubleshooting in general, turn to Chapter 24, "Cures for the PalmPilot's Most Common Problems."

Beaming Up with the Infrared Beaming Port

The infrared beaming port, which is located at the top of the Palm III and higher, is covered by a little red piece of plastic. Get ready for science fiction time—except this is real, not make-believe. If you have a Palm III or higher, you can actually beam information to other Palm III and higher owners. Want to exchange business cards with another Palm owner? Forget about old-fashioned paper; just point your Palm in the right direction, and all your contact information is sent straight to his or her Palm and shows up in the Address Book. You can beam anything over—memos, to-dos, even entire programs.

That's the good news. The bad news is that you can't use the infrared port with other kinds of equipment; for example, you can't beam information to a computer that has an infrared port. If you own a WorkPad, however, you can create a HotSync by using the beaming port and the IR port of an IBM ThinkPad.

The Battery Door

Your PalmPilot runs on two ordinary AAA batteries. To put them in your PalmPilot, just open the little door, pop in the batteries, and you're done. Just one word of advice: Don't linger when you're replacing your batteries. If you take batteries out and then take too long to put new ones in, you lose all your data; it's kind of like doing a hard reset. Because of that, doing a HotSync (see details in "Rocking the Cradle") is always a good idea before you replace your batteries. That way, if you lose everything, you still have a copy on your desktop computer and can get it back into your PalmPilot.

By the way, get used to opening and closing this door because you're going to use it a whole lot. If you use your PalmPilot with any regularity, you'll be shuttling batteries in and out of there real fast. For advice on how to keep power consumption to a minimum, head to Chapter 25, "Care and Maintenance of Your Digital Companion."

Remembering the Memory Door

Now let me see. What was I going to write about? I can't seem to remember.... Oh, that's right, the memory door. You can add more memory to your PalmPilot, and you can also upgrade an older version of the PalmPilot to a newer version by putting in a special card. You do so by opening the memory door, taking out the old memory card, and putting in a new one. In Palm III and higher models, you open the memory door by unscrewing the four tiny screws at the four corners at the back of the Palm. In earlier models, you put a straightened clip into a small pinhole in the center of the memory door.

The Contrast Wheel

One thing is not so great about PalmPilots: Their screens can be hard to read. Being able to read the screen is especially a problem when you use it in different kinds of light—for example, in a dim room versus in full sunlight. You therefore should become best friends with the contrast wheel. Using it, you can change the contrast to best suit the lighting you're currently working in. I suggest adjusting it every time you turn on your PalmPilot.

You also might find that if you regularly use the contrast wheel, you don't have to use the backlighting as often. When you use backlight, you drain your batteries quickly, so using the contrast wheel saves you time and money. And isn't that the main reason you bought a PalmPilot in the first place?

The Serial Port

No PalmPilot is an island; it's best used along with your desktop computer. To send stuff back and forth between your computer and your PalmPilot, you need to connect your PalmPilot to something. The serial port comes into play for this task. It connects your PalmPilot to the world. You can place your PalmPilot onto a cradle (see the next section) that hooks into the serial port, and that cradle then connects to your computer (the hip bone's connected to the leg bone; the leg bone's connected to the thigh bone; the thigh bone's connected...).

You also can buy a neat little modem that plugs into your serial port and then use your PalmPilot to cruise the Internet, send faxes, and send and receive email. You can also buy a modem cable that connects your serial port to a regular modem.

The PalmPilot has such a devoted following that people have come up with all kinds of crazy things to hook into the serial port. I've tried a Global Positioning System (GPS), for example, that tells me exactly where I am on Earth. (Of course, I know that already, but having a satellite and a PalmPilot tell me things I already know is a whole lot more fun.) You can even buy a little gizmo called a TaleLight that, in essence, turns your PalmPilot into a teeny-tiny flashlight. The wonders of technology! Who would ever have thought it would be so easy to make a $300.00 piece of hardware do everything that a $2.95 penlight could do?

Rocking the Cradle

As I mentioned before, you can hook up your PalmPilot to your desktop computer and then synchronize all the data between the PalmPilot and your computer. That way, whether you're working on your computer or your little digital device, all the information you have will match. So, if you put a to-do item on your computer, for example, it automatically is sent to the PalmPilot. And if you put a contact in your Address Book, it automatically is sent to your computer. This process is called *doing a HotSync.*

This magic works by using the cradle, shown in the following figure. You put your PalmPilot into the cradle, connect the cradle to the serial port on your computer, press a button, and voilá, you've done a HotSync. You should HotSync at least once a day, not only to make sure everything's up-to-date, but also to make sure that you have all the information you need should your PalmPilot require a hard reset.

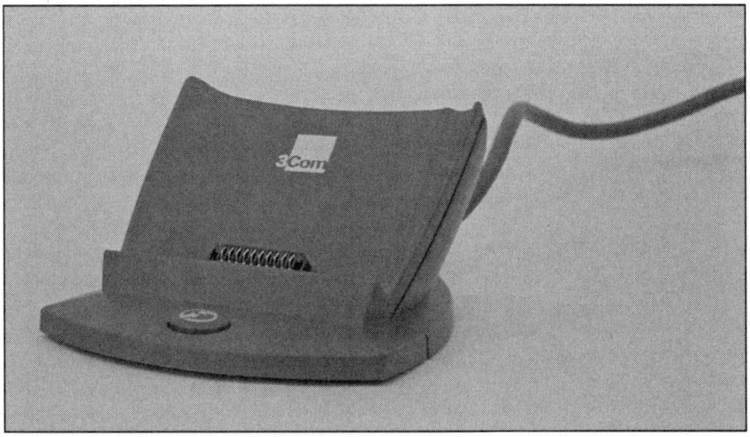

The cradle lets you synchronize the information between your PalmPilot and your computer.

The Least You Need to Know

- To run any of the programs on the PalmPilot, press or tap on the right button. The application buttons turn on the PalmPilot as well as run programs.
- You use the stylus to input data into your PalmPilot, but you can use other things on the touch screen as well.
- The backlight feature makes the screen more readable, but it uses a lot of battery power.
- You can use the contrast control to make the screen easier to see and to cut down on having to use the backlight feature.
- You use the infrared port to exchange information with other Palm III and higher users, but you cannot beam information to desktop computers.
- The serial port and cradle allow you to HotSync information between your PalmPilot and desktop PC.

Chapter 3

Time for Takeoff: Starting Your PalmPilot for the First Time

In This Chapter

- Installing the battery and turning on the PalmPilot
- Calibrating the PalmPilot's screen
- Using the contrast wheel
- Customizing the PalmPilot's main preferences for the way you work and live

By now, you know what a PalmPilot can do, and you've taken the grand tour of its outer case. So now it's time for takeoff; you're ready to launch the PalmPilot to help you get your life under control. Before you can use it to help organize your life, though, you first need to turn the thing on and fire it up.

So let me tell you what you need to know and do when you start your PalmPilot for the first time.

Let's Start at the Beginning: Take It Out of the Box

You've got your new PalmPilot. You've taken it out of the box. Now what?

The first thing you'll probably notice is that reading your PalmPilot's screen is difficult. That's because the screen has a film over it. Peel it off. Okay, the screen is easier to read now. That was simple, wasn't it? Time to move on.

Add the Juice: Installing the Batteries

Before your PalmPilot can do anything, it needs some juice. (Most mornings, I must admit, I feel the same way.) So you need to install the batteries. Turn the PalmPilot onto its back and find the battery door. It has a little plastic tab there. Press on it with your finger, and take the door off. Now put in two AAA batteries. (3COM kindly provided some for you when you bought the PalmPilot.) Make sure that you put the + and – ends in the proper places inside. Just look for the labels. Make sure not to force the battery door closed. If it doesn't close smoothly, you might have put the batteries in incorrectly, so take them out and try putting them in again.

"Ultra" batteries can mean a longer battery life on your PalmPilot.

One of the most annoying things about the PalmPilot is that batteries don't go a long way, especially if you use the backlight on your screen very much. A new breed of batteries can help. Duracell has released what it calls the "Ultra" line of AAA batteries, designed specifically for electronic equipment. People who have used these batteries in their PalmPilots (including yours truly) report that they last longer than normal batteries, so you don't have to keep popping open the battery compartment and installing new batteries.

Although batteries don't last very long on a PalmPilot, you can at least always tell how much battery juice you have left. On the top of the applications screen is an easy-to-read battery gauge.

The battery gauge tells you how much juice is left. Here, you see a full gauge—a rare sight on a PalmPilot.

By the way, you don't need to worry that your batteries will run out without your knowing about it. You get a warning when your batteries are low, advising you to change them. When you get the warning, follow the advice so that you don't lose any data.

When you add new batteries, make sure that you put them in fairly quickly. If the PalmPilot is without batteries for more than several minutes, it loses all your data.

Why doesn't the PalmPilot lose all its data the second you take out its batteries?

Built into the PalmPilot is a little electronic gizmo called a *capacitor*. A capacitor can hold an electric charge for a certain amount of time. When you take out the battery, the capacitor takes over and supplies power to the PalmPilot. Its charge runs down after several minutes, though, so if you take a long time putting in the batteries, your data goes kaput.

Switching On Your PalmPilot

Now let me tell you about another easy part. After you put the batteries in, it's time to turn on the PalmPilot. Press down on the **on/off** button to turn on the PalmPilot. It turns on instantly. If you hold down the button for two seconds or more, the backlight turns on if you have a Palm III or PalmPilot. (No backlight screen is available on a Pilot 1000 or Pilot 5000.) The backlight makes the PalmPilot screen easier to read but also uses up the battery more quickly—so as the saying goes, you makes your choices and you takes your chances.

Calibrating the Screen

As soon as the PalmPilot turns on for the first time, you see a screen asking you to tap with your stylus in the center of a target three different times. You need to follow this direction to *calibrate* the screen—to make sure that when you tap somewhere on the screen, the PalmPilot interprets it properly.

After you calibrate your screen, you'll probably never need to calibrate it again. If you do need to recalibrate it, though, you can do so easily enough. To find out how, check out "Bend the PalmPilot to Your Will: Setting the Preferences," later in this chapter.

Techno Talk

Why does the screen need to be calibrated?

The screen on your PalmPilot is made up of two layers: one that displays all the text and graphics, and another, invisible one that detects where your stylus is touching, tapping, and writing. For the PalmPilot to correctly interpret your taps, it needs to understand how to synchronize these two different layers. Because everyone holds the PalmPilot at a slightly different angle, and because some people are right-handed and others left-handed, you need to go through the calibration routine before you start using it.

Can We Have Some Light Here? Adjusting the Contrast

The PalmPilot's screen is less than stellar. In certain lighting conditions, reading it can be pretty tough; you might find yourself squinting at the thing and turning it to all kinds of different angles to read anything. Before turning on the backlight, however, you should adjust the contrast on it. Move the contrast wheel until you find a contrast that's comfortable for you. Also, make sure to adjust the contrast every time you use the PalmPilot, not just when you turn it on for the first time, because the kind of light you're working in affects how well you can read the screen. Your eyes will thank you for it.

Bend the PalmPilot to Your Will: Setting the Preferences

You want to be master of the universe. Nations should bow down to you. Planets should accede to your wishes. The cosmos should obey your commands.

Well, maybe that's aiming a little high. Why don't you settle instead on bending the PalmPilot to your will? You'll find that controlling the PalmPilot can do more than give you an ego boost; it also makes organizing your life much easier. As you'll see, you can easily customize the PalmPilot for the way you live and work.

You can customize virtually every aspect of the PalmPilot—down to even what the buttons do when you press them. In this chapter, though, I just cover the basics of customizing this little tool the first time you turn it on. For information about how to make every aspect of the PalmPilot work the way you want, turn to Chapter 21, "Customizing Your PalmPilot for the Way You Live and Work."

So where to begin? Well, right after you finish calibrating the PalmPilot, the Preferences screen appears, as shown in the following figure. Here, you can become master of the universe—or at least czar of your PalmPilot.

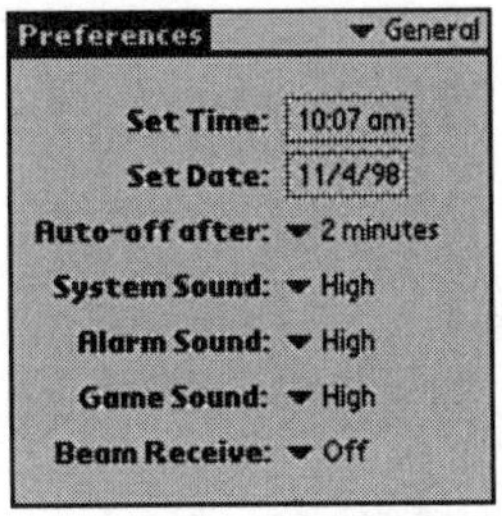

Bend the universe to your will, or at least customize your PalmPilot to your liking. You do so by working from the Preferences screen.

As you can see, this screen lets you customize the following:

- The time
- The date
- The auto-off feature
- The system sound
- The game sound
- Whether to enable your PalmPilot to receive beamed data from other PalmPilots

Next, let me tell you what you need to know to customize each of the general preferences.

Customizing the Time and Date

Don't be surprised if the PalmPilot has the time and date wrong when you first turn it on. I've unpacked and installed a good number of them, and the time and date have been wrong every time. Considering that you want to keep your life on schedule, you should first set the time and date.

Getting the time and date right on the PalmPilot is a breeze. To set the time, tap on the time, and you see the following screen. Tap on the number you want to change, or use the arrows to change the time, and tap on **AM** or **PM**. That's it; you're done.

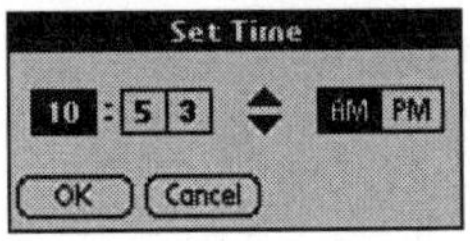

You can set the time here on the Palm III.

Setting the date is as easy as setting the time. Tap on the date, and a calendar pops up, as shown in the following figure. Tap on the current month and then the current date, and tap on **Today**. The time is now set.

Before you travel to another time zone, reset the time.

When you're traveling, you can easily forget to reset the time on your PalmPilot. If you don't reset the time, any alarms and reminders you've created for yourself will go off at the wrong times. When traveling, make sure that you're always where you need to be when you need to be there by resetting the time *before* you head off on your trip.

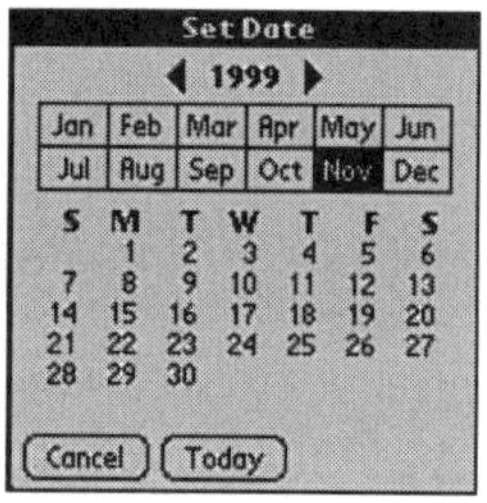

You set the date on the Palm III by using this calendar after you tap on the date in the Preferences screen.

Does the PalmPilot suffer from the "Year 2000" bug?

Some computer programs have a bug that doesn't allow them to operate properly or work at all when the date gets to the year 2000. PalmPilot owners need not worry; the PalmPilot will work fine well into the next century and beyond.

Setting the Auto-Off Delay

You can easily forget to turn off your PalmPilot, which can be a big problem, because it uses so much battery juice when it's turned on. If you leave it turned on and forget about it, the battery winds down, and you lose everything you have stored there.

Because of this potential danger, the PalmPilot has a clever auto-off feature. After a certain amount of time, it switches off automatically. Don't worry; when the PalmPilot switches off, all your information is saved. You have a choice of having it switch off automatically after one, two, or three minutes. Tap on the little down triangle next to Auto-off After on the Preferences screen, and you get the choice, as shown in the following figure.

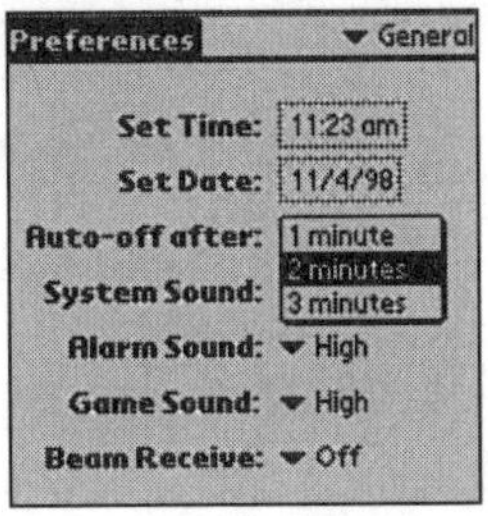

As easy as one, two, three: customizing the auto-off feature.

Which number you choose depends on the way you use your PalmPilot. If you often read documents that don't require that you tap the screen, or if you find yourself staring at the screen for a while, lost in thought (wake up, already! There's work to be done!), then set it for three minutes. If, on the other hand, you're the kind of person who takes out your PalmPilot, and with a tap, tap, tap gets your work done fast, set it to one minute.

Sound Off: Setting the System, Alarm, and Game Sounds

Use your PalmPilot enough, and it'll soon seem to you like a living thing—especially because it can make a variety of sounds, including a kind of cheeping or chirping, a little "click," and even a tiny melody when you do a HotSync. (See Chapter 5, "Keeping Your Life in Sync: HotSyncing Your PC and PalmPilot," for more information about HotSync.)

Your PalmPilot makes three kinds of sounds:

- **System sounds** These sounds are the clicks it makes when you tap with your stylus and the melody that plays when you do a HotSync.
- **Alarm sound** This sound is made when you've asked to be alerted when an event is about to occur such as an upcoming meeting.
- **Game sounds** These sounds play—yes, you guessed it—when you play games.

You can easily turn on or off these sounds. On the Palm III and higher, you also can set how loud these sounds are—low, medium, or high.

To turn on or off the system sounds in anything lower than a Palm III, check or uncheck the appropriate sound box on the Preferences screen. To set the sound level or turn it off on a Palm III, click on the little triangle next to the sound you want to change, and choose the level of the sound, or turn the sound off, as shown in the following figure.

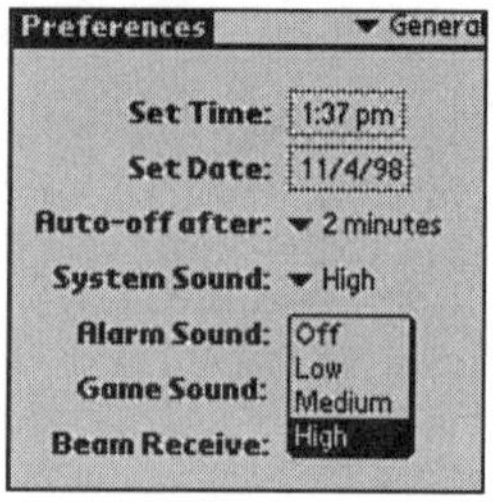

A sound decision: Changing the sounds that the Palm III makes.

You can set your PalmPilot to make all kinds of sounds, not just the ones it ships with.

Special programs called *hacks* can make your PalmPilot do all kinds of crazy things, including making many different sounds. The SystemSoundHack, available from `www.palmpilotsoftware.com`, is a good one for doing that. To use any hack, you also need HackMaster, which is available at `www.palmpilotsoftware.com`. Turn to Chapter 20, "Installing New Software on Your PalmPilot," for more information about how to install software such as HackMaster and SystemSoundHack.

It's Beaming Time: Setting the Palm to Receive Infrared Beams

You're sitting in a conference room, checking your schedule on your Palm III. All of a sudden, your Palm beeps at you and asks whether you would like to receive information. No, you're not about to receive a message from an extraterrestrial being. (At least, I *think* you're not.) Instead, someone nearby has pointed his or her Palm III at you and wants to send you some information. You've been beamed.

The Palm III and higher allows people to send each other information such as business cards, addresses and phone numbers, memos—even entire programs. When someone wants to send you information, his or her Palm beams your Palm (kind of like a fraternity or sorority handshake, minus the knuckles). You're then asked whether you want to receive the info. If you say yes, you get it from the infrared port.

If you don't ever want to receive this kind of information, you can block it out. To do so, you must turn your Beam Receive off. On the Preferences screen, tap on the triangle and choose **Off**, as you see in the following figure. For more information about beaming, turn to Chapter 19, "Beam Me Up, Scotty! Using the Palm III's Infrared Port."

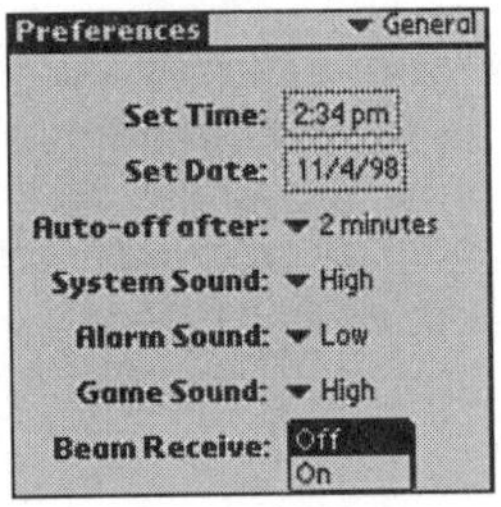

Don't beam me up, Scotty: Turning off the Beam feature in the Palm III.

Time to Get Started

So you've made it through starting your PalmPilot for the first time. Now you're ready to start organizing your life. Start with the next chapter, "Organization 101: Touring the PalmPilot's Main Screen," to start getting your life under control.

Your PalmPilot also includes some software you can run on your computer's desktop. For information on installing and using it, turn to Chapter 6, "Oh, Yeah...You Have a Computer, Too. Using the Palm Desktop." And for understanding how to synchronize your data between your computer and your PalmPilot, turn to Chapter 5, "Keeping Your Life in Sync: HotSyncing Your PC and PalmPilot."

The Least You Need to Know

- Make sure that the batteries match up properly with the + and – in the battery compartment, and don't force the compartment closed.
- "Ultra" batteries designed for electronic equipment last longer than do normal batteries in the PalmPilot.
- Adjusting the contrast control regularly makes reading your PalmPilot screen much easier.
- Before you travel to another time zone, reset the time so that your alarms go off when they're supposed to.
- If you don't want to be bothered by owners of other Palm IIIs beaming you information, turn off the Beam Receive feature.

Chapter 4

Organization 101: Touring the PalmPilot's Main Screen

In This Chapter

- Using the Application Launcher to run all the PalmPilot's programs
- Learning how the Date Book can keep you on schedule and on time
- Using Expense to keep track of your business and personal expenses
- Writing memos with the Memo Pad
- Keeping track of all your tasks with the To-Do List
- Using the PalmPilot's other main programs to get your life under control

Congratulations! You've started your PalmPilot for the first time, and you've set up your preferences so that it's no longer merely a digital companion and instead has become your digital slave. (If you've followed my advice, you can almost hear it say, "Yes, master. Your wish is my command.") Now you're ready to start organizing your life with it.

To do so, you need to start where it all begins: on the PalmPilot's main screen. Get used to this screen because you'll be looking at it a lot. Think of it as the command center for your life. On this screen, you go to get to all the features of the PalmPilot that help you set your calendar, to-dos, addresses and phone numbers, and more. So come along. We're going take a guided tour of the PalmPilot's main screen.

The First Stop on the Guided Tour

The first thing you need to do is check out the lay of the land and see what's on the main screen. Wherever you are in the PalmPilot, to get to its main screen, tap on the **Applications** silkscreened button. When you do that, you see the screen shown in the following figure.

The command center for your life: The main screen of the PalmPilot.

As you can see, everything you need to organize your life is in one place. Let me explain what's on the main screen and what it'll do for you:

- **Address Book** Keeps track of names, addresses, and contacts.
- **Calculator** Lets you do math calculations (no great surprise).
- **Date Book** Lets you keep track of all your meetings, appointments, and schedule (a calendar program).
- **Expense** Tracks your personal expenses or business expense reports, and is especially useful when you're traveling.
- **HotSync** Synchronizes all the information on your PalmPilot with information on your desktop computer.
- **Mail** Lets you read and create email. You cannot send email directly from the PalmPilot. You have to hook it up to your desktop computer with the HotSync cradle and get and receive messages through your normal email program.
- **Memo Pad** Allows you to write memos.
- **Preferences** Allows you to customize just about every aspect of the PalmPilot. You use Preferences to match the PalmPilot to how you live and work.
- **Security** Lets you lock out anyone else from using the PalmPilot, and allows you to keep whatever information you want private so that no one else can see it.
- **To-Do List** Lets you keep a list of tasks that you need to perform. This program is especially powerful because you can put your to-dos into categories and rank how important they are to you.

Stay tuned; later in the chapter, I cover what these programs do in more detail and how you can use them to organize your life. By the way, if you've installed any other programs onto your PalmPilot, such as from bonus packs or other places, they show up on the screen as well.

Prepare for Takeoff: Using the Application Launcher to Run Programs

To run any of these programs, you tap on their icons with your stylus. Then, if you want to switch to another program, you can press its button. So, for example, if you are adding an item to your To-Do List (bring home alfalfa treats for your pet rabbit), and receive a phone call alerting you to a meeting you need to attend (monthly meeting of the Rabbit Breeders Association), you just press on the **Date Book** button on the lower left of your PalmPilot's case. The Date Book pops up, and you can then schedule the date and time for that hare-raising meeting.

By the way, when you switch from one application to another, you don't need to save what you're doing. As soon as you put something in your PalmPilot, it's automatically saved; you don't need to do anything further.

If the program you want to run doesn't have a button—or if you prefer doing things differently, just for the heck of it—you can instead tap on the **Applications** button, which brings you back to the Application Launcher screen. Then you can tap on the program you want to run from there. Again, you don't need to save what you're doing.

If you've installed a lot of extra software into your PalmPilot (see Chapter 20, "Installing New Software on Your PalmPilot," for information on how to do so), all those cute little icons might take up more than one screen. If they do, you can scroll through them by using the scroll buttons or by tapping on the scrollbar on the right side of the screen to scroll through them.

You can easily jump straight to the application you want to run.

If you have more than a screen full of applications you want to run, scrolling down until you find the one you want to run can be a pain. A simpler solution is to write the first letter of the application in the Graffiti area of your PalmPilot. The Launcher then immediately jumps to the icon of the first application that begins with that letter.

If you're not the visual type, you might like to see your applications in a list-kind of format, like that shown in the following figure. As you can see, the icons in this format aren't merely tiny, they're teeny-tiny. This view is especially good if you have several applications installed because then they all fit on one screen.

Lots of little icons: This list view of the Application Launcher is especially useful if you have a lot of programs installed.

You can easily get your programs in a list like this. From the Application Launcher screen, tap on the **Menu** button. From the **Options** menu, choose **Preferences**. Then tap on the triangle, and choose **List**, as you can see in the following figure.

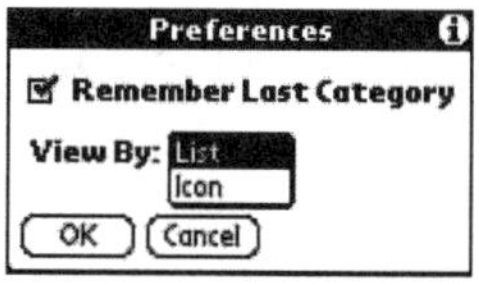

You can get your applications to show up in the list view by choosing this option.

By the way, the PalmPilot offers a very powerful way for you to group applications that you often use in concert with another. You can group them by categories and then view only programs in that particular category, putting the rest temporarily out of view.

For example, say that when you travel, you mainly use the email program, Expense, Memo Pad, and Date Book, but you rarely use any other applications. When you travel, working would be much easier if you didn't have to scroll and search through other applications to find the ones you use the most. By categorizing these four applications into a Travel group, you can show only those that you need when you're traveling. And if, for example, when you do your expense reports, you use only Expense, Calculator, and Date Book, you can group them into an Expense group. To learn how to group applications this way, turn to Chapter 9, "Using PalmPilot Categories to Organize Your Life," and Chapter 21, "Customizing Your PalmPilot for the Way You Live and Work."

Tracking Names and Addresses with the Address Book

I used to own a Rolodex. It was so fat, and had names crossed out and scribbled back in so many times, and was filled with so many sticky notes and misalphabetized business cards that I stopped using it. I cringed every time I looked at the ugly, unwieldy, unusable thing.

Then the PalmPilot came along, and I was an immediate convert. Its Address Book is everything a Rolodex should be: You can track every piece of information about someone, including not just the basics such as name, address, and phone number, but also email address, pager number, and mobile phone number.

Better yet, it's easy to search; you don't have to search only by last name. If all you remember about someone is the name of the company he or she works for, type the company name in Find, and you get full contact information for that person.

What are custom fields in the Address Book?

On the Options menu of the Address Book is a confusing menu item: Rename Custom Fields. What in the world, you're probably wondering, is a *custom field*? The Address Book contains categories of information you can enter about each of your contacts—such as Last Name, First Name, Company, and so on. Each of these categories is called a *field*. If you want to enter a category of information that's not already listed, you can create a custom field for it; for example, you can create a custom field for Web page addresses so that you can have at hand the Web addresses of businesses and individuals.

To run the Address Book, tap on its icon, or press the button with the picture of a telephone on it. You then see the following screen.

Like a Rolodex, but much better: the PalmPilot's Address Book.

For more information about using the Address Book to help you keep track of all your contacts, turn to Chapter 12, "Keeping Track of Contacts with the Address Book."

Some people find that they can more easily type in their contacts on their desktop computer and then use HotSync to get those contacts into their PalmPilot than they can enter those contacts right into the PalmPilot. Turn to Chapter 5, "Keeping Your Life in Sync: HotSyncing Your PC and PalmPilot," for more information on how to use HotSync.

A Calculating Mind: Using the Calculator

Quick, what's 86,432.4 times 9.9? Got you, didn't I? If you had a PalmPilot in hand right now, you would know the answer. (No, you don't need to do the numbers; the answer is 855,680.76.)

The PalmPilot works just like a normal calculator. The buttons are even large enough so that if you're so inclined, you can press them with your fingers instead of the stylus. (I don't suggest using your fingers after you've just eaten a sticky dessert, though. You'll gunk up your screen.) The Calculator's great for figuring tips, for example, and it's especially useful when you travel and need help with your expense report.

One great thing about the Calculator is that you can use it to paste the results of calculations into notes, memos, expense reports, and anything else you create on the PalmPilot—and again, you'll probably use it most when doing expense reports. To paste the results of a calculation into Expense, for example, you would proceed this way. After you've done the calculation, tap on the **Menu** button, and choose **Copy** from the **Edit** menu. You've now put the number into the PalmPilot's built-in Clipboard. Now switch over to Expense, and tap on the spot where you want to put the number. Next, tap on the **Menu** button, and choose **Paste** from the **Edit** menu. Voilá! Your number is in there.

You can correct number entry mistakes without having to start your calculations over.

Talk about frustrating. You've just typed in a string of calculations and realized that the last number you typed was wrong. Time to start over at the beginning...or is it? Not if you use the CE button on the Calculator. When you tap the **CE** button, it erases the last number you put in and puts the correct number you input into its place. For example, if you tap **56 + 817 × 978** but realize that you meant to type 988, you can tap the **CE** button and then **988**, and your calculation would be the one you want.

A little-known feature of the Calculator is that you can see a record of your most recent calculations. Tap on the **Menu** button, and choose **Recent Calculations** from the **Options** menu. You then see a list of your most recent calculations, as shown in the following figure.

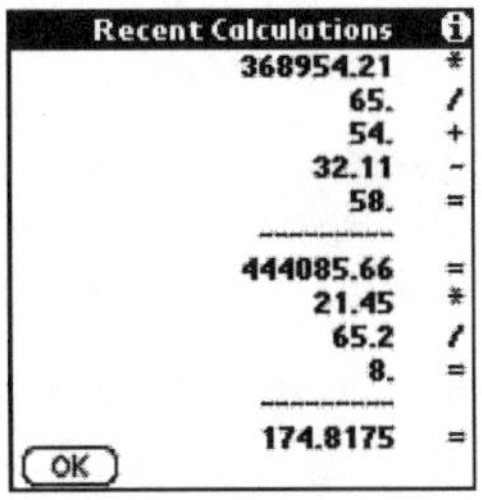

You can easily see a record of your most recent calculations in the Calculator.

Keeping Your Schedule with the Date Book

How can you be in two places at one time if you're not anywhere at all? If you've asked yourself that question or one like it, you need the Date Book. For the time-stressed and calendar-driven, it's a lifesaver.

You can schedule appointments easily. You also can easily schedule events or appointments that occur on a regular basis, such as a weekly staff meeting, a monthly luncheon, or a budget meeting that takes place on the third Thursday of every month.

Using the Date Book, you can look at your calendar either by the day, the week, or the month so that you can easily see schedules either up close or over the long haul. This way, you can easily spot conflicts as well. The following figure shows the weekly view.

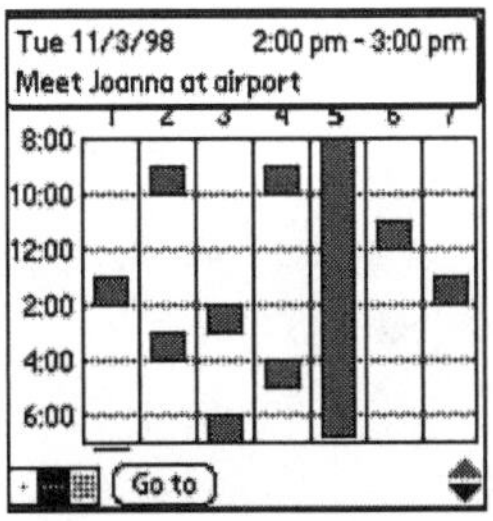

You've got the whole week in your hands: the weekly view in the Date Book.

You also can create reminders about things that happen on a specific day of the year, such as your mother-in-law's birthday. (Maybe that's something that you would prefer *not* to remember, though.)

The Date Book lets you attach notes to events as well. So, for example, if you've thought of a great birthday present for your mother-in-law, such as five pounds of rutabagas, tap in a note next to her birthday, and then get set to go to the grocery store.

Best of all, you can set alarms to remind you when events are about to occur. That way, you should never again be late for the monthly meeting of Root Vegetable Lovers Anonymous (RVLA).

For more information about how to keep your life on schedule using the Date Book, turn to Chapter 11, "Juggling Your Busy Schedule with the Date Book."

Tracking Expenses with Expense

Money, money, money. It may be the root of all evil, but for most people, to quote those famous philosophers, the Beatles, "That's what I want."

You might need to track your expenses to fill out your expense account at work, to prepare your own tax records because you run your own business, to track your family budget, or maybe for the heck of it because that's the kind of person you are.

Expense makes it easier to track your expenses for any reason at all. I've found it especially useful when traveling on business. Normally, when I travel, I shove all my receipts into my wallet, and two weeks after I return home, I dig through the wallet, pulling out bits and scraps of paper, trying to reconstruct my expenses for my expense account. This system never works. I'm always out money because I always forget to put down some expenses.

Thanks to the PalmPilot, I don't have that problem any longer. Whenever I spend anything, I immediately whip out my little digital helper and tap in the details about what I've spent. Then, when I return home, I sync my PalmPilot with my computer, send all my expenses into an Excel spreadsheet, and get my expense report, ready to be filed.

With Expense, you can track expenses every which way from Sunday, and then some. The following are some of the ways you can use this feature:

What if your company requires a specific format for filing expense reports?

Some companies require that expense reports be in a specific format, or even in a specific spreadsheet. Not to worry: You can customize the spreadsheet that your expenses get exported to when they get synced over to your computer. Turn to Chapter 14, "Time Is Money: Tracking Your Expenses with the PalmPilot," for details.

- You can track expenses by category, such as by a specific trip, kind of expense (such as meals), or any other category you can dream up.
- You can track expenses by companies you deal with and individuals at those companies.

- You can track which payment method you use to pay each individual expense.
- You can see how much in expenses you've spent between certain dates.
- You can record expenses in the local currency of the country you're visiting. (Say hello to the Eiffel Tower for me.)
- You can sync all your expense information with an Excel spreadsheet on your computer and massage that information any way you want.
- Let me put it this way: You can pretty much track your expenses any way you want.

The following figure shows an example of a single expense being recorded.

I love New York: Tracking expenses paid for a big meal in the Big Apple.

Syncing Up Your Life with HotSync

The great odds are, you use a computer as well as a PalmPilot. When you're sitting at your computer, you would like to be able to add contacts, keep track of your to-dos, and schedule your time from your computer. When you're not at your computer, you probably want to do all that in your PalmPilot.

This scenario sounds like a recipe for disaster. (Just add salt, a pinch of pepper, and some marjoram. Stir well.) How will you get information back and forth, and make sure everything on both your computer and PalmPilot are up-to-date and in sync?

Enter HotSync. This clever, exceedingly useful feature of the PalmPilot does what it says: It synchronizes all the information between your PalmPilot and your computer. It shuttles all the information in your Date Book, Address Book, To-Do List, Memo Pad, and Expense back and forth between the two so that they're identical. It does so by using the cradle to exchange information between your PalmPilot and your Palm Desktop software on your computer (which I'll cover in Chapter 6, "Oh, Yeah…You Have a Computer, Too. Using the Palm Desktop.")

Syncing your PalmPilot like this has a very big extra benefit as well: It means that you can always have a copy of your information somewhere, in case disaster strikes. So, for example, if for some reason you have to do a hard reset on your PalmPilot (don't even *think* of that happening), and your entire life vanishes—all the contacts, memos, to-dos, appointments, and everything else—you don't need to worry because all the information is there on your Palm Desktop. Just do a HotSync after the hard reset, and you don't lose an iota of data.

What's a conduit?

HotSync works by syncing data from each of the programs on your PalmPilot—Date Book, Address Book, and so on—with data from the same program on the Palm Desktop. You can customize how it syncs data from each of those programs so that it might sync data from your Address Book differently from how it syncs data from your Date Book. Each of these individual synchronizations is a piece of software called a *conduit*, so you have a Date Book conduit, an Address Book conduit, and so on. You can also buy separate conduits that sync your PalmPilot with personal information managers such as Outlook.

For more information on how to use HotSync, turn to Chapter 5, "Keeping Your Life in Sync: HotSyncing Your PC and PalmPilot."

Staying in Touch with Mail

Mail is one of the odder programs on the PalmPilot. On one hand, it does what it says: It lets you read email and create email messages. On the other hand, it does so in a truly peculiar way. You can't use the PalmPilot to connect to the Internet to send and receive email with Mail. Instead, you have to HotSync Mail with your computer's email program, and that email program sends and receives mail. The whole process is kind of like a relay race.

Despite that, Mail can be a very useful program. It's ideal to use when you're traveling, for example, and want to catch up on writing or reading email. Before you leave on your trip, sync Mail with your desktop computer to get all your latest email messages into your PalmPilot. Then, when you're on your plane or train or boat or rickshaw, read the messages on your PalmPilot and respond to them. When you get to your computer, sync everything back up, and your mail is sent using your normal email program.

One of Mail's better features is its capability to grab email addresses out of your Address Book. With a few taps of your stylus, you can get an address automatically. Mail also lets you group messages into categories that you create—for example, Personal and Sales and Follow-Up (in essence, any categories you want). It also includes many of the features you would expect in an email program, such as being able to send blind copies (no, they're not copies that need seeing-eye dogs; it means that the primary recipient doesn't know you're sending the message to other people). The following figure shows you some of the sending options you have with Mail.

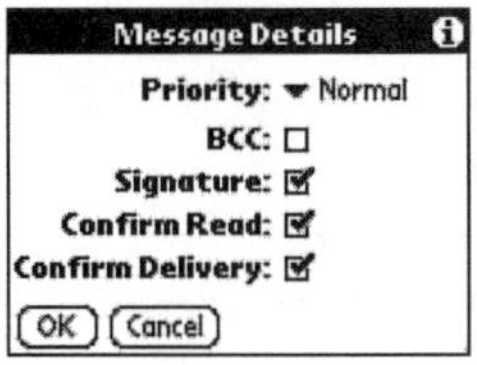

Mail gives you many of the features you would expect in a fully featured email program, such as all kinds of options covering sending messages.

For more information about using Mail, turn to Chapter 16, "How to Stay in Touch with Email."

You can get add-on programs that can send and receive email from your PalmPilot.

Although Mail can't directly send and receive email from your PalmPilot, several programs can, if you use your PalmPilot with a modem. You can buy a snap-on modem or a special cable to connect your PalmPilot to a normal external modem. Popular PalmPilot email programs include MultiMail and HandMail. You can try both for free at `www.palmpilotsoftware.com` before deciding whether to buy them.

Jotting Notes with the Memo Pad

I'm always getting ideas at odd times. When I wake from a dream at 4 a.m. When I'm about to start my car to drive to work. Right after a workout at the swim club. (Actually, I usually get my ideas at the swim club while I'm swimming, but because the PalmPilot doesn't yet come with a waterproof case, the pool is about the only place I can't bring it.)

My PalmPilot is always at hand, so when inspiration strikes (or when I think of a more mundane matter, like putting together a grocery list), I can whip out the Memo Pad and tap, tap, tap away to my heart's content.

You don't need to tap on New to create a new item in the Memo Pad, To-Do, and Date Book.

Instead, use this timesaving tip. Just start entering text by writing with your stylus on the Graffiti area. When you do that, a new item is automatically created, with the text in it that you've entered.

The Memo Pad is great for jotting down ideas, thoughts, lists, and notes of all kinds. You can easily categorize the notes so that finding any of them is easy; for example, you might have a category for budget memos, one for school-related memos, one for travel-related memos, and so on.

What makes the Memo Pad most useful is that you can easily paste memos into other places in your PalmPilot. For example, if you put together a memo about your next year's budget, you can paste the memo into a note that you attach to your budget meeting schedule in the Date Book. To paste a memo into another note or program, tap on the **Menu** button when you're in Memo Pad, and choose **Copy** from the **Edit** menu. Then switch to the place where you want to paste the memo, tap on the **Menu** button, and choose **Paste** from the **Edit** menu. That's it. You're done.

For more information about using the Memo Pad, turn to Chapter 10, "Write On! Taking Notes with the Memo Pad."

Customizing Your PalmPilot with Preferences

One of the reasons that you can organize your life with the PalmPilot is that it's so flexible; you can customize just about every aspect of the way it works. In Chapter 3, "Time for Takeoff: Starting Your PalmPilot for the First Time," you saw how to customize the basic functions of the PalmPilot. But you can customize just about anything you can imagine about the PalmPilot—everything from the way buttons work to which day the week starts. (Yes, it's true. You can have your week start on either a Sunday or a Monday. How's that for power?)

You do much of your customizing from the Preferences screen, shown in the following figure.

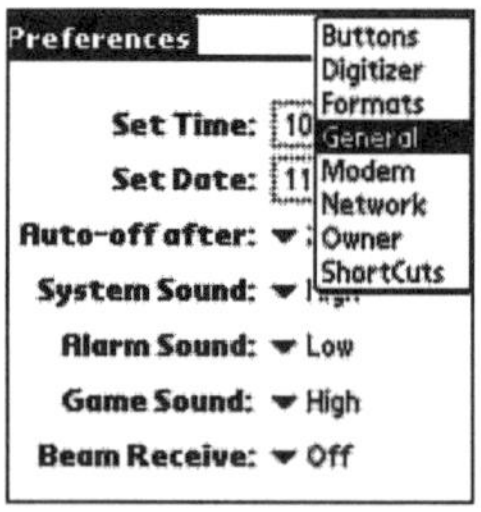

Bend your PalmPilot to your will from the Preferences screen.

For more information about how to customize your PalmPilot, turn to Chapter 21, "Customizing Your PalmPilot for the Way You Live and Work."

Keeping Safe with Security

Your whole life is locked inside your little digital companion. The last thing you want is to have prying eyes peeping in there.

Security gives you two ways to keep your information private:

- You can mark specific information as "private" so that no one except you—or someone you've given a password to—can read it.
- You can password-protect your PalmPilot so that only you—or someone you've given your password to—can run the PalmPilot.

You do both things by using Security, shown in the following figure. Tap on **Hide** to allow you to keep certain information private; then tap on the **Unassigned** box next to Password, and enter a password that will unlock those private records. Then, when you're creating a piece of information, you can mark it private, and only someone with access to your password can read those records.

Protecting your privacy with Security.

Keeping Track of Important Tasks with the To-Do List

How much do you have to get done in a given day? If you're like me and most people, just beginning to think about it all makes your head spin. Work, family, entertainment, recreation, grocery shopping...too much to do, too little time, and too few spare brain cells to keep track of it all. It's enough to make you want to retire to a monastery.

The PalmPilot's To-Do List may not be able to give you any extra brain cells, but I can vouch from personal experience that it certainly feels like it does. Use this feature, and no longer will your life make you feel as if you've been lifted up by a tornado and are being spun at high speed across the U.S. Plains. I can't vouch that it will make your life less complicated, but I can tell you that you'll at least be able to know all the things you have to get done—and maybe your head and entire body won't spin quite so fast.

So how can the To-Do List do all this for you? The following are some of the ways it can help:

- **You can set priorities for every one of your tasks.** That way, the most important ones show up at the top of your list and the least important ones at the bottom.
- **You can group them into categories, such as Personal, Budget, Travel, and so on.** This way, instead of having a huge, daunting To-Do List so big you'll never start on it, you can break it down into smaller, doable tasks in specific certain portions of your life.

- **You can assign due dates for your tasks.** As anyone who's ever created a To-Do List knows, you can easily let all your to-dos slide so that they never get done. Assigning due dates reminds you when they need to be done—and prods you into action.
- **You can view your to-dos in many different ways, such as by due date, by category, and by their priority level.** Need to find out everything in your life that needs to get done on a specific day? No problem. How about seeing all the top priority items? It can be done. And you can easily view them all by categories as well.

The following figure shows an example of a To-Do List sorted by category—in this case, Personal.

Yes, picking up your daughter from her ballet class today is more important than taking your rabbit to the vet. How do you know? The To-Do List tells you.

The Least You Need to Know

- You can group programs into categories in the Application Launcher to make it easier to find the programs you want to run.
- You can set alarms in the Date Book to remind you when important events are about to occur.
- When you travel, you should write down your expenses as soon as you get them to make it easier to create expense reports with Expense.
- You can paste entire memos from the Memo Pad into any event or document on the PalmPilot.
- If you're worried about your personal privacy, you can password-protect your PalmPilot and also hide certain pieces of information stored on it.
- By grouping To-Do List items into categories, you'll find that keeping track of everything that needs to be done is easier.

Chapter 5

Keeping Your Life in Sync: HotSyncing Your PC and PalmPilot

In This Chapter

- Understanding how HotSync works
- Installing the Palm Desktop software for the PC and the Mac
- Performing your first HotSync
- Customizing HotSync for the way you work

Your computer and your PalmPilot. They go together like Abbott and Costello. Like love and marriage. Like a horse and a carriage. Any time, any weather, your computer and your PalmPilot go together—to coin a phrase.

Of course, if you really wanted to, you could use your PalmPilot all by its lonesome. You could just pack it in your pocket and tap away whenever the urge hit. In fact, if you don't own a computer, that's the only way you can use it.

If you do have a computer, though, you'll soon find that using your computer and your PalmPilot together is helpful. That way, when you're sitting at your computer, you can enter information, and when you're away from your computer with your PalmPilot, you can enter data there. You then can get them to trade information back and forth—*HotSync* it, in PalmPilot parlance—and you've synced their data so that they each have the same information on them.

HotSyncing provides an extra benefit beyond making your life easier (which it most certainly does). It also ensures that you have a backup of everything in your PalmPilot. That way, if your PalmPilot goes kablooey (*kablooey:* technical term for "crash and burn"), and you lose all your data, you don't need to consider committing hara-kiri; instead, you can just HotSync all your data from your PC to your PalmPilot, and it's as good as new. I've had to do back up this way a few times myself, so believe me, it's a lifesaver. I haven't had to commit hara-kiri yet. I've got my fingers crossed.

In this chapter, I show you how to set up your cradle for HotSyncing, how to install the software you need to HotSync, and then finally, how to do the deed. Along the way, you get some inside tips to help you customize the HotSync for the way you work.

Understanding HotSync

HotSyncing is an amazing process. It's the closest thing I can think of to *Star Trek*'s Vulcan Mind Meld ("emafa suru" in the Vulcan language, by the way—but unfortunately the Vulcan language has no words for HotSync, so I can't show off any more of my extraterrestrial linguistic ability.)

When you HotSync, your PalmPilot and computer do some pretty neat magic. Every single piece of information on the PalmPilot and the computer is compared to one another, and then information is exchanged. At the end of the process, all the data matches. So, for example, if you've put three new contacts into your PalmPilot, you've put two new meetings into your PC, you've deleted a memo on your PalmPilot, and you've changed the category of a To-Do item, HotSync looks at all those changes and keeps the information on both the PC and PalmPilot up-to-date and matching.

First, Connect the HotSync Cradle to Your PC

Your PalmPilot needs some way to connect to your computer so that they can HotSync—and that's where the cradle comes in. It's a little plastic device that connects your PalmPilot to your computer. Before you can start to install the HotSync software, you have to connect your cradle to your computer.

A long wire snakes out of the PalmPilot cradle, and it has a plug at the end of it. Take that plug, and connect it to the serial port on your computer, after turning off your PC. Now you're ready to start installing your HotSync software—after you turn your PC back on, that is.

Well, *maybe* you can start installing your HotSync software. You might have a problem, though. Most serial ports have 9 holes in them, and the 9 pins on the plug on the end of the cradle's wire fit neatly into them. However, you may have a serial port with 25 pins instead of 9. (Thank you, computer engineers, for figuring out such thoughtful ways to waste our time and make all our lives more difficult. What would we ever do without you?)

Hold on, though; don't despair. Luckily, this problem has a simple answer. Inside the box that your PalmPilot came in is a little doohickey (*doohickey:* a technical term for a widget-like thing) that you can attach to the cradle's plug. One end of the doohickey connects to the plug. The other end, which has 25 pins on it, attaches to a 25-pin serial port. Success! Now you're ready to install the software.

What's a computer's serial port?

A computer needs some way to connect to other devices like modems and mice, so it uses a serial port. Data travels back and forth along the serial port one piece of information—or bit—at a time (although at very high speeds). That's why it's called a *serial port;* communication takes place serially, one piece of information after another.

I'm Glad *That's* Over. Now Can We Start Installing the Software?

For your PalmPilot to HotSync with your computer, you're going to have to install the Palm Desktop software. Installing any software is never any fun, but you'll find that installing this software is easier than most. Still, you might want to follow the four steps I always take before installing any software for the first time:

1. Take a deep breath.
2. Say a silent prayer.
3. Quit any programs running on your PC, including virus scanners and screen savers.
4. Pop the CD into your CD drive.

There, that wasn't so hard, was it? When you put the CD into the drive, a Palm Desktop Installer menu appears. Click **Install**, and you get the usual kind of Welcome message that you get with most software. Then the installation begins. Unlike most software you'll use, this software is easy and straightforward. Just follow the recommendations and defaults, and you'll be fine. When you're done, Palm Desktop will be ready to run. As with any other program, you can run it by double-clicking its desktop icon.

Techno Talk

Save PC disk space by not installing the Palm Quick Tour.

When you install the Palm Desktop software, you're given the option of whether to install the Palm Quick Tour, which is basically an introduction to the PalmPilot. I find it not at all useful and a waste of hard disk space. Consider not installing it to save some space.

You should know a few details about the Palm Desktop installation. You should keep in mind these points:

- Your cradle should be connected to your PC before you begin.
- You'll be asked to type in a username. You don't have to use your real name; you can make up one (Rumplestiltskin might be a good one), or use a name such as Preston's PalmPilot.
- Make sure to put your PalmPilot into the cradle when you're prompted. The software needs to test the connection between your computer and PalmPilot before it can finish the installation.
- If you don't set up PalmPilot Mail during installation, you can always do so at some later time.

Techno Talk

What's the Palm Desktop software?

The Palm Desktop software that runs on your computer matches the software that runs on your PalmPilot. In Palm Desktop, you can find an Address Book, a Date Book, and so on. You can put information into these programs, and when you do a HotSync, that information is transferred to your PalmPilot. Likewise, when you put information into your PalmPilot, that information is put into your Palm Desktop; that way, your data matches on your computer and your PalmPilot.

Hold On a Minute Here. I Use a *Mac!*

Whoa! Sorry about that. Didn't mean to offend you. If you're a Mac user, you install the Palm Desktop and HotSync almost identically to the method used if you're a PC user, outlined in the preceding section. However, you need to know a few additional points:

- The software you need for your Mac, Pilot Desktop for the Macintosh, doesn't come on the CD that ships with the PalmPilot. (You've always known about the conspiracy against Mac owners. Here's the proof!) You have to buy the MacPac from 3COM to get the software. It costs $15. Go to `www.palmpilot.com` for details.

- If you use Pilot Desktop 1.0, and you've upgraded to the Mac OS 8.5, Pilot Desktop might not work. You need to get a copy of MacPac 2. Head to `www.palmpilot.com` for details.
- The Mac has two serial ports: one for a printer and one for a modem. You can connect the cradle to either port, using the special adapter included in the MacPac. If you have an internal modem, you probably have a modem port free, so use it. If not, you're probably going to have to take turns plugging and unplugging your cradle and either printer or modem into a port. Bad news, but it's worth the effort.

Using HotSync for the First Time

Before you can HotSync for the first time, you need to perform three tasks:

- Make sure your cradle is connected to your computer.
- Put your PalmPilot into the cradle. To put your PalmPilot into the cradle, you slide it onto the cradle, making sure that the connector on the bottom of the cradle fits neatly into the slot on the bottom of the PalmPilot.
- Run the HotSync Manager software.

When you installed the Palm Desktop software, you also installed the HotSync Manager software. Next, let me describe how to use it.

Make sure to turn off AppleTalk.

If you plan to plug your cradle into the Mac printer port, make sure to turn off AppleTalk; otherwise, it won't work. AppleTalk is the Mac's feature for networking and using a laser printer. If you don't use a laser printer, you might have it turned off already. Check before installing.

Using the HotSync Manager Software

When the HotSync Manager runs on your computer, it just sits there, doing nothing most of the time, waiting for something to happen. (That reminds me of the old Woody Allen line that 90 percent of life consists of just showing up.)

What HotSync is doing is waiting for the PalmPilot to start talking to it. After it detects the PalmPilot trying to communicate, it springs into action, shuttling data back and forth between your computer and your PalmPilot.

You can set up HotSync in the following ways. How you set it up depends on how often you synchronize your PC and PalmPilot.

- **HotSync Manager runs all the time.** You can have HotSync Manager running all the time on your computer, from the moment you turn it on until the moment you turn it off. The good part about this arrangement is that you never need to remember to turn on HotSync Manager; it's always there waiting (and waiting and waiting and waiting...). The bad thing about it is that HotSync Manager is using up your computer memory all day long, even though you may use it for only three minutes in the entire day. I recommend you use this option only if you spend a lot of time HotSyncing. Otherwise, you're using up precious system memory for no good reason. Of course, if you're absent-minded, you might want to use this option as well, because then you'll never be forced to remember to run the program.

- **HotSync Manager runs whenever you run Palm Desktop.** With this option, HotSync hardly ever runs; it's sitting there waiting only when you run the Palm Desktop. If you use the Palm Desktop regularly, this is a good option to choose.
- **HotSync Manager runs only when you specifically tell it to.** With this option, you have to remember to turn on HotSync Manager whenever you want to do a HotSync. It does mean that you don't use any memory most of the day because the program isn't running most of the day. It's the option I use because I usually HotSync about two to three times a day and often don't run the Palm Desktop.

To customize how you want HotSync to run, double-click the Palm Desktop and choose **Setup** from the **HotSync** menu. You then see the following dialog box. Choose the option you want, click **OK**, and you're ready to roll.

Waiting, waiting, waiting...Here, you can tell HotSync Manager when it should run on your computer and when it should go away.

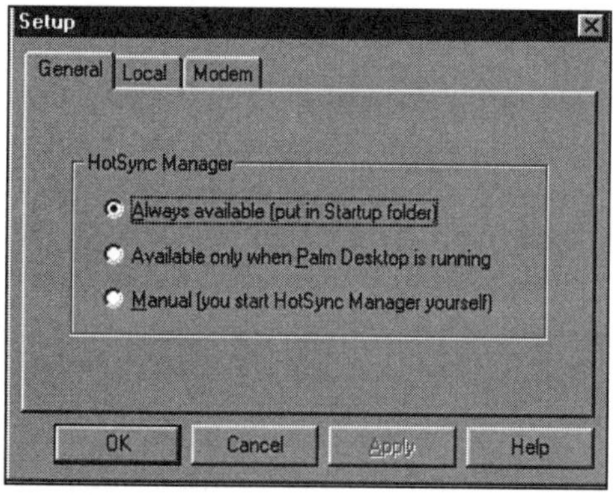

Put a shortcut to the HotSync Manager on your desktop.

If you choose the option of having the HotSync Manager run only when you tell it, let me tell you a quick way to get to the program whenever you want: Put a shortcut to it on your desktop. To add a shortcut, in Explorer, go to the \Palm directory. Right-click the hotsync.exe file. Choose **Create Shortcut** from the menu that appears. Then drag the shortcut (it appears at the bottom of the directory) onto your desktop. Now, whenever you want to run the HotSync Manager, it's there waiting for you.

Doing Your First HotSync

Whichever way you decide to use HotSync Manager, make sure it's running. Then put your PalmPilot in its cradle, but you don't need to bother to turn it on. It's finally the moment you've been waiting for—time to do your first HotSync.

Now that you're all set up, be prepared to do one of the simplest tasks in the entire computer world. Here you go: Press on the little button on the base of the cradle. That's it. You don't need to do another single thing. You've just initiated your first HotSync. When you do a HotSync for the first time, you are asked the name of the PalmPilot you want to sync with. Your name is listed there, so choose it.

Thereafter, whenever you HotSync, you'll see a screen like the following to show that the PalmPilot is connecting with your computer.

Making the connection: what you see on your PalmPilot when you start a HotSync.

As your HotSync proceeds, it copies information back and forth between your PalmPilot and your computer. It tells you what it's doing, too; the PalmPilot screen and the computer screen both tell you what application they're synchronizing—Memo Pad, To-Do, and so forth. Watching this process is kind of like watching a tennis match, but without the pock, pock, pock of the ball on the court. The following screen illustrates what your PC tells you as it's synchronizing Expense information.

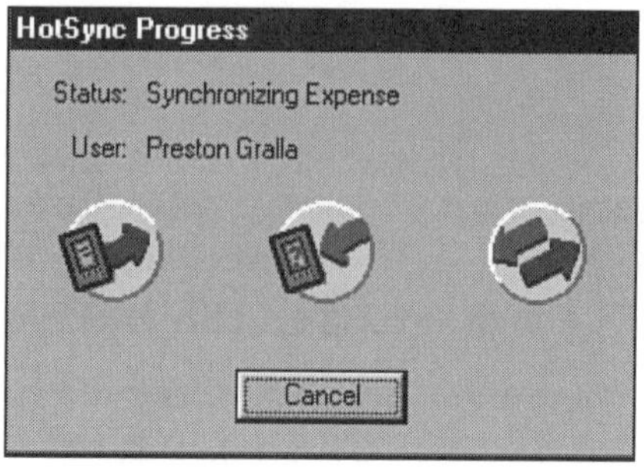

HotSync doing its work of synchronizing data between your computer and your PalmPilot.

After the synchronization is done, you see a screen, like the one on the left, telling you that the HotSync is complete. If you experience a problem of some kind, instead you see a screen like the one on the right. For advice on what to do if something goes wrong with a HotSync, turn to Chapter 24, "Cures for the PalmPilot's Most Common Problems."

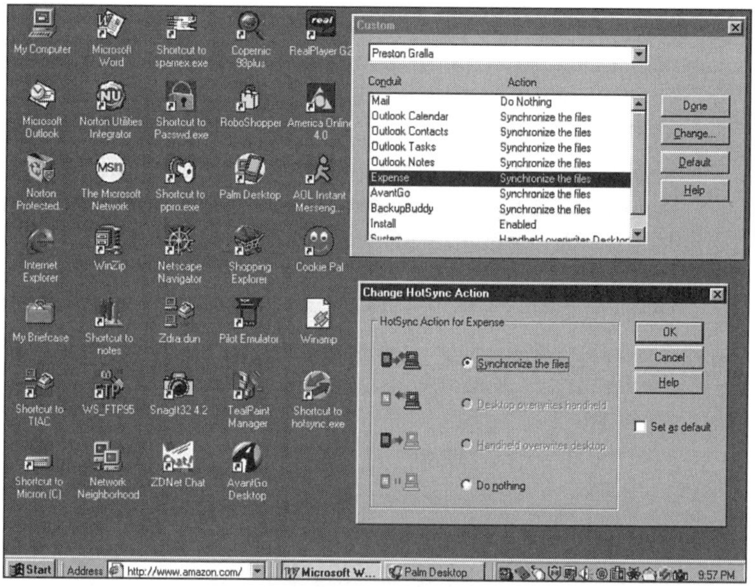

Congratulations, your HotSync has gone well.

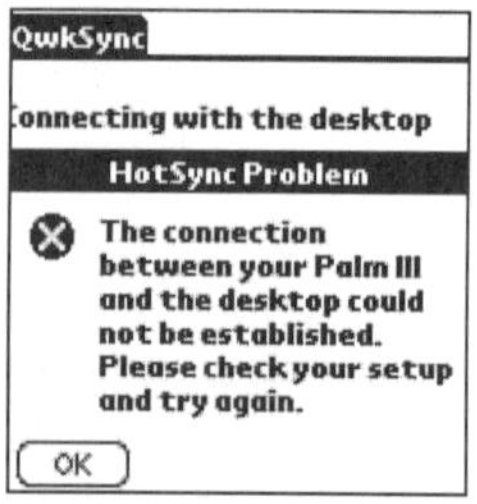

You get the booby prize: Something's gone wrong.

Customizing HotSync for the Way You Work

Normally, when you do a HotSync, data flows in both directions: Whatever you've put into your PalmPilot gets sent to your computer, and whatever you've put into your computer gets sent to your PalmPilot. And *everything* gets synchronized—your Memo Pad, your Contacts, your To-Do List—the whole schmear (that's Yiddish for the whole nine yards).

However, you don't have to be straightjacketed like this. Remember what I told you in Chapter 3, "Time for Takeoff: Starting Your PalmPilot for the First Time." You can be master of the cosmos, or at least czar of your PalmPilot. You can make this little puppy jump through hoops.

Notice that HotSyncs can take several minutes, which can be annoying if all you want to do is synchronize the Memo Pad so that you can get into the computer the memo you just wrote about the crying need for grilled goat to be a choice for lunch every day in the company cafeteria.

To customize HotSync, you customize what are called *conduits*. A conduit is a connection that governs a specific kind of information. The To-Do List has its own conduit, the Memo Pad has its conduit, and so on. You can customize each of these conduits by turning some off and some on, for example.

To customize the conduits, run Palm Desktop, and then choose **Custom** from the **HotSync** menu. You get a list of all your conduits. The main way you customize these conduits is to turn off some of them. When you turn them off, the HotSync goes faster, so the rest of your information gets synchronized more quickly.

You can HotSync your PalmPilot and PC via long distance.

If you need to do a HotSync while you're traveling, you can still get to the computer in your office. To do so, you can hook up a modem to your PalmPilot and have it dial into your PC at the office and do a HotSync. Everything works pretty much the same, except that the data transfer is slower.

To turn off a conduit, highlight it and then click **Change**. You then see a figure like the following. Choose **Do Nothing**. (Choosing Nothing is always a safe choice for most anything in life, I've found. Life is so much more peaceful that way.) The next time you do a HotSync, that conduit won't be synchronized, and the HotSync will go much more quickly. By the way, when you turn off a conduit like this, you change it only for the next HotSync. The time you HotSync after that, the conduit will go back to HotSyncing. If you want to change the conduit from now on, click the box that says **Set as Default**. From then on, the conduit won't be HotSynced. You can also customize your HotSyncs so that you can synchronize your PalmPilot information with personal information managers such as Outlook. I show you how to do that later in this chapter.

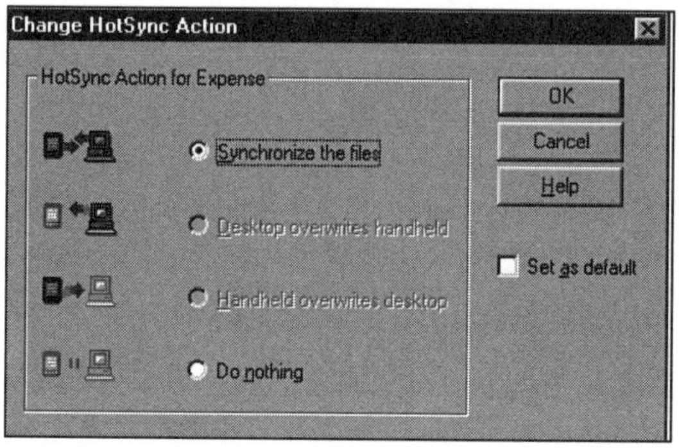

Here, you can customize the way HotSync works.

Changing the Direction of the HotSync

HotSyncs normally flow in both directions. Sometimes, though, you might want the data on your PalmPilot to overwrite the data on your computer, or vice versa. For example, if you accidentally delete all your appointments on your Palm Desktop Date Book, when you do a normal HotSync, all those appointments are wiped out on your PalmPilot. True, that's one way to simplify your life, but your boss may not appreciate your missing your weekly meeting with him, and your spouse certainly won't appreciate your forgetting to pick him or her up after work for a candlelight dinner.

So what can you do? You can tell the conduit for Date Book to have the information in your PalmPilot overwrite the information in your computer. That way, the information on it is up-to-date. For any conduit, you can tell it to have information on the PalmPilot overwrite information on your PC, you can have information on the PC overwrite information in your PalmPilot, or you can synchronize the two, which is the default. And, of course, you can simply turn off the conduit.

Before changing the direction of a conduit, check, check, and check again.

You can accidentally wipe out data on a part of your PalmPilot if you change a conduit incorrectly. If you accidentally delete data in your Address Book on your computer, for both example, and you tell the conduit to have the computer overwrite the PalmPilot, you wipe out vital information. So, whenever you change a conduit, check, check, and check again.

Customizing HotSync for Personal Information Managers

The Palm Desktop is a nice piece of software, but the truth is, it's not as powerful or useful as personal information management software such as Microsoft Outlook or ACT.

This lack of power puts you in a bind. What if you've been using or want to use one of these programs, and you have a PalmPilot? How in the world are you going to get information back and forth between them and your PalmPilot?

Luckily for you (and me), getting information back and forth is easy. Specialized conduits can be created to synchronize information between your PalmPilot and your personal information manager. That way, every time you do a HotSync, data is shuttled back and forth, just like it normally is with the Palm Desktop.

Keep in mind that you have to buy these specialized conduits. Many are available. I use one called Desktop to Go that's been specifically designed to work with Outlook. Others also work with Outlook and other personal information managers. A few popular ones are Intellisync and Pilot Mirror. The following figure shows Desktop to Go.

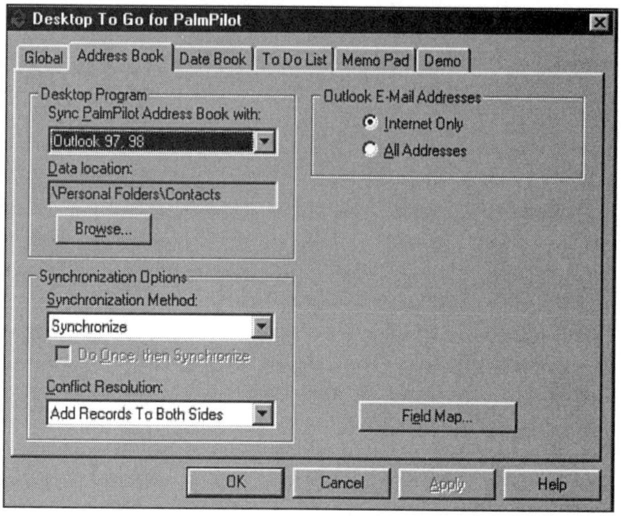

You can HotSync personal information managers such as Outlook to your PalmPilot with software like Desktop to Go.

The Least You Need to Know

- Before you can do a HotSync, you have to install the Palm Desktop software and connect the cradle to your computer.
- If you do frequent HotSyncs, you should keep the HotSync Manager running at all times. Otherwise, consider turning it on manually every time you do a HotSync.
- To speed up HotSyncs, turn off conduits you don't need.
- If you accidentally delete data on your Palm Desktop software, change a conduit so that information from the PalmPilot overwrites information on the computer. If you accidentally delete data from the PalmPilot, change a conduit so that the computer overwrites the PalmPilot.
- You can buy specialized conduits that synchronize your PalmPilot with personal information software such as Outlook and ACT.

Chapter 6

Oh, Yeah...You Have a Computer, Too. Using the Palm Desktop

In This Chapter

- Why you should use the Palm Desktop and when
- How to use the Palm Desktop's Address Book, Memo Pad, To-Do List, and Date Book
- How to drag items into Microsoft Word, Excel, and the Clipboard
- How to print from the Palm Desktop
- How to retrieve items that you've deleted from the PalmPilot or Palm Desktop but saved in an archive

As much as I love my little PalmPilot (top of To-Do List: send it a Valentine this February), I use a computer, too—and the odds are that you do, too. One of the neatest things about the PalmPilot is the way it transfers information back and forth to your computer.

When the PalmPilot shuttles information this way, it's sending stuff and receiving stuff from the Palm Desktop software. The Palm Desktop software does pretty much the same thing that the PalmPilot does: It helps you organize your life. Its main sections—Date Book, Address Book, To-Do, Memo Pad, and Expense—correspond exactly to the main applications of your PalmPilot. When you do a HotSync, all the information in these applications is synced between the PalmPilot and the Palm Desktop.

Even if you rarely use the Palm Desktop, it still can help you get your life under control, when used with the PalmPilot. In this chapter, I tell you all the reasons you should use the software, give you some strategies on when to use the Palm Desktop and when to use the PalmPilot, and give you the complete rundown on how to use the Palm Desktop software.

By the way, Mac people, I know that the Mac version is called the Pilot Desktop, but bear with me here. You've unfortunately gotten used to being in the minority, so what I say for the Palm Desktop holds true for the Pilot Desktop as well.

My PalmPilot Is Perfect. Why Should I Use the Palm Desktop?

No matter how attached you are to your PalmPilot and how much you like using it to the exclusion of anything else, the Palm Desktop can help you get your life under control. The Palm Desktop works with the PalmPilot in the following ways to help you:

- **It provides a convenient way to back up all the data on your PalmPilot.** Like it or not, you might one day need to reset (*reset:* technical term for "do a crash and burn") your PalmPilot, and then you'll lose everything in there. Considering that your whole life is in there, you can't afford to lose everything. When you HotSync with your Palm Desktop, you copy all your information to it. So, if your PalmPilot loses all your data, you can copy all the information from the Palm Desktop to it, and it'll be as good as new.
- **When you're sitting at your computer, using the Palm Desktop is often easier than having to take out your PalmPilot and switch it on.** In that way, it's a time-saver. And isn't saving time one of the main reasons you bought a PalmPilot?

You can use the Palm Desktop to install extra software onto your PalmPilot.

The PalmPilot comes with all the software you need to organize your life. Keep in mind that you can install a lot of other software as well, including software to send faxes, manage projects, and get travel information. Check out the CD at the back of this book for more software. Then head to www.palmpilotsoftware.com for thousands of other pieces of software you can install as well. You install software onto your PalmPilot using a feature of the Palm Desktop. Turn to Chapter 20, "Installing New Software on Your PalmPilot," for information on how to install programs.

- **Inputting text using a keyboard is easier than using Graffiti.** If you need to write a memo or a note that requires a lot of text input, Graffiti isn't particularly easy or convenient. Using the keyboard is much easier and faster.
- **You can keep archived copies of to-dos, memos, and other items that you've deleted on your PalmPilot.** That way, even when you delete items on your PalmPilot to save space and to clean up the clutter, you still have copies of them you can refer to. So should a special prosecutor ask to examine every detail of your private life for the past two years, you'll have records at hand for him to...uh, wait a minute; maybe that's a reason *not* to archive all that stuff. But apart from the problem of special prosecutors (and unless you're the president, you're free and clear), keeping archived items is a good idea, as I explain later in the chapter.
- **You can print from the Palm Desktop.** You can't print from your PalmPilot. So, if you need to print a travel itinerary, for example, you have to use the Palm Desktop. (You can, by the way, buy special software and hardware to let your PalmPilot print, but using the Palm Desktop is easier.)

When Should I Use the PalmPilot and When Should I Use the Palm Desktop?

You would be wise to come up with a smart strategy for deciding when to use the Palm Desktop and when to use the PalmPilot for organizing and planning your life. Otherwise, you'll spend as much time trying to decide which to use as you'll actually spend getting any work done. Follow this advice, and you can't go wrong:

- **If you're writing a memo of more than a sentence or two, use the Palm Desktop.** Using Graffiti is much slower than typing, and you're more prone to making errors when writing by hand.
- **When you need to see names and addresses at the same time you use your Date Book, use the Palm Desktop.** Your computer screen offers you a whole lot more screen real estate than your PalmPilot does. You can see both your Address Book and Date Book at the same time—something you can't do in the PalmPilot.
- **If you tend not to keep the Palm Desktop running most of the time, use your PalmPilot for most tasks.** Doing a few taps with your stylus is much easier than double-clicking an icon to start the Palm Desktop and then hunting and clicking for the program you want to run.
- **Use your PalmPilot for tracking your expenses.** The Expense button on the Palm Desktop doesn't run a program; instead, it launches Excel and puts your PalmPilot Expense data into a spreadsheet. So always use the PalmPilot for expense tracking.

You can use a personal information manager such as Outlook instead of the Palm Desktop.

Outlook and other personal information managers are much better than the Palm Desktop at managing your life. You can use Outlook and other similar software instead of the Palm Desktop. Specialized conduits can HotSync the information between this kind of software and your PalmPilot. See Chapter 5, "Keeping Your Life in Sync: HotSyncing Your PC and PalmPilot," for details. If you do use a personal information manager such as Outlook, you might want to use it instead of the PalmPilot when you're working at your computer because personal information managers often have extra features that the PalmPilot doesn't.

- **If you need to print something, use the Palm Desktop.** The PalmPilot can't print. Enough said.

Touring the Palm Desktop

Although the Palm Desktop works a lot like the PalmPilot, it looks a lot different, as you can see in the following figure.

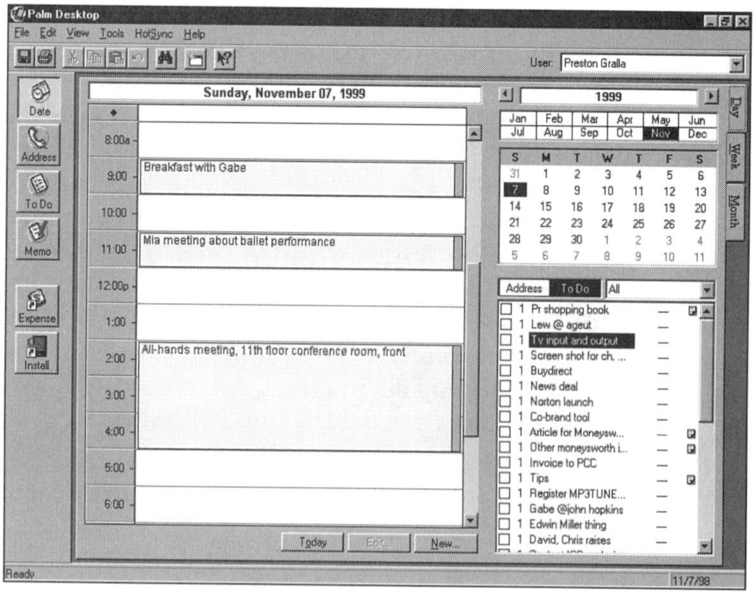

The same, but not the same: The Palm Desktop works much like the PalmPilot but looks completely different.

Down the left side of the screen are the applications you use; just click an icon to run any of them. Across the top of the screen is a toolbar that you use for printing, copying, cutting, pasting, and creating a new item.

As you go merrily clicking away on the Palm Desktop, notice that it changes depending on the application you click and run. Makes sense—the Date Book looks and works differently from the Address Book. Most of the applications divide the screen into two parts, called *panes*. The left pane shows you information in a form a whole lot like you see it on the PalmPilot. The right pane includes more details, such as the category, if any, into which you've put the information, the due date if any, the priority you've assigned to it, and so on, as you can see in the following figure.

Several different versions of the Palm operating system are available, and each of them has its own version of the Palm Desktop.

The one shown here is version 2 or higher. Earlier versions don't have the Expense icon or the Install icon. (I'll cover installing in Chapter 20, "Installing New Software on Your PalmPilot.")

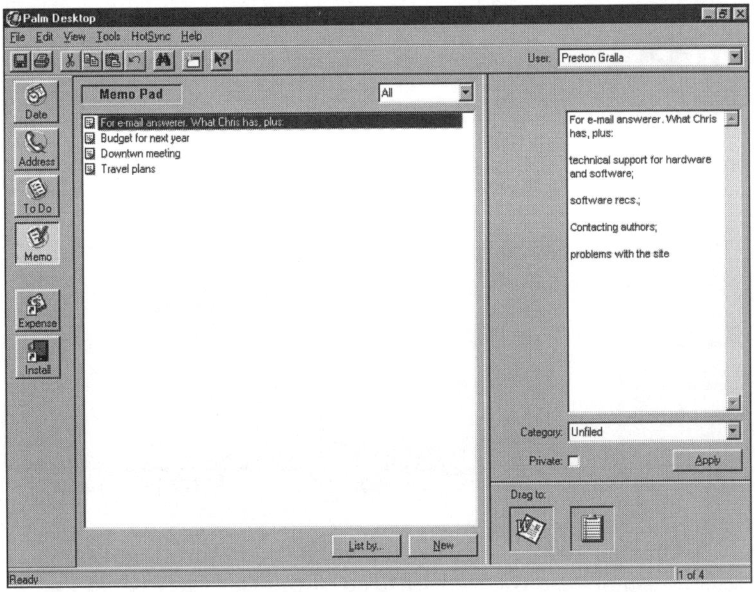

In the Memo Pad, as in most Palm Desktop programs, the left pane shows a list of all your items, and the right pane shows details about each item, such as its category and other information.

Now that you know what the Palm Desktop looks like, it's time to see what each of the applications on it can do and how they can help you organize your life better.

Keeping Your Schedule with the Date Book

The Date Book application on the Palm Desktop works a whole lot like the Date Book on your PalmPilot. (For more information on how to use the PalmPilot Date Book, turn to Chapter 11, "Juggling Your Busy Schedule with the Date Book.") You'll find differences between them because your desktop computer has a whole lot more space than your PalmPilot does, so the Palm Desktop shows you more details onscreen.

On the Palm Desktop, as with the Date Book on your PalmPilot, you can use three views, depending on what you need to see at that moment, your mood, and the phases of the moon, for all I know. You get to each of them by clicking the small tabs on the right side of the Date Book. Let me tell you what you need to know about each:

- **The Day view** Yes, you know when you'll use this view: when you want to see your schedule for an individual day. What I like about this view is that it shows you not just your day's schedule, but also shows a little calendar for the month and either your Address Book or To-Do List, whichever you would rather see. Notice that just above the Address Book or To-Do List is a little box with the words *Address* or *To Do* in it. To switch between the To-Do List and the Address Book, click the one you want to see. The following figure shows the Day view.

And how has your day been? You can easily tell with the Day View.

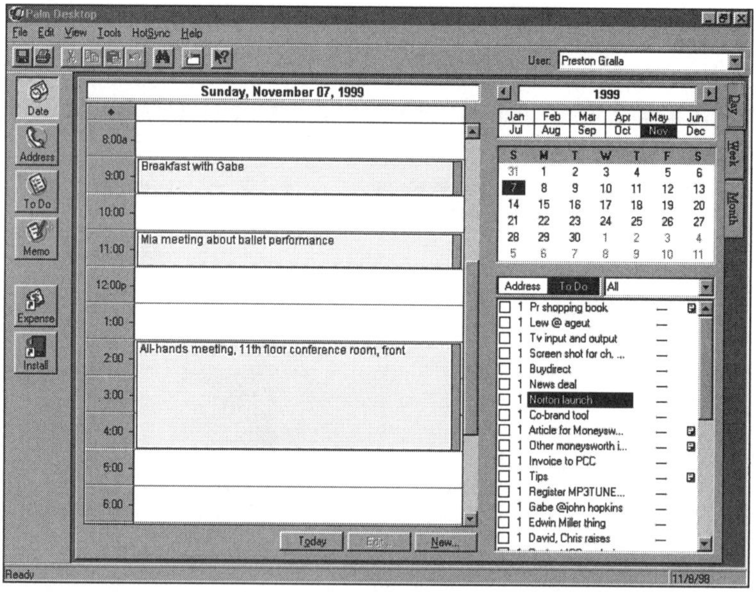

- **The Week view** As the name says, use this view when you want to see an entire week's schedule. I usually use this view instead of the Day view when I'm putting new events or appointments in my calendar. I use it because it gives me an overview of an entire week, so I'm better able to balance my schedule that way.

Moving appointments is easy in the Day view.

Let's say you've scheduled an appointment for today, but at the last minute you need to reschedule it for the same time two weeks from now. You can easily make that change in the Day view. Just click the appointment, and drag it up to the calendar date where you want to reschedule on the upper-right portion of the screen. Unfortunately, though, you can reschedule the appointment only some time in the current month.

- **The Month view** Use this view when you want to see an entire month at a time. The problem with this view, though, is that you can't see every appointment you have on every day of the month; your screen simply doesn't provide enough room for that. Because of these limitations, I rarely use this view.

Adding Appointments in the Date Book

Adding events in the Date Book also is easy. You can do so in a number of ways, but these two are easiest. When you're in the Date Book, you can

- **Click the time you want to schedule the appointment in either the Day or Week view.** This is the simplest way to add an appointment. Use it when you schedule a typical appointment—one that doesn't repeat. Type what the appointment is. By default, the appointment lasts an hour. To lengthen it or shorten it, grab the bottom of the box that your appointment is in, and drag it up or down until it shows the proper time.
- **Click New at the bottom of the screen.** You then see a little box pop up, as in the following figure. From here, you can schedule repeating events, set alarms, attach notes to the event, and do many more things as well. Use this way of creating a new appointment only when you need to have it repeated or add a note or alarm. This method takes longer than just clicking the time.

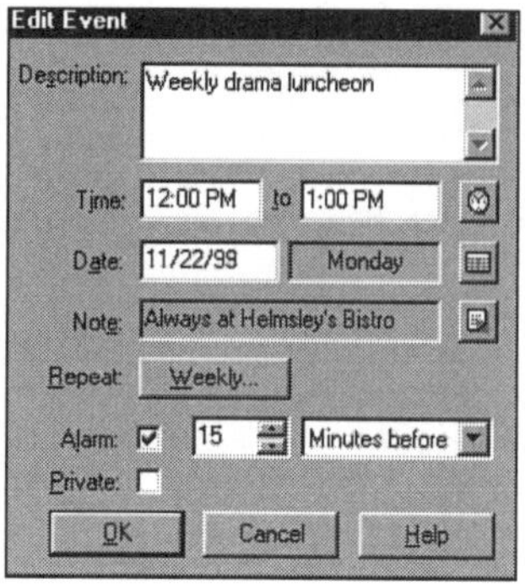

Again and again and again...When you want to create an appointment that repeats—or set alarms, for example—start from this little box.

What do you do if you've created an appointment and want to edit it for some reason? Let's say that you want to turn it into a repeating appointment or add a note or set an alarm. Easy. Right-click the appointment; then choose **Edit** from the drop-down menu. When the little box in the preceding figure shows up, use it to change the appointment in any way you want.

To schedule an appointment with one of your contacts, just drag the name from the Address Book to the time you want to make an appointment in the Date Book.

When you're in the Day view, you can easily schedule an appointment with one of your contacts in the Address Book. Simply click the person's name, and drag it to the day and time you want to schedule the appointment.

Keeping Track of Contacts with the Address Book

Names, addresses, people, phone numbers—keeping track of all of them is tough. Just like your PalmPilot's Address Book, the Palm Desktop's Address Book is for keeping track of this information.

The Palm Desktop's Address Book looks and works a whole lot like the PalmPilot's, with one big difference: On the Palm Desktop, you see more than the simple listing for each contact that you see on the main screen of the PalmPilot's Address Book. On the Palm Desktop, on one screen, you see all the information about that contact as well. You see the address, the phone numbers, the email addresses, the notes, the category it's in—in short everything, as you can see in the following figure.

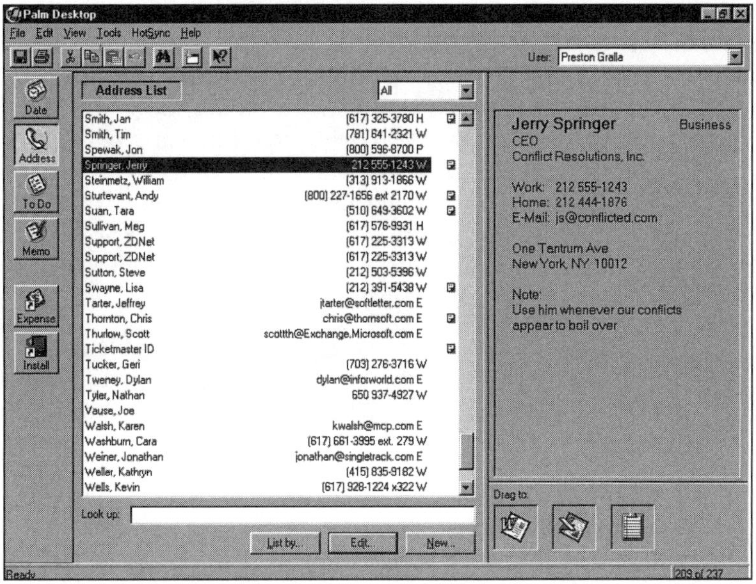

The Palm Desktop's Address Book lets you see all the information about a contact at a glance.

To see all this information about someone, just click the person's name. All the personal information appears in the right pane.

Adding a New Name in the Address Book

Adding a new name to the Address Book is a breeze: Just click **New** at the bottom of the screen. You then see the screen shown here.

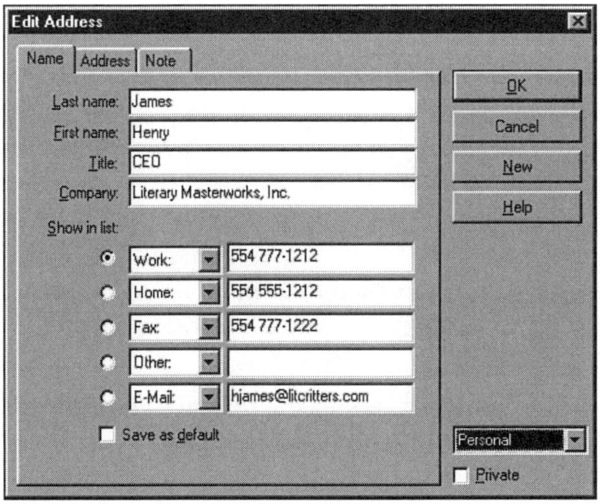

Point and type: To add a new entry to your Address Book, fill in this form.

You can fill in three tabs on the form. The first tab is for the most basic information: name and title, phone numbers, company name, email address. The second tab is for address information and for something called *custom fields*. These fields work just like the custom fields on your PalmPilot. Don't worry about them yet; I'll cover them in greater detail in Chapter 12, "Keeping Track of Contacts with the Address Book." The third tab lets you attach a note to the entry. These notes can be anything you want. For example, you could put down the names of someone's children or pet iguana here.

You can change the program that the Palm Desktop shows at startup.

When you start the Palm Desktop, it shows you the Date Book. If you would rather it start up with a different program, such as the To-Do List or Address Book, choose **Options** from the **Tools** menu. Then choose which program you want to see at startup.

To edit an entry in the Address Book, double-click the entry. The same form that you use to create a new entry pops up. Edit it, save it, and your work is done. (All of life should be so simple.)

Finding Names Is Easy, Too

Jumping to a person's name works on the Palm Desktop just like it does in the PalmPilot. At the bottom of the Address Book screen, you can type the name of the person whose information you're looking for. Type a letter, and you go immediately to the record of the first person whose name begins with that letter. If several people have names beginning with that letter, just keep typing; as you do, the screen moves to the record of the person whose name has letters you type. Of course, if you have a lot of Smiths in your Address Book, you'll have to scroll to the name at some point.

What to Do with the To-Do List

As with the other Palm Desktop programs, the To-Do List looks just like its counterpart on the PalmPilot, as you can see in the following figure. The exception is the right pane, which shows you all the details about an individual to-do, such as the category, the priority you've assigned to it, the date it's due, and notes you've attached to it.

The To-Do List works just like the PalmPilot's To-Do List in pretty much every way. For more details about organizing your life with the To-Do List, see Chapter 13, "Take Control of Your Life with the To-Do List."

Adding a new entry to your To-Do List is a bit confusing on the Palm Desktop. (First item on your To-Do List: Learn how to put to-dos into your To-Do List.)

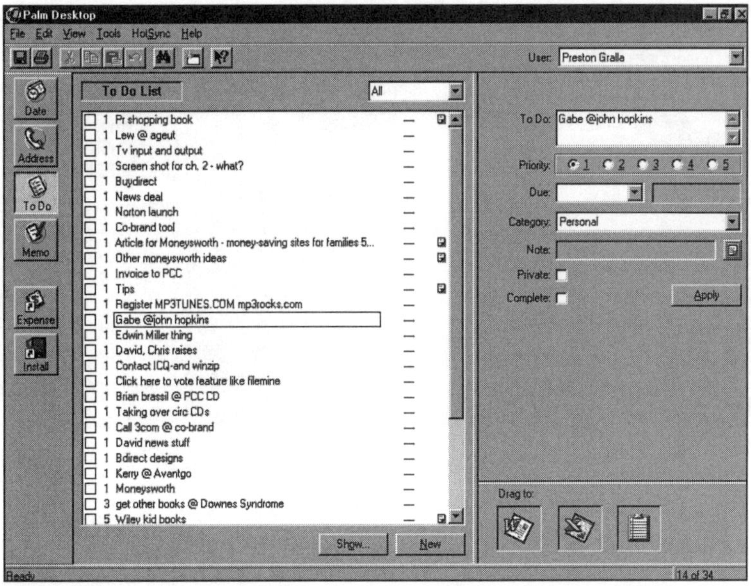

To do or not to do: The To-Do List looks like this in the Palm Desktop.

To start, click **New** at the bottom of the screen. Easy enough. So far, so good. A blank entry then appears in your To-Do List. Now fill in information about the to-do in the right pane. The words you put in the top of the right pane near the words *To Do* appear in the list in the left pane when you're done with the entry. Makes sense, too. Keep filling in the form by putting down the priority, the category, the due date if any, and adding a note and similar information.

Okay, you've done all that. But wait a minute; what's going on here? The entry in the left pane is still blank? What do you have to do to get it to fill in, anyway?

Click **Apply**. That'll do it. After you click this button, the to-do appears. Everything else on the Palm Desktop works so easily. Why did 3COM make just this one thing so confusing? Don't ask me. I'm just writing the book, not creating the software.

If this process isn't confusing enough, you actually don't have to use the Apply button to make your entry show up. Just do something else on the Palm Desktop, like switch to a different program, and the entry is automatically put in.

Creating Memos with Memo Pad

The Palm Desktop's Memo Pad has one big advantage over the PalmPilot's: You can type your memos instead of writing with your stylus and using Graffiti. Now, I have nothing against Graffiti; it's just that typing is so much easier than using Graffiti.

As with the other Palm Desktop programs, Memo Pad looks and works like the PalmPilot's version, except that the right pane shows all the details about the memo, as you can see in the following figure. (Turn to Chapter 10, "Write On! Taking Notes with the Memo Pad," for advice on how to use the PalmPilot's Memo Pad.)

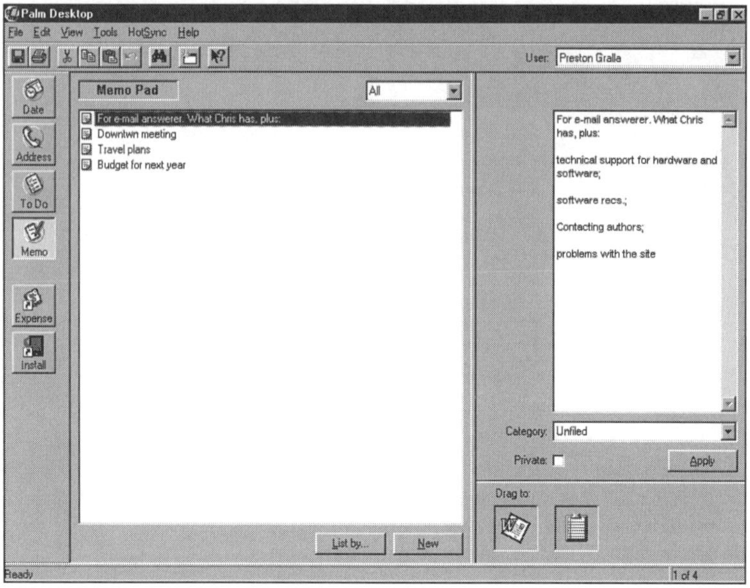

Write on! Using the Palm Desktop's Memo Pad is a lot like using the Memo Pad on the PalmPilot.

To create a new memo, click **New** at the bottom of the screen, and fill out the resulting form. You're going to run across the same problem with the Memo Pad that you did with the To-Do List: Until you click **Apply**, the memo doesn't show up onscreen. (Memo to 3COM: Change this feature, please! It doesn't make sense.)

You can see your memos in alphabetical order.

Normally, your memos are listed in the order in which you created them. Sometimes, though, that order can be unwieldy, and finding the exact memo you want can be difficult. Let me fill you in on a neat little trick: Click **List By** at the bottom of the screen in Memo Pad on the Palm Desktop, and choose **Alphabetical**. Your memos then show up in alphabetical order. This way, if you remember what the memo was about, you can scroll to the letter of the alphabet that starts the first word of the memo.

What About Expense and Install?

Down the left side of the Palm Desktop are two other buttons: Expense and Install. As you might guess, Expense helps you handle expenses, and Install installs programs.

When you click **Expense**, it takes your PalmPilot expense information and puts it into a spreadsheet. I'll cover Expense in more detail in Chapter 14, "Time Is Money: Tracking Your Expenses with the PalmPilot." When you click **Install**, you can install new programs on your PalmPilot. (Clicking this button doesn't install anything into your Palm Desktop, though—just on your PalmPilot.) To understand how to install programs with this button, turn to Chapter 20, "Installing New Software on Your PalmPilot."

Working in Drag: The Virtues of Dragging in the Palm Desktop

When you run the Address Book, the Memo Pad, or the To-Do List in the Palm Desktop, several large icons appear on the lower-right corner of your screen: one for Microsoft Word, one for Microsoft Excel, and one for the Clipboard. (The Excel button doesn't show up in the Memo Pad, though.) Above those icons are these mysterious sounding words: *Drag To*.

Drag To? What in the world can these words possibly mean? They mean that you can drag items from the rest of the Palm Desktop to the icons, and the program to which you're dragging it opens with that item inside. For example, if you drag a memo to the Word icon, Word launches, and the text of the memo appears in a Word document. Drag an address from the Address Book to the Excel icon, and Excel opens with that address entry. You can even drag multiple items at once to the icons. (Yes, Mac owners, I know, I know; you don't see these icons. They're not available in the Mac version of the software. Yet another example of the vast conspiracy against you.)

Very nice technology, you're probably thinking. But who cares? You should. It can help you in the following ways:

- When you drag memos and other items into Word, you can then add fonts and other formatting and print them.
- When you drag multiple entries from your Address Book into Excel, those entries are neatly put into the proper cells with all the fields in the right places. You can then print a neat-looking address book from Excel.
- You can create form letters, mailing lists, labels, and envelopes when you drag items from the Address Book into Word. See Chapter 12, "Keeping Track of Contacts with the Address Book," for detailed information.

You don't have Excel or Word installed on your computer?

The icons won't show up on the Palm Desktop if the programs are not installed on your computer. You can, however, drag items to the Clipboard.

Printing from the Palm Desktop

Because you can't really print from the PalmPilot, one of the main reasons to use the Palm Desktop is to print. Printing from the Palm Desktop is as straightforward as it gets. Highlight the item you want to print, and then click the **Print** icon on top of the screen or press **Ctrl+P**.

You don't get a whole lot of options when you print. You can't choose fonts or other fancy printing stuff. Depending on what you're printing, you sometimes have the option of printing notes or not, and some of the information in the entry or not. The whole process is pretty straightforward and simple.

Old Records Never Die...They Just Get Archived

Your PalmPilot doesn't have a whole lot of space on it, so you would be wise to keep only those items and records that you really need. When you no longer want something, delete it to make space for the stuff that you do want.

In the ideal world, it would be nice to be able to keep only those records and information you want in the PalmPilot but still somehow to have access to them when you wanted them.

Welcome to the ideal world, at least in this case. Whenever you delete something from your PalmPilot or your Palm Desktop, you're asked whether you would like to save an archived copy of it on your PC, as you can see in the following figures. If you think you want to see that information at some point later, just say yes and keep the archive box checked. That way, the information is gone from your PalmPilot and your Palm Desktop but saved in a special place on your computer where you can view it later if you want. If you know you don't ever want to see the record again, uncheck the box.

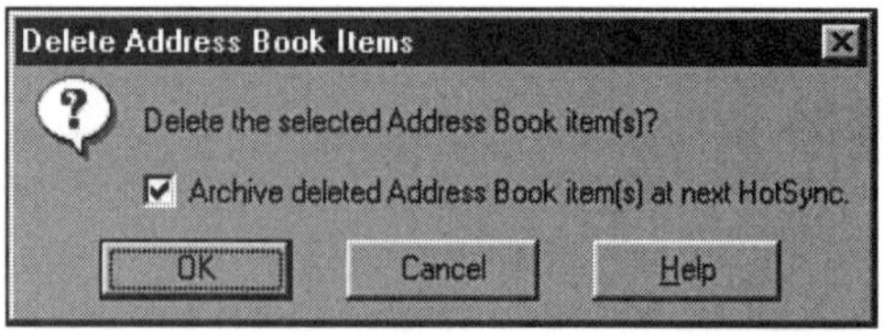

You see this message when you delete a record in the PalmPilot (left) and the Palm Desktop (right). If you want to archive the record and view it later, keep the Archive box checked.

When you delete but archive a record in your PalmPilot, the next time you do a HotSync, the archived record is sent to a special file, but it vanishes from the PalmPilot and the Palm Desktop. Similarly, a record vanishes from the Palm Desktop if you delete it from the Palm Desktop and will be deleted from your PalmPilot the next time you do a HotSync. However, it will be sent to a special file you can view later.

How to Retrieve Archived Data

To retrieve archived data, fire up the Palm Desktop. That's the easy part. Now things get a little hairy. For some reason known only to them, the makers of the PalmPilot seem to have gone out of their way to make it difficult to let you retrieve archived data.

Let me give you the lowdown: Archived data isn't kept in one spot on your PC. Instead, it's kept in many different places. Separate archive files are used for each of the PalmPilot main programs—the Memo Pad, the Address Book, the To-Do List, and the Date Book.

"Four files," you're probably thinking, "Okay, that's a bit confusing, but not overly so." Well, it gets worse because the PalmPilot actually creates more than one archive file for each of the main programs. It creates separate archive files for each *category* of each main program. So, if you delete and archive records from three categories in the Memo Pad, four categories in the Address Book, three in the To-Do List, and four in the Date Book, you will have *14 separate* archive files.

What does this mean? It means that before you retrieve archive files, you should remember first what kind of record it was (Memo Pad, To-Do, and so on) and then what category it was in. When you know that information, you're as good as gold.

When you know what you want to retrieve, launch the Palm Desktop. Now click the icon of the program whose information you want to retrieve, such as the Memo Pad. After you've done that, choose **Open Archive** from the **File** menu. When you choose this option, you see the Open Archive dialog box, as shown in the following figure.

Good luck hunting: Using this dialog box, you can open an archive file from the Palm Desktop.

Find the file you're looking for, and then open it. After you open it, your screen looks like you're in the normal Palm Desktop program, but you're really not; you're in a special screen that lets you retrieve archived information. From this screen, select the entries you want to retrieve. Then choose **Copy** from the **Edit** menu.

No, you're not done yet, but you're close. Hang on, you're getting there. Next, return to the normal Palm Desktop program. Choose **Current** from the **File** menu. (Weird. This menu item shows up here only if you're retrieving archived information. Usually, you never see it.) Choose the category where you want to put the retrieved information. (You can choose the one it started in or a different one. Makes no difference. It's up to you.) Now choose **Paste** from the **Edit** menu. There! Finally! The information is in your Palm Desktop. The next time you do a HotSync, it will show up in your PalmPilot as well.

The Least You Need to Know

- Use the Palm Desktop instead of the PalmPilot when you want to print or when you want to write a long memo using the keyboard instead of your stylus and Graffiti.
- Even if you never use the Palm Desktop, it's useful as a way to back up all your PalmPilot data in case something goes wrong with your PalmPilot.
- If you want to print memos, to-dos, and other items with special fonts and other formatting, drag the items to Microsoft Word, and then print using Word.
- To schedule an appointment with one of your contacts, just drag the name from the Address Book to the time you want to make an appointment in the Date Book.
- If you want to delete items but think you might want to refer to them someday, archive them. That way, you can retrieve them from the Palm Desktop.

Part 2

Organizing Your Life with Your PalmPilot

So, you know how to fire up your PalmPilot, tap with the stylus, run the major programs, and do a HotSync. Good start. But you're still not completely sure how it's going to make sure you don't turn up at the next budget meeting in your Bozo mask again, forgetting that it's not the Halloween party.

Well, that's why you've come to this section. Here's where you'll learn how your diminutive digital companion can help you take control of your life. You'll see how each major program—the Address Book, the Date Book, the Memo Pad, the To-Do List, and Expense—will help you organize your too-busy life. And you'll learn the secrets of how little-known features such as Categories can help get your life under control, and how you can find anything fast when you need it. In short, here's where you'll turn to find out how the PalmPilot can organize your life.

Chapter 7

Digital Magic: Taking Notes with Graffiti

In This Chapter

- Basic tips for learning how to write Graffiti
- Special characters drawn with Graffiti
- The Command stroke and ShortCuts for saving you time
- The built-in Graffiti cheat sheet
- Alternate strokes for best Graffiti recognition

One of the neatest, coolest, most useful—and at times most maddening—aspects of the PalmPilot is the way that it lets you write by hand with a stylus instead of using a keyboard. It's one of the main reasons that the device is so useful. You can carry it around in your pocket like a notepad, and when you need to jot down a To-Do item, schedule an appointment, or write a memo about your latest business brainstorm (selling stock in pick-your-own pumpkin franchises—Pik-A-Pumpkin; there's a killer idea), just whip out your PalmPilot and your trusty stylus and write away.

The good news is that writing by hand on your PalmPilot actually works. The bad news is that it might not always work in the way you expect. When you look at a To-Do item and read "ppinc honc cpocspies," you might not necessarily know that what you thought you were writing when you tapped in the note was "bring home groceries."

In this chapter, you learn how to use Graffiti, the handwriting-recognition software that comes with the PalmPilot. You learn tips and shortcuts so that not only will your notes be dead-on accurate, but you'll spend a whole lot less time writing and a whole lot more time able to concentrate on the work at hand. As I just wrote in my PalmPilot, "I dpomisc if!" ("I promise it!")

Understanding Graffiti Basics

Software like Graffiti that understands handwriting has been around for a while. But the one problem with this kind of software was that it rarely worked. For example, anyone who owned the Apple Newton, the ill-fated precursor to the PalmPilot (*precursor* because so many Newton owners cursed at the little device because it was so flaky) can tell many horror stories about how rarely the Newton accurately transcribed their keystrokes into letters, characters, and numbers.

Graffiti works pretty well, though, if you spend the time learning to use it, and if you follow a few tips. Keep these points in mind, and Graffiti should do a pretty good job recognizing what you write:

- **You need to learn the Graffiti alphabet.** With the PalmPilot, unlike the Newton and some other handwriting-recognition systems, you don't teach it to understand your own idiosyncratic handwriting. Instead, you have to learn Graffiti's idiosyncratic method of writing. It's not very hard, though. Spend a few hours, and you'll be a pro. Use the stickers and cards that 3COM provided when you bought the PalmPilot, check out the tear card on the inside cover of this book, and use the PalmPilot's own built-in cheat sheets.
- **When you write with Graffiti, you don't lift your hand.** Each letter and number is formed with a single, continuous stroke. If you lift the stylus, you write a different letter.
- **Graffiti boils down each character and number to its most basic form.** An *A*, for example, is formed by drawing two sides of a triangle, pointed up, with no bottom—in other words, like a regular *A* but without the cross stroke.
- **You have to pay attention to where you start each stroke.** That starting point has everything to do with whether Graffiti recognizes your letter properly. Draw a *U* with your stylus starting on the upper-left side, and Graffiti recognizes it. Draw that same *U* with your stylus starting on the upper-right side, and Graffiti assumes it's a *V*.

Using the Graffiti Writing Area

You do all your writing in the Graffiti writing area, shown in the following figure, which is the rectangular area at the bottom of the PalmPilot's screen. You write letters on the left side (logically enough, you see a little *abc* there) and numbers on the right side (yes, you guessed it, you see a little *123* there). If you look closely, you can see two tiny triangles at the top and bottom of the writing area. Those triangles mark the dividing line between where you can write letters and where you can write numbers. Most people write more letters than numbers, so the area for writing letters is larger. You can write with Graffiti only when the program you're running lets you enter text, such as the Memo Pad. So next time you're playing Chess or Space Invaders on your little friend, don't try writing "I give up!"

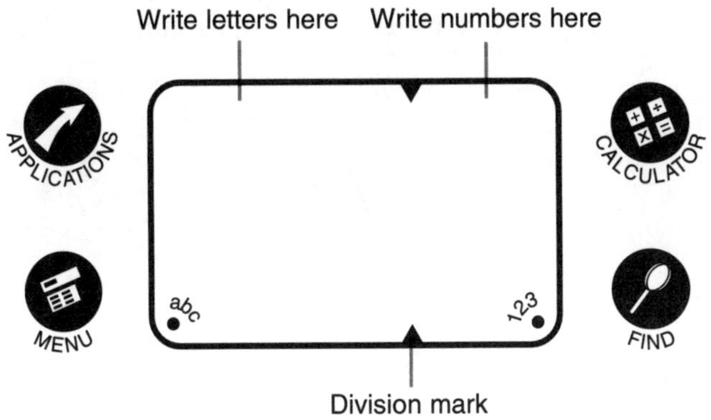

Let the writing begin: the PalmPilot's Graffiti writing area.

Two tiny dots appear in the writing area, one underneath the *abc* and one underneath the *123*. Tap on the dot beneath the *abc,* and a little keyboard pops up with letters on it, as you can see in the following figure. Tap on the dot beneath the *123,* and a keyboard pops up with numbers on it instead. You can tap on the letters and numbers and have them input into the PalmPilot. Use this keyboard only in a pinch. Writing for any length of time using this keyboard is almost impossible; it's kind of like trying to tap-dance in a two-foot square area. Sure, maybe it can be done, but why bother? You can pop up the keyboard only if you're running a program such as Memo Pad that accepts text input.

Use only the stylus or a similar device made for the PalmPilot to write in the Graffiti area.

The stylus has been specifically designed so that it doesn't scratch the surface of the writing area. If you use a sharp object or a pen, for example, it could scratch the Graffiti area, which would make it very hard for the PalmPilot to do a good job of character recognition.

Tap, tap, tap...You can input text by using the built-in keyboard.

Learning How to Write Graffiti Letters and Numbers

The best way to begin writing in graffiti is simply to begin. Using either the sheets provided by 3COM or the alphabet on the inside covers of this book, follow the directions for writing each letter. Notice that each stroke has a thick dot. That dot is your starting point. To draw the letter *A*, you start at the lower left, as shown in the following figure.*

The alpha but not the omega: drawing the letter A in Graffiti. The large dot tells you where to start your stroke.

That's Very Nice, But How About Drawing Capital Letters?

To draw a capital letter, you have to use what amounts to a virtual Shift key. To draw a capital letter, put your stylus at the bottom of the screen, and draw an upward stroke. An arrow then appears at the bottom-right corner of the screen. It tells you that whatever letter you draw next will be capitalized.

Fine. But what if you want to write several capital letters in a row? Having to keep using that extra stroke between letters is kind of a pain. No problem. Instead of drawing a single upward stroke before writing a letter, draw two single upward strokes, one after another. *Two* arrows now appear. All the letters you draw next will be capital letters JUST LIKE THIS. (This stroke acts like a Caps Lock key.)

OKAY, BUT HOW DO I SHUT OFF THE CAPITAL LETTERS? JUST DRAW A SINGLE UPWARD STROKE. The two arrows disappear, and the capital letters are turned off.

Learn the Graffiti alphabet by playing Giraffe.

One of the programs that comes with your PalmPilot is called Giraffe. It's a game that teaches you the Graffiti alphabet; think of it as Space Invaders meets the "Alphabet Song." It's fun, it's fast, and it's a quick way to learn Graffiti. It doesn't come installed on your PalmPilot; you have to install it from the accompanying CD. Playing this game is worth the effort.

Don't Curse at the Cursor

Just like when you use word processing software on a computer, you see a little blinking line at the point where you're entering text. That's the PalmPilot's cursor. Sometimes you might want to move the cursor forward or backward—to make a space between letters, for example, or to backspace.

Moving the cursor is easy. To move the cursor forward one space, just draw a line, from left to right, in the Graffiti area. To move the cursor back a space, draw a line from right to left in the Graffiti area. Both of these strokes are shown here.

From here to there and there to here, you can make the cursor move anywhere. The forward space (left) and the backspace (right) in Graffiti.

You can also easily move the cursor down to the next line of text—for example, if you're writing in the Memo Pad—and want to start writing on a new line of text. This stroke works like the Return key on a computer (and for those of a certain age, like the Return key on a typewriter). The following is the return stroke in Graffiti.

The return stroke in Graffiti.

Entering Special Characters with the Extended Shift

Sometimes you need to enter special characters into your PalmPilot (and no, I'm not talking about Groucho Marx), such as the copyright symbol (©) or the trademark symbol (™). You do so by using the Extended Shift stroke, as shown here.

To enter special characters such as the copyright symbol (©), you use this Extended Shift stroke.

After you draw the Extended Shift stroke, you use another stroke, such as an *M* stroke, which gives the trademark symbol. For a list of these strokes, turn to the tear card in this book.

Using the Command Stroke to Master Your PalmPilot

Heel, PalmPilot, heel! If you want to take total control over your PalmPilot, use the Command stroke, as shown here.

Use the Command stroke, and make your PalmPilot jump through hoops.

Using this stroke, in fact, is a quick way of using the PalmPilot's menu commands. For example, to delete a record, you can tap on the **Menu** button and then choose **Delete** from that menu. Alternatively, you can do it much faster by using the Command stroke and then writing **D**. The menu commands change according to what PalmPilot program you're currently using. For more information about menus, turn to Chapter 8, "Taking Control of the PalmPilot's Applications, Menus, and Records."

To delete several letters, numbers, or words, highlight them, and then use the backspace or Space stroke to delete them.

Highlight the characters on the touch screen by drawing a line directly through them with your stylus. Then move your stylus to the Graffiti area, and draw a Space stroke or Backspace stroke.

Using Punctuation

Periods, question marks, commas, and otherpunctuation marks are good things. Without them, writing anything that makes much sense would be impossible. You can easily use punctuation with Graffiti. Just tap once in the Graffiti area, and then enter a punctuation character. For example, for a period, tap once, and then tap again. When you tap once, a dot appears in the lower-right corner of the PalmPilot's display. For a list of punctuation, turn to the tear card.

Taking ShortCuts with Your PalmPilot

One of the most useful of all Graffiti strokes is the ShortCut stroke, shown in the following figure. ShortCuts are abbreviations that are expanded into longer words or phrases through PalmPilot magic. You enter a ShortCut by first using the ShortCut stroke and then writing in the letters of the ShortCut. On my PalmPilot, for example, I have a ShortCut that automatically expands the letters *cig* into *The Complete Idiot's Guide*.

Use this shortcut stroke, and save yourself a whole lot of time.

A number of ShortCuts are already built into your PalmPilot, such as *me* for the word *meeting*. Check out this list of built-in shortcuts:

- **br** Expands to *breakfast*
- **lu** Expands to *lunch*
- **di** Expands to *dinner* (Hmmm, does someone have a food fixation here?)
- **me** Expands to *meeting*
- **ds** Automatically puts in today's date
- **ts** Automatically puts in the current time
- **dts** Automatically puts in the current date and time

You can create new shortcuts yourself easily. To add your own, go to Preferences from the Applications screen. Then choose **ShortCuts** from the upper-right corner of the screen, and follow the directions. Turn to Chapter 21, "Customizing Your PalmPilot for the Way You Live and Work," for more information about creating and using ShortCuts.

Getting Help by Using the Built-In Graffiti Cheat Sheet

If you're still having trouble writing Graffiti, don't despair. We've all been there. You can use the built-in Graffiti cheat sheet, shown here, to give guidance on how to write Graffiti.

Help is on the way: You can use this built-in Graffiti cheat sheet.

You can call up the Graffiti cheat sheet in several ways. Because of the peculiarities of the PalmPilot, not all of them work in all applications.

- Tap on the **Menu** button, and then choose **Graffiti Help** from the **Edit** menu.
- Enter the Command stroke, and write the letter **G**.

Writing large makes it easier for Graffiti to recognize your letters.

When you write small in the Graffiti area, more errors occur. Larger is better and more accurate.

➤ Starting from near the bottom of the Graffiti writing area, draw a slash up the entire PalmPilot, all the way up to the screen area. (This approach works only in Palm OS 2.0 or higher.)

Different Strokes: Shortcuts to Better Graffiti Writing

Some characters (such as *A* are easier to write than other letters (such as *Y*). You can use different strokes than 3COM recommends and get better character recognition. See the list in Table 7.1.

Table 7.1 Different Strokes for Better Graffiti Recognition

Character	Graffiti Stroke	How to Draw It
B	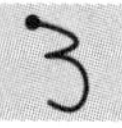	Draw a *3* on the letter side of the Graffiti writing area.
E		Draw a *W* turned on its side.
G		Draw a *6* on the letter side of the Graffiti writing area.
J		Draw a backward *L*. Start from the top, go down, and then left.
K		Make it look kind of like a fish. Make the loop big.
N		Round the corners, like a sine symbol, instead of making them sharp.
P		Start at the bottom. You can make the top loop small.
Q		Pay attention to making a very long tail. It's okay if you don't close the *O* shape.
R		You can start at the bottom, as with the *P*. You can make the top loop small.
S		Draw a *5* on the letter side of the Graffiti writing area.
V		Draw a *U*, but start from the right.
X		Draw a fish swimming in the opposite direction as a *K*.

Character	Graffiti Stroke	How to Draw It
Y		Draw a downward-facing loop, starting on the upper left.
2		Draw a *Z* on the number side of the Graffiti writing area.
4		Draw a *C* on the number side of the Graffiti writing area.
5		Draw an *S* on the number side of the Graffiti writing area.
7		Draw a backward *C* on the number side of the Graffiti writing area.
9		Draw an *h* on the number side of the Graffiti writing area.

The Least You Need to Know

- ➤ When you're writing Graffiti characters, don't lift your stylus from the writing area.
- ➤ You can call up a tiny keyboard by tapping the dots beneath the *abc* or *123* in the Graffiti area.
- ➤ Playing the built-in game Giraffe can help you learn Graffiti faster.
- ➤ Use ShortCuts to write frequently used words and phrases with only a few strokes.
- ➤ Use the built-in Graffiti cheat sheet to get help with writing characters and numbers.

Chapter 8

Taking Control of the PalmPilot's Applications, Menus, and Records

In This Chapter

- How to run PalmPilot applications
- How to use the PalmPilot application controls
- How to attach notes to records
- How to make records private
- How to use menus

Before you can get your life organized with the PalmPilot, you need to first take control of the PalmPilot itself. In this chapter, you find out how to master the heart of the PalmPilot's software: the applications, menus, and records. Hey, don't turn the page. Believe me, you need to know these basics before you can get your life under control with your little digital companion. In this chapter, you find out the inside scoop on these important features:

- How to attach notes to records so that you can not merely schedule appointments and to-dos, but also include important information, such as details about who you're meeting, and more details about your to-dos
- How to use the menus to edit, cut, and paste, and rearrange the way your PalmPilot looks
- How to use built-in tips so that you're never at a loss for what to do when you need help

Up and Running: Starting a PalmPilot Application

Just a reminder: You can start a PalmPilot application in two different ways. One is to press one of the four "hard" buttons at the bottom of the PalmPilot screen, if you want to launch the Date Book, Address Book, To-Do List, or Memo Pad. If your PalmPilot isn't turned on, this action turns it on; if it's already on, this action switches to the application whose button you pushed. The other way to start an application is to tap on its icon in the PalmPilot's main screen.

Want to launch any program from a "hard" button? It's easy.

You can have any of the "hard" buttons at the bottom of the PalmPilot launch any program you want, not just the ones they're preprogrammed to run. To remap the buttons to launch different programs, tap on **Preferences** from the main screen, and then choose **Buttons**. You then can remap the buttons. Turn to Chapter 21, "Customizing Your PalmPilot for the Way You Live and Work," for more information on customizing the buttons.

What you probably don't know (don't feel bad, not many people know this) is that those "hard" buttons at the bottom of the screen serve another purpose as well. They cycle you through the different categories and views for each application. For example, press on the **Date Book** button once, and it shows you the Day view. Now press again, and you see the Week view. Press one more time, and you're shown the Month view. With the To-Do List, the Address Book, and the Memo Pad, you start the application when you press once. Then each time you press the hard button again, you cycle through the different categories of data in that application, such as Business, Personal, and so on.

Taking Control of the Application Controls

Spend any time in a PalmPilot application, and you'll notice a variety of little buttons, scroll arrows, and tiny little widgets of all sorts. In the following list, you can see what they look like and learn what they do:

A check in a check box means that the option is active; no check means the option is inactive. Tap on a check box to put a check in it. If a check already appears there, tap on it to remove the check.

To see a previous page of information, tap on the up arrow; to see the next page of information, tap on the down arrow. Simple, yes?

Tap on the pick list, and you see a list of choices you can make. Tap on the choice you want, and you've chosen it.

These babies are all over the place. Tap on this type of button to perform an action, such as create a new item, or to give an OK, Cancel, or Done command in a dialog box.

Use this bar to easily scroll through a document. Drag it and you can move it one line—or more—at a time. Tap on the arrow at the top of the bar, and you move up one line at a time; hold your stylus on the arrow, and you continue to scroll. Tap on the arrow at the bottom of the bar, and you move down one line at a time; hold your stylus on the arrow, and you continue to scroll. Tap on the bar itself to move several lines at a time.

This type of box tells you that you can tap inside the box and take an action of some sort, such as setting the time.

Attaching Notes to Records and Making Records Private

A record is any event or item in your PalmPilot—for example, a memo, a To-Do item, an appointment, or an address entry. You can attach a note to any record on your PalmPilot, except you can't attach a note to a memo. This makes sense because a memo is really just a note, and you don't need to attach a note to a note.

This ability to attach notes may seem simple, but it's one of the most useful features of the PalmPilot. Let me tell you some of the ways you can use it:

- When you're scheduling an appointment in the Date Book, you can attach a note with the person's contact information and with other information relevant to the appointment.
- In your To-Do List, you can add a good deal of detail about each specific to-do, instead of having just a simple list. You also can use notes to group many To-Do items into a single entry. For example, under the single to-do "Pick up groceries," you could attach a note with your entire grocery list.
- In your Address Book, you can add personal information to the usual name, address, and phone number information about someone—for example, his or her birthday or names of his or her children or favorite food.

How to Attach Notes to Records

Attaching a note to any record is quite easy. First, go to the entry where you want to enter a note. At the bottom of the entry, tap on the **Details** button, which you can see in the following figure. Tap on the **Note** button, type your note, and tap **Done**. Your note is then put in your list. Whenever an item has a note attached, a little Note icon appears next to it, as you can see in the figure.

*To add a note, tap on **Details** and follow the instructions. When you're done, a little Note icon appears next to the entry.*

How to Make a Record Private

Sometimes you might want to mark certain records private, which means that they disappear until you type in a secret password. Why would you want to hide records? Well, let's say you're going to a job interview on your lunch hour. You want to have information about that interview in your PalmPilot, but you don't want your boss to accidentally see it. And if you want to remember to buy a specific gift for your spouse on your anniversary, you want to keep that a secret as well. And, of course, you just might be flat-out paranoid. Whatever the reason, you can hide information from other people.

Marking a record private is easy. First, go to the record you want to keep private. Tap on the **Details** button, and then tap on the **Private** check box. Doing so marks the record as private. In the Address Book, after you go to the record, you have to tap on the **Edit** button and then the **Details** button before you can mark the record as private.

The process seems simple, but in fact, it might not work yet. Sometimes when you mark a record as private, it still appears. Why is that? Because you also need to tell your PalmPilot to hide all private records. Unless you take this extra step, your private records don't become private; they are still public. I guess that makes them public private records, which is about as confusing as things get.

To tell your PalmPilot to hide all private records, go to the Security program by tapping on the **Applications** button and then tapping on **Security**. You then see the following figure. Tap on **Hide**, and your records are all hidden.

Can I have my privacy, please? This Security screen lets you make sure that your private records stay private.

If you want to be super-secure, also add a password using this screen. That way, the only way to show your private records is if someone first types the password here.

Pick One from Column A: Using Menus

If you want to cut and paste, change your font, create new entries, set preferences, or do a whole lot of other neat stuff, you need to use menus. The PalmPilot menus look and work a lot like the ones you're familiar with from the PC and the Mac. They drop down from the top of the screen, and you choose an option by tapping on it.

So far, so good. But one thing is kind of confusing about the PalmPilot menus. They change according to the program you're running. Therefore, the menus for the To-Do List are different from the ones for the Address Book. And making things even more confusing, the menus can change even in the same program, depending on what you're doing. For example, the menus you use in the To-Do List are different from the menus you use when you're writing an attached note in the To-Do List. The following figure shows a menu pulled down.

A typical menu on the PalmPilot.

To open a menu in any program, tap on the **Menu** button. A menu then appears at the top of the screen. Generally, you'll find these three kinds of menus:

- **The Record menu** Using this menu, for example, you can create and delete records, attach and delete a note to a record, or beam a record to another Palm III or higher.
- **The Edit menu** You use the Edit menu for cutting, copying, and pasting text; undoing editing commands; and calling up the keyboard so that you can enter text without using Graffiti.

- **The Option menu** You use this menu when you want to change the font or change the way you display information, such as by company name rather than last name in the Address Book.

Use the Command stroke to enter menu commands quickly.

If you want to save time, use the Graffiti Command stroke instead of menus. The Command stroke lets you perform menu commands without having to tap, tap, tap. To use the Command stroke, draw an upward slash, starting at the lower-left area of Graffiti and ending near the upper-right area. Then write a single letter, such as **D**, which deletes a record, or **X**, which cuts a selection of text. The menu shows you the letters to use with Command strokes to perform each menu function. For more information on using Graffiti, turn back to Chapter 7, "Digital Magic: Taking Notes with Graffiti."

Changing Your Font with Menus

The PalmPilot screen is small and often hard to read, especially under many different kinds of lighting. For that reason, I find myself changing fonts often. On the Palm III, you can use three different fonts: small, medium, and large. I use the small font for most things, for example, but often use the medium font in memos and notes because I find it hard to read much text in the small font. To change a font, choose **Font** from the **Options** menu, or use the Command stroke followed by the letter **F**. You then see the following screen. Just choose the font size you want, tap on **OK**, and you've done the job.

Pick a peck of fonts. Choose small, medium, or large.

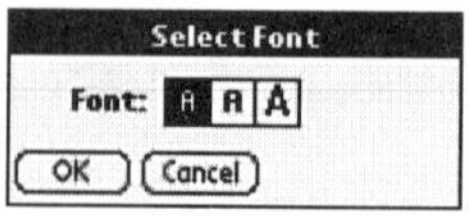

Cutting, Copying, and Pasting Text

The other menu feature I use all the time is for cutting and pasting text. It works a lot like Windows or the Macintosh. To cut or copy text, highlight it by drawing your stylus through it. When the text is highlighted, choose **Cut** from the **Edit** menu to delete it and put it into the PalmPilot's built-in Clipboard. (The Clipboard works just like a computer's Clipboard: Whatever you put in there can be pasted somewhere else, although you can have only one thing in there at a time. When you put in a new clip, the old one vanishes.) To paste the text somewhere else, tap with your stylus on the place where you want it pasted, and choose **Paste** from the **Edit** menu. The text then is pasted in. If you want to copy text but not delete it, choose **Copy** instead of **Cut** from the **Edit** menu.

Psssst! Using the PalmPilot's Built-In Tips

No matter how much of a pro you become at mastering your life with your PalmPilot, you're still going to need tips at some point. Let me share the good news: Tips are built right into the PalmPilot. You just have to know where to look.

When you tap on the **Details** button on any record, you get a screen that lets you enter information about that record. At the top of the screen is a little *i* button (which stands for "information"), as you can see in the figure on the left. Tap on it, and you get tips about working with that particular record, as you can see in the figure on the right.

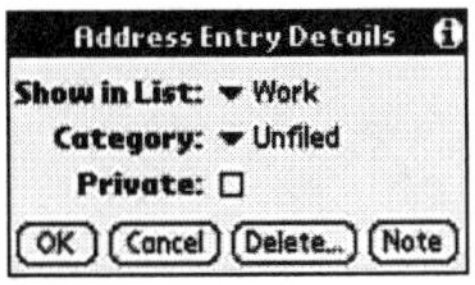

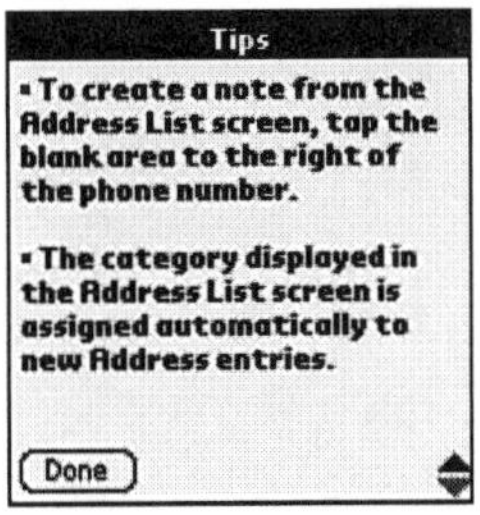

*Tap on the little **i** in this screen, and you get a tip about how to use the record.*

The Least You Need to Know

- If you keep pressing a "hard" button for a particular application, it cycles you through the different categories and views for that application.
- You can remap the "hard" buttons so that they can launch any program you want, not just the ones they were originally programmed to do.
- You can attach notes to records so that you can get more information about your appointments, contacts, and to-dos.
- You can mark records as private so that only you can read them. You also can password-protect them so that only someone who knows the password can view them.
- You can use the Graffiti Command stroke as a shortcut to using Menu commands.

Chapter 9

Using PalmPilot Categories to Organize Your Life

In This Chapter

- Learning what categories are and how they work
- Assigning records to different categories
- Creating, editing, deleting, and merging categories
- Using categories to make launching applications easier
- Discovering smart strategies for organizing your life with PalmPilot categories

Think of all the different kinds of things you have to get done in a day. You write memos about your budget, attend staff meetings, handle personnel problems, plan travel, figure your expenses, drop off your kids at school, go grocery shopping, feed the dog, compete in a triathlon Iron Man event (well, maybe you compete in the triathlon only on Sundays). You do so many different kinds of things every day that sometimes you feel as if you're not one person, but instead an entire army of people, all of whom happen to be cohabiting in the same body.

Consciously or not, you divide those things you do every day into categories—such as things you do in your home life, in your business life, and for entertainment. You also might divide those categories even further; for example, at work you deal with budget issues, personnel matters, travel, individual projects, and so on.

One of the most powerful ways that the PalmPilot can help you get your life under control is its use of categories like these. You can categorize just about everything you track on your PalmPilot, such as your memos, to-dos, and names and addresses. Then, when you use those categories, seeing what jobs and work need to be done in that part of your life is a breeze. For example, in your To-Do List, tap on the Strategic Planning category that you've created, and you'll see all the things you have to do to put your strategic plan into effect. Tap on the Triathlon category, and you'll get so tired looking at all that training you should be doing that you'll instead fall into bed and call it a day—which is a good idea because we all need rest every once in a while.

In this chapter, you learn everything you need to know about categories—one of the most powerful ways you can organize your life with the PalmPilot.

Start with the Basics: How to Assign Records to Categories

Each of your PalmPilot applications already has several prebuilt categories, just waiting to be used. The Memo Pad and To-Do List have Business and Personal categories, and the Address Book has both of those categories, plus a QuickList category as well. And in a bit of wishful thinking, perhaps, Expense has two categories: Paris and New York. (Memo to my boss: Why I spent a week in Paris even though our company has no division in Paris. Item to put into my To-Do List: Find new job after boss hits the roof about getting the Paris expenses and memo.)

The Date Book doesn't use categories.

If you're using the Date Book and wondering where the categories went, don't bother looking: They're not there. The Date Book, for reasons I've never understood, doesn't allow you to categorize appointments you enter.

When you create a new record, by default, it isn't assigned to any category. It's "Unfiled," which means that it isn't in any category at all. When you create a new record, though, you can easily put that record into a category. While you're creating the record, tap on the **Details** button. Then tap on **Category**, choose the category where you want to put the record, and tap on **OK**. The job is done. The following figure shows a record being assigned to a category.

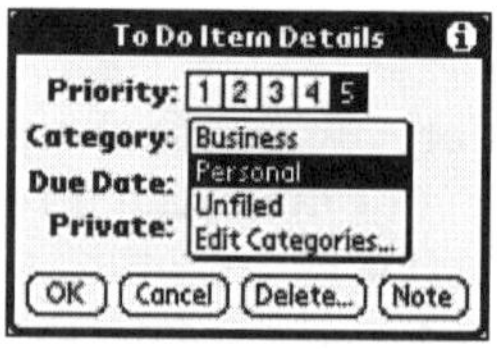

Just a few taps are required to assign a record to a specific category.

Well and good. But what if you already have a whole lot of to-dos, memos, and names and addresses, and they're all Unfiled—not attached to any category? What to do then?

Putting an existing record into a category is also a breeze. Open the record you want to put into a category. Now tap on the **Details** button, and assign the old record to a category in the same way you assigned a new record to a category. You've now categorized it. (The Address Book, being the nonconformist of the PalmPilot, does things just a tad different. There, you have to select a record, tap on **Edit**, and then tap on **Details** to categorize something.)

Let me tell you a fast way to add several new items to a category.

If you want to add several records to a category, you don't have to go through the process of individually assigning each to a category. Instead, switch to the category where you want to add the items. Then create the items. The items are automatically put into that category.

How to View Records in Categories

After you assign records to a category, you can easily view all the records in that category as a list. From the main screen of the program you're using, such as the To-Do List, tap on the triangle in the upper-right corner of the screen, and choose the category you want to view, as shown in the following figure. You then are shown all the records in that category.

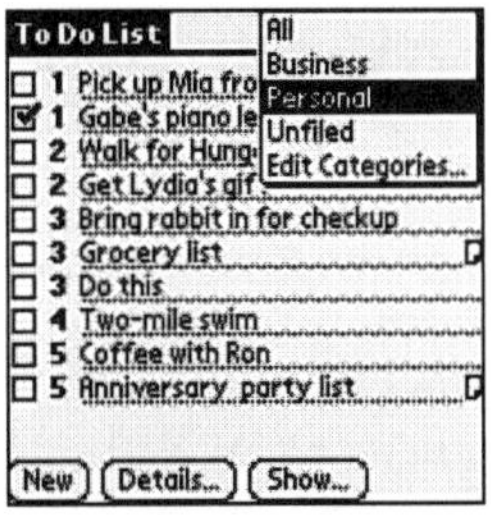

You can pick a category to view from this list.

One confusing thing you'll have to get used to when using categories on the PalmPilot is that no connection exists between the categories you set up in the Memo Pad, To-Do List, Address Book, and Expense. In other words, if you set up an Ultimate Frisbee category in each of these programs, you cannot see, on one screen, all the memos, to-dos, expenses, and names and addresses you've put in the category. Instead, you have to open the programs one at a time to see what records are in the Ultimate Frisbee category in each. (Memo to 3COM: Fix this feature, please.)

Sometimes you might like to cycle through all the categories in a particular program—to see all your to-dos, for example, first in one category, then another, and then another. You'll find it's pretty laborious to keep tapping away on your screen to go through the categories. A faster way is to use the hard buttons at the bottom of your PalmPilot. When you're working in a program, press its hard button, and you then cycle to the next category in that program. If you're in the Memo Pad and looking at your Rabbit Breeding category, for example, press on the **Memo Pad** button, and you cycle to the next category. Press again to go on to the next, and so on.

By the way, the All category is a list of every record in a particular application. When you view All, you're viewing every single record there, whether or not it's in a category.

How You Can Create New Categories

The odds are great that just using the Personal and Business categories isn't enough for you. You need to create many more categories—categories that reflect what needs to be done in your home and business life. To create a new category when you're working in a program, tap on the category triangle in the upper-right corner of your screen. Choose **Edit Categories** and then click **New**. You then see the following screen. Type the name of the new category, and you're done.

Just fill in the blank, and you've created a new category.

Yes, You Can Change Your Mind: Editing and Deleting Categories

You can create up to 15 categories for each application.

The PalmPilot lets you create many categories for each of your programs—up to 15 of them. You can't create any more than that for any one individual program. If you need more than 15, your life is far too busy. Take a vacation.

Your life changes fast. The things you need to do and track today aren't the same things you need to do and track next month or next year. In fact, the things you need to do and track this afternoon might not even be the things you needed to do and track this *morning*.

Luckily for you, only a few taps are required to change the names of categories or to delete them. To change the name or delete a category, tap on the **Categories** triangle in the upper-right corner of the screen, and choose **Edit Categories**. To rename the category, tap on the **Rename** button, type the new name of the category, and then tap on **OK**. To delete the category, tap on the **Delete** button. (Do you see a pattern here?) You then see the following warning. By the way, when you delete a category, you don't actually delete the records in that category. Instead, only the category is deleted. All the records in that category then go into the Unfiled category.

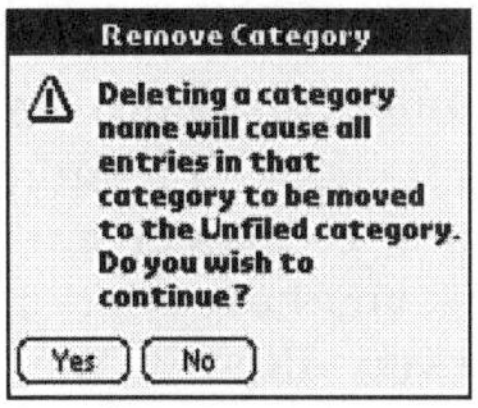

Are you really, completely, absolutely sure you want to delete that category?

All Together Now: How to Merge Categories

Sometimes you might want to merge all the items in two or more different categories into one single category. For example, let's say in your Address Book, you have one category for Consultants and another for Outside Contractors. You realize that there's not much of a difference between the two categories (other than the fact that those people who put the word *consultant* in front of their name charge four times the fees of those who call themselves *outside contractors*). So you decide to combine those two categories into a single Consultant category. I'll let you in on a trick on how to merge those categories with a few taps of the stylus.

You can't assign multiple categories to a single record.

Being able to assign a single record to multiple categories would be nice—for example, to assign a memo about the 1999 budget for the Electric Fork project to both your Budget and Electric Fork categories. It would be nice, but it can't be done. The PalmPilot doesn't allow you to assign multiple categories, so don't try. You have to decide which is the main category for a record and assign it to that.

First, decide which category you're going to get rid of. In this example, you want to get rid of the Outside Contractors category. Now, tap on the **Categories** triangle, and choose **Edit Categories**, in the same way you would when you want to edit or delete a category. Tap on the category you're going to get rid of (in this example, **Outside Contractors**). Now rename it with the name of the category you're going to merge it with (in this example, **Consultants**). All the records that used to be in the Outside Contractors category are now placed into the Consultants category.

How to Use Categories to Group Your Applications

Many people who become devoted to their little digital companion often end up installing software on it. Sometimes lots of software. Believe me; I know. My Palm III is stuffed full of more software than you can imagine. (For more information on how to install new software on your PalmPilot, turn to Chapter 20, "Installing New Software on Your PalmPilot.") When, like me, you have a lot of software installed, finding the software you want to run can be very difficult. Your screen is filled with icon after icon after icon, and you don't know where to turn—or tap, that is.

If you own a Palm III, one simple way around the problem is to group applications into categories. So, in the Application Launcher, when you display a category, you see icons of only those applications in that category. As shipped, the applications come grouped into categories. For example, in the System category, you see HotSync, Preferences, and Security, as shown in the following figure.

Finding applications is easy if you group them into categories.

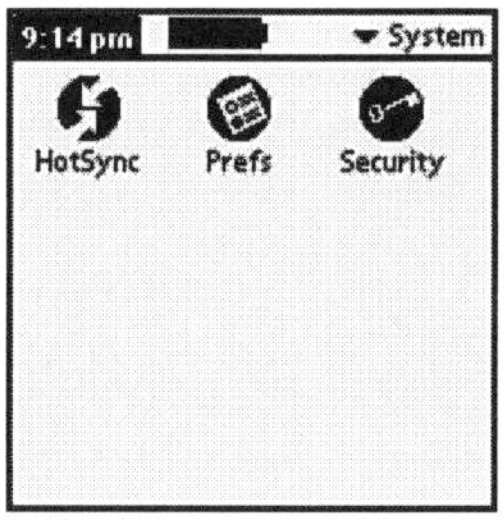

To group your applications into categories, first tap on the **Applications** button. Then tap on **Menu**, and choose **Category** from the **App** menu. (You can also use the Command stroke shortcut **/Y**.) When you do that, you see a list of all your applications and the category that they're currently in. To change the category of any one of them, tap on the triangle next to it, and choose the category where you want it to be. To create a new category, tap on a triangle next to any application, and choose **Edit Categories**. Then create a new category as you normally would.

The PalmPilot remembers which categories you've been viewing.

Let's say you're working in an application such as the Memo Pad, and you're looking at records in a category such as Soccer League. You suddenly remember you wanted to jot a note about a to-do, so you switch to the To-Do List. When you switch back from the To-Do List to the Memo Pad, you switch straight back to the Soccer League category. The Memo Pad and the To-Do List both remember what category you were last viewing and automatically start you in that category.

That's not true of the Address Book, though. In the Address Book in Palm OS 2.0 or higher, you have the option of having it remember the last category you were viewing or instead showing you all the names and addresses. To tell the PalmPilot which to do, go to the Address Book and choose **Preferences** from the **Options** menu. You then see a check box titled Remember Last Category. If you check it, the Address Book remembers which category you were last viewing and shows it to you when you come into the program. If the check box is unchecked, you instead see all the records in the Address Book.

Smart Strategies for Using Categories to Manage Your Life

You no doubt can think of many ways to use categories to help you manage your life with the PalmPilot. In addition to whatever you cook up, use these smart strategies for using PalmPilot categories to help manage your life:

- Create a category titled Projects in your Memo Pad. You can use it as a kind of master category. When a new project comes up, don't put your memos for it into the Projects category; instead, create a new category for that individual project, such as Electric Fork Launch. After you finish with the new project—in this case, Electric Fork Launch—rename it. In this example, you would rename the Electric Fork Launch category to Projects. All the memos from it are merged into the master Projects category. That way, you have a record of all your old memos concerning your projects in one place, but you don't clutter up your Memo Pad with too many categories. Periodically, go through the Projects category and delete memos you know you'll never need again.

- Create a category called Private in each of your applications as a way to keep track of all the appointments, contacts, memos, and other information that you've decided to keep private. One problem when you mark any record as private is that even you can't see it until you change your settings to be able to see those private records. And when you do that, you might not even remember where all the private records are. Putting them into a Private category helps you find them all easily.
- When you're creating new categories, keep them detailed enough so that they're of use to you but broad enough so that you don't clutter up your applications with too many categories—or hit the limit of 15 categories per application.
- In the Address Book, don't create categories that are names of individual companies. You might think that doing so will help you keep track of people, but in fact, it's a waste of categories. The Address Book contains a field in which you put company information. Because you can search by company name in the Address Book, you can find everyone and anyone in a particular company easily enough without having to use up categories.
- At least once a day, go through every category in each of your applications, making sure that you've done what needs to be done and adding any new things you need to do. Take this extra step because when categories proliferate, you can easily forget to check them all. Getting into checking them as a daily habit will help you make sure you keep your life under control.
- In the Application Launcher, create a Travel category, and put into it applications such as Expense, Email, and any other software you've installed that has to do with travel, such as faxing software. That way, when you're on the road, you can have a single place where all your travel-related applications can be found.
- You can use categories to beam many related pieces of information to a person with a single beam. In an application, group all the information you want to beam to someone into a single category. Then go into that category, and from the **Record** menu, choose **Beam Category**. All the records in that category then are beamed over. For information on how to beam information using the Palm III, turn to Chapter 19, "Beam Me Up, Scotty! Using the Palm III's Infrared Port."

The Least You Need to Know

- Until you assign records to a category, they remain unfiled, but you still can see them.
- To cycle through all the categories in an application, keep pressing the appropriate hard button. Pressing the button repeatedly brings up the records for each category in that application one after the other.
- When you need to create several records in a single category, first switch to the category, and then create the records. Every record you create is automatically put into that category.
- When you delete a category, you don't delete the category's records; you delete only the category itself. The records in that category become unfiled.
- In the Application Launcher, group categories of related applications together to make it easier to find the program you want to launch.

Chapter 10

Write On! Taking Notes with the Memo Pad

In This Chapter

- Creating new memos
- Changing the memo's font and other attributes
- Categorizing and sorting memos
- Keeping your memos private so that only you can read them
- Using the Memo Pad's shortcuts and menus
- Learning smart strategies for using the Memo Pad to make your life more productive

It's 3 a.m. You wake groggily from a dream—a dream in which a grand business plan was revealed, a business plan of such broad vision and scope, and yet presented with such utter simplicity, that it's a sure-fire bet to succeed and make you wealthy beyond your imaginings. Good-bye, boss; hello, money and freedom. Good-bye to vacations in Revere Beach and New Jersey; hello to snorkeling in Aruba and skiing in the Swiss Alps.

You grope around your night table for a pencil and paper, but there's none to be found. No problem, though. You'll never forget something this simple and obvious, you think, as you sink back into a deep, forgetful sleep....

You wake the next morning. That business plan...what was it about? Something to do with recycling the lead from pencil nubs thrown away by schoolchildren? Selling time-share parking spots in downtown Cleveland? Creating a line of electric forks and spoons? Ahhhhh! It's all gone. Still at your day job, are you?

If you had had your PalmPilot close at hand that night, all you would have had to do was press on the **Memo Pad** button, write your memo, and you wouldn't be a lifer at your current job.

In this chapter, you look at all the ways the Memo Pad can help you in your business and personal life. Whether you use the Memo Pad for jotting notes, writing full-blown memos and importing them into your PC's word processor, or keeping lists of recipes and tech support notes, you'll find it an absolutely vital part of keeping your life organized and under control.

Writing a Memo with the Memo Pad

It's 3 a.m. again. You've had the dream one more time; the plan is revealed. You're going to make your fortune by selling franchises in a new catch-your-own fish seafood chain called "You-Catch-It-We-Cook-It" that you're going to start. Ah, but this time you have your trusty PalmPilot close at hand. You fire it up, turn on the backlight so that you can see in the dark, and you're ready to go. Let me tell you how to write a memo with the Memo Pad so that the next time you have a brainstorm, you'll be able to save it for posterity (and if you use the Memo Pad intelligently enough, it'll save your posterior at times as well).

Start the Memo Pad by pushing the hard button on the lower-right corner of the PalmPilot—the one that looks like a distorted reporter's notebook. If your PalmPilot is already running, and you're at the main screen, you can instead tap on the **Memo Pad** icon.

If you've written memos before, you see a list of them. To write a new memo, tap on **New**. Then start writing in the Graffiti area with your stylus. The following figure shows a memo being written. To save the memo, tap on the **Done** button. By the way, if you shut off the PalmPilot before tapping on the **Done** button, your memo is saved. The next time you start Memo Pad, it will open with the memo that you were writing.

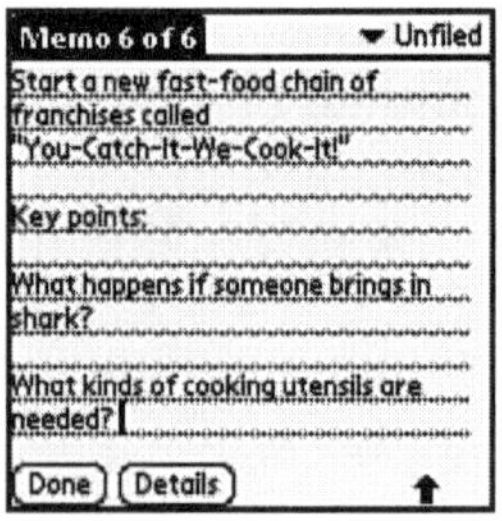

Eureka! The grand business plan revealed and captured forever in a memo in Memo Pad.

Font Madness: Changing the Fonts in Your Memo

No one is ever going to accuse the PalmPilot screen of being easy to read. The default font for memos is so small and thin that in the wrong light it looks like nothing so much as mouse scratches.

Luckily, you can change the fonts so that you can make them more readable. On a Palm III, you get three choices: the small default font, a slightly larger font, and a much larger font. To change the font on a Palm III, tap on the **Menu** button, and then choose **Font** from the **Options** menu. (You can also use the Command stroke followed by an *F*—**/F**.) You then see the following screen with three buttons on it. Tap on the font you want to use.

> **Check This Out**
>
> **When you open Memo Pad, you can create a new memo by just beginning to type.**
>
> You don't actually have to first tap on the **New** button. If you start writing using Graffiti, a new memo is automatically created, starting with the letters you're writing. The PalmPilot is smart enough so that it even capitalizes the first letter of the memo.

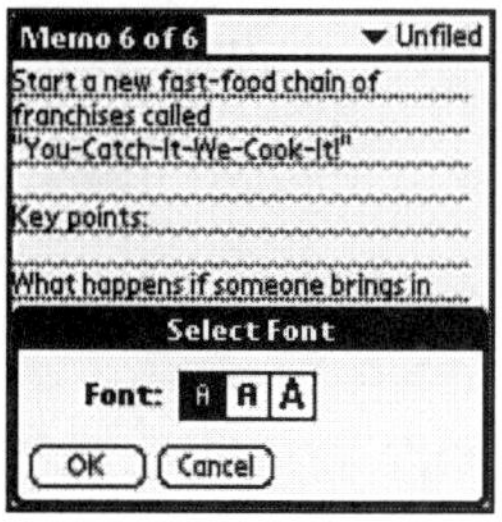

Changing the font in the Memo Pad is fantastically easy. Just tap on the button of the font you want to use.

Scrolling Through a Memo

Sometimes you have a whole lot you want to say, and it doesn't all fit into a single screen's worth on your PalmPilot—especially if you use larger-than-normal fonts. When you have more than a screen's worth of text in a memo, a scrollbar appears on the right side, as you can see in the figure that follows.

> **Check This Out**
>
> **If you have a PalmPilot Professional, you get a choice of only two fonts, not three.**
>
> On the PalmPilot Professional, the buttons for changing the fonts are always visible in a memo at the bottom of the screen.

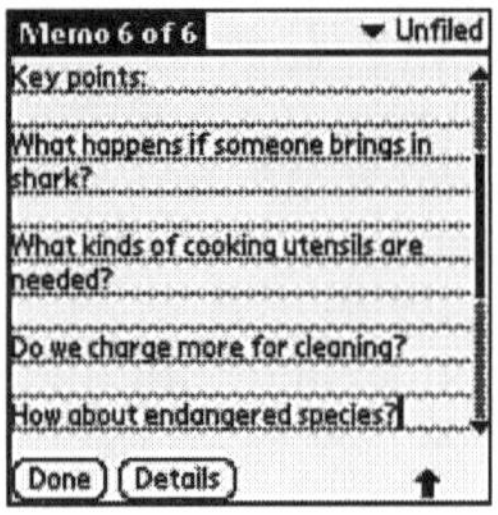

Use the scrollbar to move through long memos.

You can scroll through a memo in the following ways:

- Drag the black bar in the middle of the scrollbar up or down to move to whatever point you want in the memo.
- Tap on the little up or down arrow to move a single line at a time. If you instead hold down the stylus on either arrow, you scroll continuously through the memo.
- Tap in the gray area of the scrollbar, and you move up or down one screen. You can hold down your stylus in this area to scroll continuously.
- Press on the plastic up and down scroll buttons at the bottom of the device. Each time you press, you move up or down one screen. If you press the up button when you're at the top of the memo, you jump to the previous memo in your list of memos, if you have any. If you press the down button when you're at the bottom of the memo, you jump to the next memo in your list of memos, if you have any.

Jumping immediately to the beginning or the end of a memo is easy.

To jump, tap on the **Menu** button, and choose **Go to Top** or **Go to Bottom** from the **Options** menu.

Sorting and Categorizing Your Memos

The best way to keep track of all your memos is to categorize them. (For more detailed information on how to use categories, turn to Chapter 9, "Using PalmPilot Categories to Organize Your Life.") Unless you categorize your memos, they all appear in one long master list, like the one on the following page, when you open the Memo Pad.

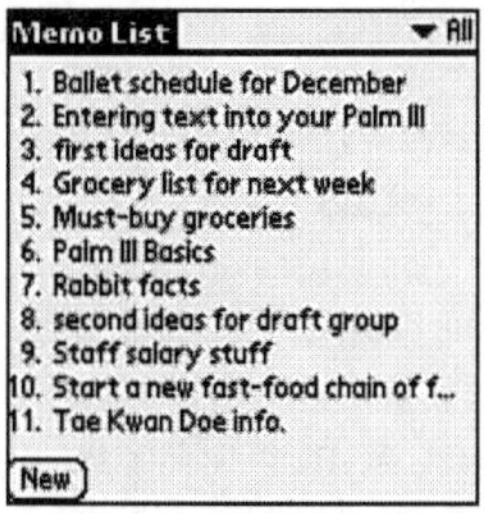

Where did you put that memo? Finding it is hard if you didn't bother to categorize it.

If you put your memos into categories, though, you can make your life much easier. You can view memos in one category at a time; for example, you might want to create one category for memos about your family budget, another for memos about your work budget, and so on. To create a category, tap on the little triangle in the upper-right corner of the PalmPilot screen, and choose the category you want to view. You then see only the memos you've written in that one category.

Categorizing your memos is easy. If you've already written memos and want to put them into categories, first call up the memo you want to categorize. From here, you can choose from two ways to put it into a category. The faster of the two is to tap on the triangle in the upper-right part of the screen, and choose the category where you want the memo to be placed.

Another way—and one you'll use if you want to do other things with the memo, such as making it private—is to tap on the **Details** button at the bottom of the screen. You then see the following screen. Tap on the triangle next to the word *Category*, choose the category where you want the memo to be filed, and you're done.

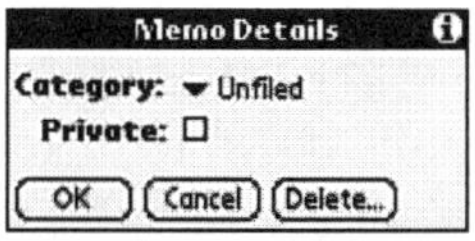

You use this screen to categorize your memos.

If you're creating a memo from scratch, categorize it in the same way. And if you want to create several memos in the same category, switch to that category, and create memos. Every memo you create is placed in the category that you're currently working in.

To view memos in different categories, when you're in the list view in the Memo Pad, tap on the little triangle in the upper-right corner of the screen. Next, choose the category you want to view. You then see a list of memos in that category.

Use this shortcut for looking through one category after another in the Memo Pad.

Don't bother to use your stylus. Instead, when you're in the Memo Pad, press the hard **Memo Pad** button. Each time you press the button, you view a different category.

How to Sort Your Memos

Categorizing your memos is a good way to help you get your memos (and life) organized. If you have a lot of memos in a particular category, though, or if you decide not to categorize your memos, always seeing your most important memos can be difficult. They might be at the bottom of the list because, by default, your memos are categorized alphabetically. So what if your most important memo is titled "Zoological implications of 'You-Catch-It-We-Cook-It'"? You'll rarely see it when you open Memo Pad.

The answer is to sort memos manually. You can move around their order in any category and put the most important ones first and the least important ones last.

To sort memos manually, when you're in the Memo list view, tap on the **Menu** button, and then choose **Preferences** from the **Options** menu. (Alternatively, you can use the **/R** Command stroke.) You then see the following screen. Choose **Sort by Manual**, and you can sort memos any way you want.

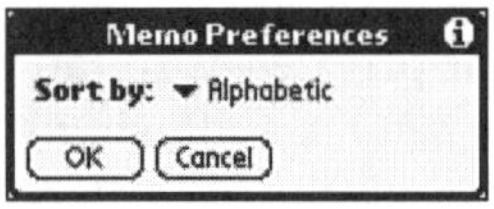

Manual labor: Here, you can decide to sort your memos manually instead of alphabetically.

After you choose this option, you can drag memos up and down the list and put them in any order you want. Just hold down with your stylus on the memo you want to move, and drag it to its new location. That's all there is to it.

That's the good news. (You knew I had to give you the bad news, didn't you?) The bad news is that when you do a HotSync, the Palm Desktop software doesn't put your memos in the order you would like. It apparently doesn't follow orders very well and therefore puts them in alphabetical order.

If you change your mind and sort alphabetically after you've done a manual sort, the order of memos in the manual sort is not remembered.

If you go back to the alphabetical sort, the sorting you did manually is lost. If you want it back, you have to sort it all by hand again.

Secret Agent: How to Keep Your Memos Private

Sometimes you might want to keep your memos private so that only you can read them. For example, you certainly don't want your boss knowing that you're in the midst of putting together a business plan for the "You-Catch-It-We-Cook-It" chain of fast-food restaurants. If he saw a memo detailing the business plan, he would know that something fishy was going on. (Sorry, but I'm a sucker for bad puns; I'm always trolling for them.)

To make a memo private, tap on the **Details** button in the memo, and then check the **Private** box. This way, you can make your memo private so that only you can see it with a password—or at least it does that if you've enabled the privacy feature on your PalmPilot. To turn on the privacy feature, go to the Security application by tapping on the **Applications** button and then on the **Security** icon. From the screen that appears, tap on the **Hide** button. You're now set. Your boss will never know about your whale of a plan.

Farewell and Good-bye: How to Delete Memos

The best-laid plans of mice and men can sometimes go awry. You pitched your "You-Catch-It-We-Cook-It" business plan to investment bankers, venture capitalists, wealthy people looking for hot investments, your best friend, your postman, your cat, and several people you dragged in off the street. For some reason, though, no one wanted to bite. No money is coming your way. Sadly, you admit to yourself that perhaps this idea is going nowhere. Time to delete the memos you've written about the venture.

To delete a memo, first call it up. Then you can delete it in one of these three ways:

- Tap on **Details**, and then tap on the **Delete** button.
- Tap on the **Menu** button, and then choose **Delete Memo** from the **Record** drop-down menu.
- Use the Command stroke shortcut **/D**.

No matter which way you choose to delete the memo, you see the following screen. Tap on **OK** to delete the memo, or tap on **Cancel** to keep the memo.

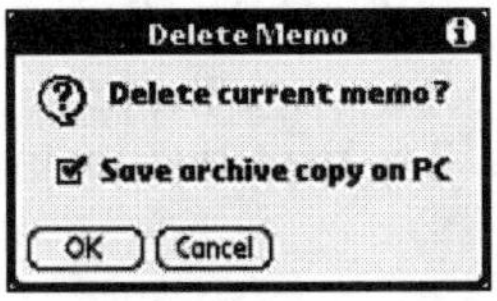

The last long good-bye: deleting a memo.

Hope always springs eternal, so perhaps you're thinking that you might like to revive the business plan some day. In that case, you can archive the memo and call it up later. To archive the memo, make sure the Save Archive Copy on PC box is checked. When you check it, the next time you do a HotSync, the memo will be saved in a special archive on your PC. For information on how to retrieve files from the archive, turn to Chapter 5, "Keeping Your Life in Sync: HotSyncing Your PC and PalmPilot."

How to Beam Memos to Others

If you have a Palm III or higher, you can beam memos or even entire categories of memos to other people with Palm IIIs or higher. You do so as follows:

- **To beam a single memo** Call up the memo, tap on the **Menu** button, and choose **Beam Memo** from the **Record** menu. You can also use the Command stroke shortcut /**B**.
- **To beam every memo in a category** Go to the Memo List of the category you want to beam, tap on the **Menu** button, and choose **Beam Category** from the **Record** menu. (No Command stroke shortcut is available for beaming an entire category to another Palm.)

For more information about beaming information to others, turn to Chapter 19, "Beam Me Up, Scotty! Using the Palm III's Infrared Port."

What's on the Menu? Using the Memo Pad's Menus and Shortcuts

To cut and paste text, beam memos, change the fonts, and so on in the Memo Pad, you use the Memo Pad's menus and shortcuts. The shortcuts are basically ways to perform tasks that you would normally perform with a menu, but doing so more quickly by using the Command stroke. The Command stroke is an upward slash you make with your stylus in the Graffiti area, starting at the bottom left and moving to the upper right. You follow the Command stroke by writing a letter that accomplishes the task you want done. (For more information about the Command stroke, turn to Chapter 7, "Digital Magic: Taking Notes with Graffiti.")

The menus in Memo Pad are different, depending on whether you're looking at a list of memos or instead are working in a memo itself. Let me give you the lowdown on the menus and shortcuts for each.

Menus and Shortcuts in the Memo List

When you're working in the Memo List, looking at a list of your memos, you can't do a whole lot with the menus and shortcuts. You have two main menu choices: Record and Options.

From the **Record** menu, you can

- Beam all the records in the category you're currently using by choosing **Beam Category**. That's it.

From the **Options** menu, you can

- Choose **Font** to change the Font in the list view (Command stroke: /**F**).
- Choose **Preferences** to change the way you sort your memos (Command stroke: /**R**).

Menus and Shortcuts in the Memo Itself

When you're working in a memo, you can perform many tasks with menus and shortcuts, such as cutting and pasting text, beaming the memo, and much more. You have three main options: Record, Edit, and Options.

From the **Record** menu, you can

- Choose **New Memo** to create a new memo (Command stroke: /**N**).
- Choose **Delete Memo** to delete the memo (Command stroke: /**D**).
- Choose **Beam Memo** to beam the memo to someone with a Palm III or higher (Command stroke: /**B**).

From the **Edit** menu, you can

- Choose **Undo** to undo the last action you took (Command stroke: /**U**). For example, if you accidentally deleted text, you can get it back by using this command.
- Choose **Cut** to delete a selection of text and put it into the Clipboard (Command stroke: /**X**). You then can paste the text somewhere else on the PalmPilot.
- Choose **Copy** to put a selection of text into the Clipboard (Command stroke: /**C**). You then can paste the text somewhere else on the PalmPilot.
- Choose **Paste** to copy text into the memo from the Clipboard (Command stroke: /**P**).
- Choose **Select All** to select all the text in the memo (Command stroke: /**S**).
- Choose **Keyboard** to call up the onscreen keyboard for entering text (Command stroke: /**K**).
- Choose **Graffiti Help** to call up a list of all the Graffiti keystrokes (Command stroke: /**G**).

From the **Options** menu, you can

- Choose **Font** to change the font in the memo (Command stroke: /**F**).
- Choose **Go to Top of Page** to go to the top of the memo (no Command stroke).
- Choose **Go to Bottom of Page** to go to the bottom of the memo (no Command stroke).
- Choose **Phone Lookup** to look up something in the Address Book (Command stroke: /**L**). You then can add information from the Address Book into your memo.

Smart Strategies for Using the Memo Pad to Make Your Life More Productive

You can probably think of a lot of ways you can use the Memo Pad to get your life under control. The following are even more smart strategies for using the Memo Pad:

- You can print memos and use special formatting such as fonts, bold text, and more by importing memos from the Memo Pad into your computer's word processor. To do so, do a HotSync. Then open the Palm Desktop, and click on the **Memo Pad** icon. Now drag the memo you want to print to the **Word** icon. Word automatically opens, with your memo in it, waiting for you to do whatever you want.
- The Memo Pad is a perfect place to keep your favorite recipes; that way, they are always at hand so that you can pick up groceries for them on your way home from work. Type the recipes into a word processor (or paste them into a word processor from a Web site). Then open the Palm Desktop. Now cut and paste the recipes from your word processor into the Palm Desktop Memo Pad—one recipe per memo. When you next do a HotSync, the recipes are all on your PalmPilot. You can even put them into categories, such as desserts, main dishes, and so on.
- If you're working on a project, and you need to contact many people in concert with it, put all their names into a memo titled Contacts in the same category as your other memos on that project. Paste their names in by choosing **Phone Lookup** from the **Options** menu (or use the **/L** Command stroke shortcut). This way, you don't have to search through the Address Book every time you need to find someone's phone number for the project; just open the Memo Pad.
- If you're a collector—whether it be sports cards, Beanie Babies, old bottlecaps, license plates, or anything else—use the Memo Pad to keep track of them. You can create a single category for all your collectibles. If your collection is large enough, you can create several categories (such as baseball cards, football cards, and so on). Then, for each object you've collected, create a separate memo with all the important details about it.

The Least You Need to Know

- You can create a new memo by starting to type when you're in the Memo list view; you don't have to tap on the **New** button.
- Make the fonts on memos larger (to make them easier to read) by choosing **Font** from the **Options** memo or by using the **/F** Command stroke shortcut.
- To sort your memos manually so that they're in the order you want, choose **Preferences** from the **Options** menu, and then choose **Manual**. Then drag your memos in the list to the place where you want them.
- To print your memos, use special fonts and other attributes, first HotSync your PalmPilot; then go into the Palm Desktop. Drag your memo to the **Word** icon, and Word is opened with your memo already in it.

Chapter 11

Juggling Your Busy Schedule with the Date Book

In This Chapter

- Scheduling new events with the Date Book
- Scheduling repeating events and setting alarms
- Keeping certain appointments, events, and reminders private
- Using the Day, Week, and Month views
- Discovering smart strategies and tips for organizing your time with the Date Book

It's 3 p.m. Do you know where you're supposed to be?

Are you supposed to be at a meeting with your boss about your request for a salary increase? Maybe you are supposed to pick up your son to take him to his piano lesson. Or are you supposed to lead a staff seminar on better time management? Perhaps you have to watch your daughter play goalie in her soccer finals. And you have this nagging feeling that you are, in fact, supposed to be in a different state entirely, participating in a conference on the newest mushroom-growing technology.

Why do all these events sound so familiar? Probably because you're supposed to be at all of them at the same time. You've done it again; you're overbooked, overpromised, and overextended.

If you had been using your PalmPilot's Date Book, none of this would have happened. With a few taps of your stylus, you could have scheduled your time properly, so you wouldn't be in this bind. Piano, salary raise, soccer, mushroom technology—you would be able to do them all, with no conflicts at all. So check out this chapter to see how you can juggle your busy schedule with the Date Book, and you'll never overbook, overpromise, and overextend yourself again.

How to Schedule a New Event

Press on the **Date Book** hard button on the lower left of the PalmPilot to switch to the Date Book. (If your PalmPilot isn't yet turned on, pressing the button also turns on the PalmPilot.) Assuming that you've set your preferences so that it's the proper day (see Chapter 3, "Time For Takeoff: Starting Your PalmPilot for the First Time," for information on how to set your preferences), you see a screen that displays today's date and all the hours of the day, mercifully free, because you haven't yet scheduled anything. How nice. If only life really were that way—a clean slate every day. This view, shown in the following figure, is called the Day view.

A rare sight: your Date Book's Day view with nothing scheduled.

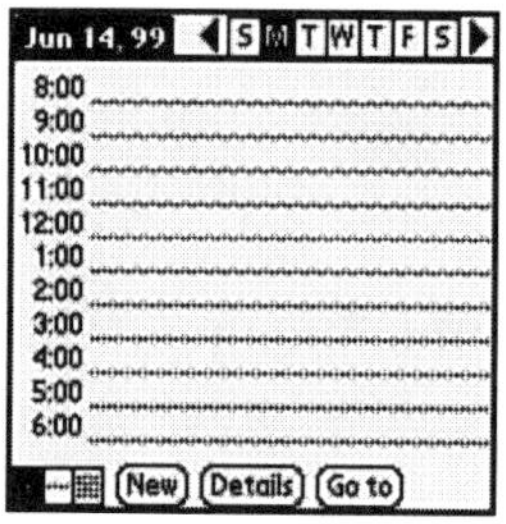

Nothing could be simpler than to schedule an event or appointment. Choose from one of these two ways to do it:

- ➤ Tap on the time when you want to schedule an event, write in what the event is, and you're done. It's that simple. By default, the appointment or event is scheduled to last for one hour. If you want to start or end at a different time, tap on the time on the left side of your screen (for example, 10:00), and you can use the Set Time screen, as shown in the following figure.

Here, you can pick a time for an event you're scheduling.

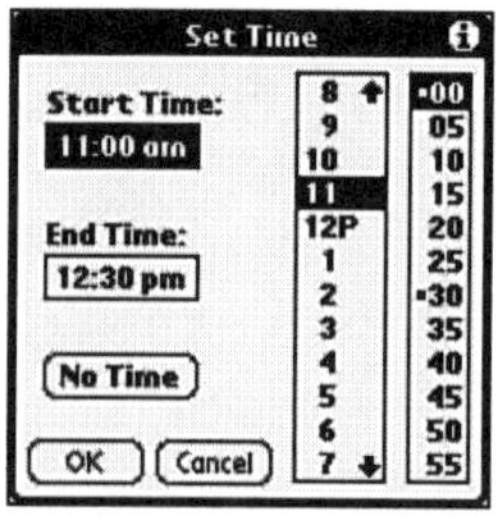

- Tap on the **New** button. You then see the Set Time screen, shown in the preceding figure, which lets you choose the starting and ending time for the event. Tap on the proper buttons, choose the times you want, and you're done. Note that you can also schedule an event that has no fixed time—for example, someone's birthday or a deadline of some sort.

Schedule an event by writing the starting time with Graffiti.

You can schedule an event in yet another way: Simply write the starting hour of the event in the right side of the Graffiti writing area. You then can use the Set Time screen to schedule the event. After you set the time, you have to write in what the event is when you return to the Day view.

Scheduling an Event on a Different Day Than the Current One

As you can see, you can easily schedule an event on your current day. But let's get real: How often do you *really* do that? Not very often, I bet. Mostly, you schedule events that occur on a different day, month, or even year (and based on some of the meetings I've had to schedule, sometimes I think they even occur in a different *universe*).

You can schedule an event on a different day than the current one in the following ways:

- If the event takes place during the same week as the current one, on the top of the screen, tap on the day the event will take place. You are sent to that day. Now schedule the event as you normally would.
- If the event takes place on a day within a few weeks of the current one, on top of the screen, tap on the forward or backward arrows until you get to the week in which the event takes place. Then tap on the day the event will take place, and schedule the event as you normally would.
- For any date, tap on the **Go To** button on the bottom of the screen. When you see the following screen, you can navigate to the right date. Then schedule the event as you normally would.

Pick a date, any date. Here, you can navigate to another date in the Date Book to schedule an appointment.

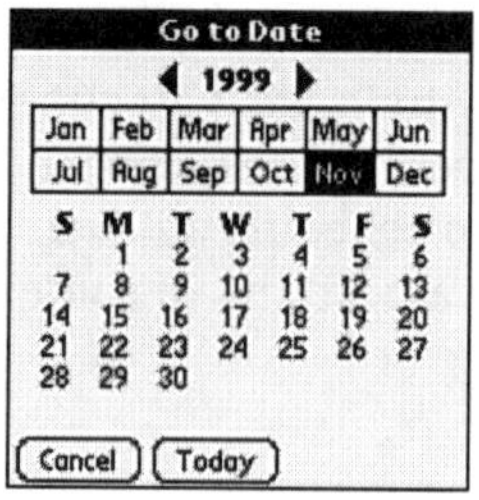

It's Déjà Vu All Over Again: Scheduling Repeating Events

A lot of things in your life occur at the same time every day, week, month, or year. You have birthdays and anniversaries, staff meetings, luncheon appointments, Tai Chi lessons, mid-life crises…no, delete the last one. That one hits at unscheduled times, unfortunately.

The PalmPilot makes it easy to schedule repeating events. When you create an event, tap on the **Details** button at the bottom of your screen. You then see the Event Details screen, as shown in the following figure. You'll use this screen a lot, for making events private, setting alarms, and so on, so get used to it.

The Event Details screen lets you schedule repeating events and keep events private.

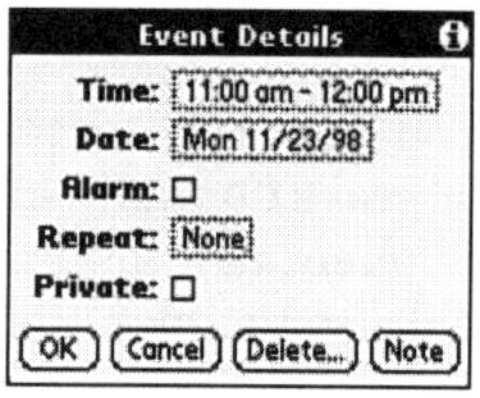

To make the event repeat, tap inside the **Repeat** dotted rectangle. You then see the screen on the left. Now choose whether you want to repeat the event daily, weekly, monthly, or yearly. When you do, you see the screen on the right.

Here, you can make an event repeat over and over and over…by filling in the details of when you want the event to repeat.

On this screen, you fill in the details of how you want the event to repeat. For example, if you choose the Week option, do you want it to repeat every week, every second week, every third week, or even less often? Tap next to the **Every** option, and put in a number to determine the frequency the event repeats.

You can also pick an end date for the time you want the event to stop repeating, on which day of the week you want it to repeat (or which day or date of the month if you've chosen an event that repeats according to the month), and other details. This process is pretty straightforward. Just keep tapping away. If you get confused, just fiddle with it some. It doesn't take very long to figure out.

Schedule vacation time by using recurring events and the No Time feature.

The PalmPilot doesn't give you any built-in way to schedule any event that spans several days or weeks such as a vacation. To schedule such an event, create it as an event that recurs for every day of your vacation. Also, schedule it as an event that has No Time attached to it; that way, you can still use your PalmPilot to schedule beach trips and lunches with friends during your vacation.

I Want My Privacy: How to Keep Events Private

Sometimes you want to keep events private—for example, a surprise birthday for a friend or co-worker. To make an event private, tap on the **Details** button of the event to get to the Event Details screen. Then tap on the **Private** box to add a check mark there. This way, you can make your event private so that only you can see it with a password—or at least it does that if you've enabled the privacy feature on your PalmPilot. To turn on the privacy feature, go to the Security application by tapping on the **Applications** button and then on the **Security** icon. From the screen that appears, tap on the **Hide** button. The event is now private.

Adding Notes to Events

Often, when you set an appointment or create an event, you want to add a whole lot of details. However, the small space you're given to write information about an appointment doesn't do you much good. If you want to jot down ideas about the presentation you're planning to give at the Mushroom Growers Technology Conference, you are out of luck—or so it might look.

In fact, you're in luck because the PalmPilot lets you attach notes to any event. To attach a note to a document, tap on **Details**, and then from the Event Details screen, tap on **Note**. You then can jot down a note about the event.

When you add a note to a repeating event, you have the option of whether to add it only to the current event or to every instance of the repeating event. When you want to add a note to a repeating event, you see the following screen. When it appears, just choose whether you want the note to be attached only to this one occurrence or to every occurrence of the event.

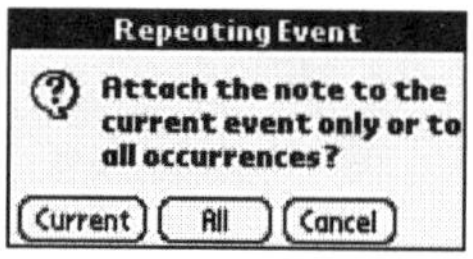

Once or many times? You can decide whether to attach a note to every occurrence of a repeating event.

Use the Address Book as a birthday reminder—and to remember which gifts to buy.

You can use the Address Book not just to help you remember someone's birthday, but also to know what gift to buy. First, create a repeating Address Book event for someone's birthday. Then attach a note to it, recording what you've bought for presents in the past and what you plan to buy this year. That way, you'll never buy someone the same gift twice. Make sure to mark the event as private so that the birthday boy or girl can't see it. And use the Alarm feature to remind you when to buy the present. You learn how to use the alarm later in this chapter.

By the way, I've discovered an annoying little "feature" (a nice way to say "bug") of the PalmPilot. If you attach a note to a repeating event when you first create it, you don't get the screen asking whether to attach a note only to this occurrence of the event or to every occurrence. The PalmPilot blithely attaches the note to every occurrence of the event. So, if you're creating a repeating event for the first time and are attaching a note—and you don't want that note to show up for every occurrence of the event—first create the event and then tap on **Done**. Then, when you're done, go back into the Event Details screen, and tap on **Note**. Now you'll get the preceding screen to allow you to decide whether to attach the note to every occurrence or just this one.

Cause for Alarm: Setting Alarms in the Date Book

If you're like me, you tend to be a bit absent-minded. I've been known to put the car keys in the refrigerator, for example—although so far I haven't tried to start my Toyota with broccoli. I've also been known to forget buying presents for people on time or to forget about luncheon appointments. (Memo to Keith: Sorry. I really did forget that I was going to be on vacation on the date when we had our luncheon appointment scheduled.)

There's good news for people like me and for anyone who needs a gentle reminder when events or appointments are coming up. You can use the Address Book to set alarms. When you set an alarm, your PalmPilot doesn't quite dance and sing, but it certainly does make its presence known. If the PalmPilot is turned off, and it's time to sound the alarm, it turns itself on, chirps and beeps at you, and then flashes an alert on the screen.

To set an alarm for an event, tap on the **Details** button to bring up the Event Details screen, as shown in the following figure. Check the **Alarm** box. When you do that, you get a choice of how far in advance you want to set the alarm, either in minutes, hours, or days.

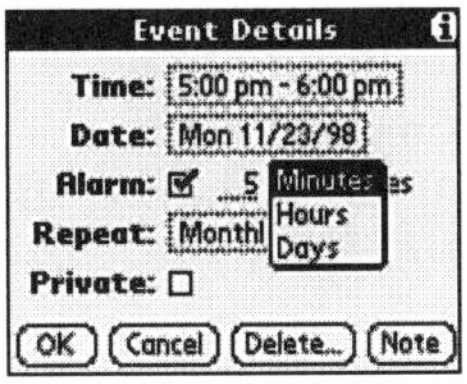

You can set alarms in the PalmPilot here.

After you set the alarm, the PalmPilot waits before springing into action. Then, at the appointed date and time, it turns itself on, if it isn't on already, and plays sounds in its chirpy little voice. On the Palm III or higher, you get a choice from a variety of chirpy sounds. On the earlier PalmPilots, you get ding-dong type sounds. You also get a full screen alert telling you that you have business to attend to.

You can also set alarms for untimed events, such as birthdays and anniversaries. Do so in the same way that you set alarms for any other kinds of events. The only difference is that the PalmPilot doesn't sing and dance when the alarm goes off; the alarm doesn't make any sound when it goes off for an untimed event. The alarm screen appears, and that's it. And the PalmPilot doesn't turn itself on to show you the screen; it appears only if you turn on the little thing yourself.

Position your PalmPilot properly to hear its alarms.

The PalmPilot isn't blessed with an especially powerful speaker; anemic would be the best description of it. So, you could easily miss an alarm when it goes off. The speaker inside the PalmPilot faces the back of the device. To make the speaker louder, turn it upside down onto its face; that way, the speaker isn't quite as muffled than it is when the speaker is pointed into your desk.

Editing and Deleting Appointments and Events

Your boss has scheduled your salary review with you—about seven times. Each time you're about to find out about your new raise, she puts off the appointment so that you have to reschedule it. Or your best friend canceled lunch on you because he had to watch his pet opossum run in a race. Welcome to life. Appointments were made to be changed or broken.

You can easily edit an appointment—for example, to change its time, change the note you've written about it, or make it private. To do so, tap on the appointment you want to change, and then tap on the **Details** button. The now-familiar Event Details screen appears. Just make any changes you want from here, whether it be about the time, to set an alarm, or to change anything else about the event. You can delete the appointment or event from this screen as well. By the way, you can also move appointments and events around another way, by using the Week view. See "Using the Day View, the Week View, and the Month View" for details on how to do it.

You also can delete an appointment or event in another way. Tap on the appointment you want to delete. Then tap on the **Menu** button, and choose **Delete Event** from the **Record** menu. (You can also use the Command stroke shortcut **/D**.)

Using the Day View, the Week View, and the Month View

The whole point of making appointments with the Date Book, of course, is that you can see your schedule. You can view your schedule in three different views:

- **The Day view** Shows you all the appointments and events on a single day. This view is the only screen from which you can create and edit events.

- **The Week view** Shows you an entire week's schedule. You can move appointments and other events from one day and time to another in this view. However, you can't create or otherwise edit appointments and events.
- **The Month view** Shows you an entire month's schedule. You can't create, edit, or move events from this view. It's for viewing purposes only.

To move from view to view, just tap one of the three adjoining squares on the lower left of the screen, as you can see in the following figure. The one on the left is for the Day view, the middle one is for the Week view, and the right-most one is for the Month view.

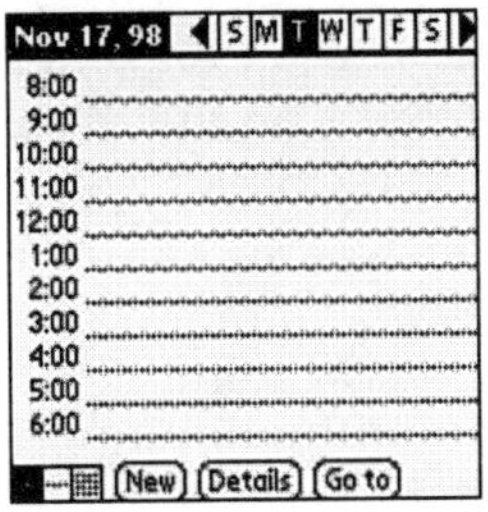

By tapping one of these three squares, you can move among the three different views in Date Book.

Using the Day View

The Day view is what you'll use most of the time in the Date Book. It looks a lot like many desk calendars—only very, very small. It lists your schedule for the day. As I've already explained (you've been listening, haven't you?), in this view you create new events and edit old ones. Those are the tasks we've been looking at in this chapter so far.

In the following figure, notice the interesting little icons and widgety-looking things in the Day view. The diamond shape by the top of the screen indicates that the event next to it is an untimed event—in this case, a birthday. The little icon of what looks like a sheet of paper with a folded-down corner next to an appointment or event means a note is attached to it. The little icon of two squares on top of one another means that it's a repeating event. The itsy-bitsy little clock indicates that an event has an alarm attached to it. And the bracket-like line next to each event shows how long the appointment or event is scheduled for.

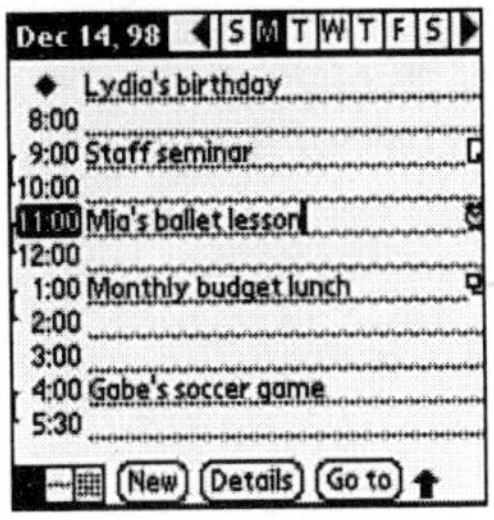

The Day view and all the little icons and widgety-looking things.

Oh, about that birthday. What you *can't* see here is the private event I've scheduled—a surprise birthday party for Lydia. I've chosen to hide private events so that only I know about them.

To see your schedule for another day of the week, tap on the day you want to view at the top of the screen. To move to another week, tap on either of the arrows. You can also move from day to day by pressing on the hard scroll button at the bottom of your PalmPilot.

Cycle through the views in your Date Book.

Let me tell you about a simple way to cycle through the views in the Date Book. Just keep pressing the **Date Book** hard button at the lower left of the PalmPilot, and it cycles through one after the other.

Using the Week View

Want to see your schedule for the week? Just tap on the **Week** view button, and you're there, as you can see in the figure on the left. Each gray block indicates that you have an appointment. Tap on any of the blocks, and you see the details of the appointment show up on the top of the screen, as shown in the figure on the right.

The Week view has a particularly neat feature that no other view has in the Date Book: You can drag appointments from one time or day to another. Just put your stylus on the appointment you want to move, and drag it to the day or time you want it moved to. Done. Unfortunately, you can drag appointments only to a date in the week you're looking at.

Busy, busy, busy. On the left is the Week view, with gray blocks showing when you're busy. Tap on any of the blocks, and you see what the appointment is about, shown at the top in the right screen.

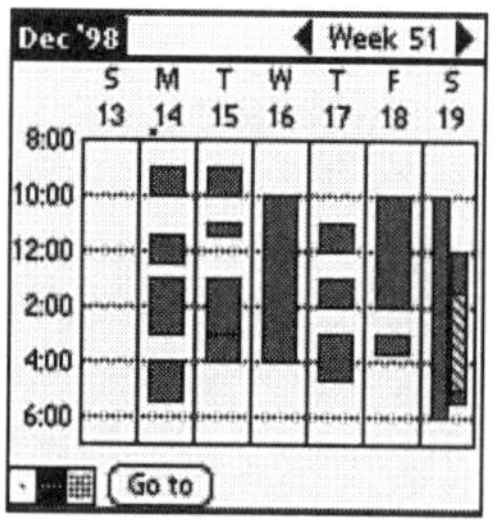

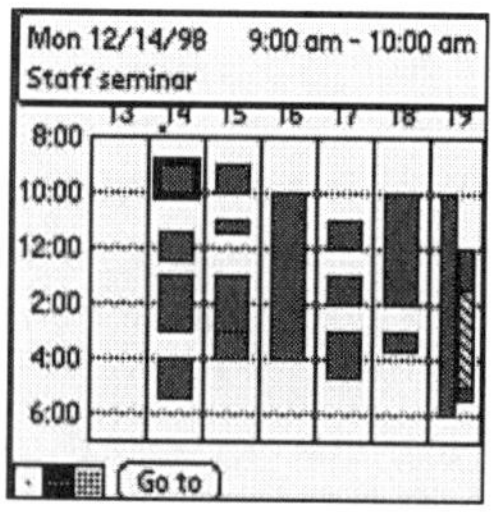

To look at a different week, tap on one of the arrows on the top of the screen, or else use the hard scroll buttons at the bottom of the PalmPilot. To go to the Day view on any individual day, tap on any blank area between the gray blocks on the day you want to see. You then are sent there.

You might want to know a few other things about the Week view:

- A small dot appears underneath any day that has a nontimed event scheduled, such as a birthday. You can see that dot on the preceding Week view figure.
- If you've scheduled two events that conflict with one another, they appear as two small gray boxes side by side. Again, look at the preceding figure of the Week view to see a conflict.
- If you've scheduled more than two events that conflict with one another, they are indicated by a striped box, as you can see in the preceding figure of the Week view. If you see a whole lot of striped boxes in your schedule, you're too busy. Take a vacation.
- Do you see the Go To button at the bottom of the screen? Guess what it's used for. Yes, you win the prize. Tap on it to go to another date. Tap on it, choose the week where you want to go, and you then get sent there.

Using the Month View

Want to see your schedule for a month at a time? Tap on the little month button, and take a look. Check out the following figure to see what the screen looks like.

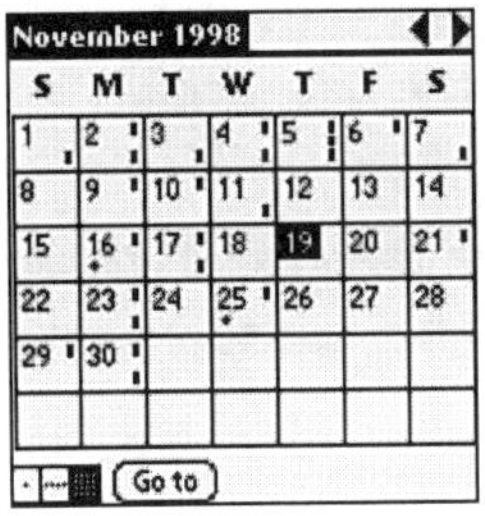

Here, you can see the Month view in the Date Book.

You can use the Month view to get an overview of your schedule for the month; it doesn't really let you do anything else. For each appointment, you see a tiny black box. If the box is at the top of the day, you have a morning appointment; if the box is in the middle, your appointment is in the middle of the day; and if it's in the bottom of the box, you have an afternoon or evening appointment.

To see the day's schedule, simply tap on it. To go to a different month, tap the arrows at the top of the screen, or use the hard scroll button at the bottom of your PalmPilot. You can also tap the **Go To** button to go to a specific month.

Show extra symbols and information in the Month view.

You can have the Month view show information about your appointments—such as whether you have a nontimed event in a given day (it shows a tiny plus sign) or a repeating daily event (it shows an underline). To have the view show this information, tap on the **Menu** button in the Month view, and then choose **Display Options**. From that screen, check **Show Untimed Events** and **Show Daily Repeating Evts**.

Smart Strategies for Using the Date Book

Too much to do, too little time. That's your life and the life of just about everyone you know these days. Well, you can use the Date Book not just to look at your schedule, but also to take control of your life and your time. How to do that? Use the smart tips and strategies I describe next for using the Date Book.

Use the Internet to Share Your Date Book—and Use Your Calendar Even Without Your PalmPilot

You can share your calendar with others—with your family, for example—and also always have access to your schedule, even if you don't have your PalmPilot. To do that, sync your Date Book with a free Web-based calendar service. Yahoo and PlanetAll both offer free calendar services that allow you to put your PalmPilot calendar on the Web.

You can decide whether to keep your calendar private or share it with others. You export your schedule to the Web, and then you can access it there, for example, if you're traveling and your PalmPilot crashes. Not only that, but you can even schedule your time on the Web calendar and export it to your PalmPilot later. And a big benefit is that storing your calendar on the Web is a great way to keep a copy of your schedule in case your computer and PalmPilot both crash (Heaven forbid).

For more details, see Chapter 23, "Traveling with Your PalmPilot." You can get to the Yahoo Web calendar by going to `http://calendar.yahoo.com/`. For PlanetAll, head to `www.planetall.com`.

Use Categories to Organize Your Schedule

One drawback to the Date Book is that it doesn't allow you to group events into categories, as do other PalmPilot programs. However, using categories is a great way to take control of your life and time; for more information on how to do so, see Chapter 9, "Using PalmPilot Categories to Organize Your Life." What to do? Let me tell you about this workaround. Decide in what ways you want to categorize your appointments and events, such as Family, Work, and so on. Then, whenever you create an appointment, put the name of the category, with a colon, at the front of the appointment, like this: "Family: Drive Mia to ballet class." That way, when you're scanning your schedule, you can easily see the categories of things you have to do that day at a glance.

Even more important, when you use the PalmPilot's Find function, you can search by that category and see all your appointments related to it. So, for example, if you search for **Family:**, you see all the family-related events and appointments you've scheduled. (See Chapter 15, "Where Did I Put That Note? Finding Information on Your PalmPilot," for more information on using Find.)

Create Regular Reminders Without Cluttering Up Your Date Book

Many times, you might want to be reminded to do something regularly, such as drive your child to piano lessons at a certain time every day of the week or to take medications at certain times of the day. You just don't want to clutter up your Date Book with all that stuff. You can easily have the PalmPilot warn you when things have to be done, but you'll never have to see the events cluttering up your Date Book.

To follow this strategy, first create an event. Because it's one that happens regularly, schedule it as a repeating event and fill in details about how much ahead of time you want an alarm to sound. Now mark the event as private. After you do so, make sure that you hide all your private records by going to the Security application and telling it to hide them.

That's all there is to it. So every day at 5:30 p.m., an alarm will go off telling you to leave work and pick up your son to take him to his piano lesson, but you'll never actually see the "Drive Gabe to piano lesson" event that you've scheduled every day.

The Least You Need to Know

- To schedule an event or appointment, you have to be in the Day view. Tap on the **New** button to create an event or appointment.
- You can use the **Details** button to schedule repeating events, to add notes to your appointments, and to keep certain events private.
- You can use the Week view to reschedule appointments and events by simply dragging them from one date and time to another.
- In the Month view, you can see your schedule at a glance but can't create new appointments or move existing ones.
- You can sync your Date Book with a free Web-based calendar such as Yahoo's at `http://calendar.yahoo.com/` to share your schedule with others, to get access to your schedule even if you forget your PalmPilot or if it crashes, and to have a backup of your schedule so that you never lose it.

Chapter 12

Keeping Track of Contacts with the Address Book

In This Chapter

- Adding names and addresses to the Address Book
- Editing and deleting names in the Address Book
- Keeping contacts private and adding notes to contacts
- Categorizing contacts and customizing the way that names and addresses appear
- Using custom fields to track any information
- Beaming your own personal business card to others with Palm IIIs
- Discovering smart strategies for managing your life with the Address Book

You met someone six months ago—someone who, you now realize, could change your life if only you could get in touch with him. He was a venture capitalist, looking for hot, new investments to pour money into, and you've come up with your latest business brainstorm: high-tech mushroom farming kits that you can sell to suburbanites who want to make extra money growing the fungi in their basements. How could the idea miss?

The only problem is that you need money—and for the life of you, you can't remember the man's name or company. Was his name Joseph Portobello? His company Shiitake Enterprises? No, that's not right. You're in the dark. You'll never remember. Another brilliant idea gone down the tubes.

If you had used your PalmPilot's Address Book, you would be sitting pretty now, the head of a vast mycological (relating to mushrooms, for those without a dictionary) financial empire. You would have been able to call up the venture capitalist's name and phone number with a few quick taps of your stylus. As it is, though, it's 6:45 a.m., and you have to head into rush-hour traffic to get to work.

In this chapter, you learn how to use the Address Book to track and find names, addresses, and other information. You also learn tips and strategies for managing all your contacts—even for using your PalmPilot to create mailing lists, for example.

Getting Started with the Address Book

Press on the **Address Book** hard button on your PalmPilot (it's the one with the picture of the telephone on it), or tap on its icon on your screen to open the Address Book in a view called the Address List. In this view, you see a list of all your contacts in alphabetical order. Tap on any of them, and you see all the information about them in what's called the Address View. Check out the following figures to see the Address List and a single contact in the Address View.

Start the Address Book to see an alphabetical list of all your contacts, as shown on the left. Tap on a contact to see all the information about him or her, as shown on the right.

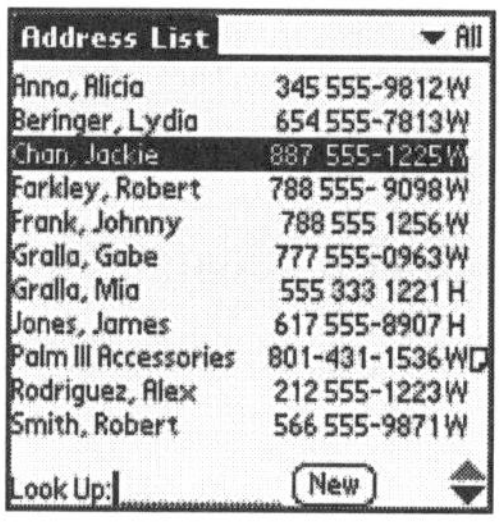

You can also add notes to any of your contacts to add more information about them—for example, personal information such as their birthdays. Whenever a note is attached to a name, you see the little Note icon next to it, as you can see in the figure on the left.

You can easily scroll through your list of contacts: Tap on the arrows, or use the up and down scroll buttons on your PalmPilot.

Normally, when you look at your list of contacts, they are sorted alphabetically by the person's name. If you would like, though, you can instead sort them by company name. To do so, tap on the **Menu** button, and choose **Preferences** from the **Options** menu. On the screen that pops up, tell your PalmPilot to sort the list by company name.

How to Add a New Name to the Address Book

Let's rewind your life. At a cocktail party, you meet Harold Crimini, a squat-looking, pasty-faced man with an over-large head, and he mentions to you that he's a venture capitalist looking to fund any hot, new startup businesses—especially any that involve dark places, fertilizer, and odd-looking fungi. You whip out your PalmPilot, press the **Address Book** button, and spring into action. You put his name into your PalmPilot.

To add his name, tap on the **New** button, and start filling in the form that appears, as shown in the following figure. Fill in any information that's applicable. Any information that isn't applicable, just leave blank. When you're finished, tap on the **Done** button. Guess what? You're done.

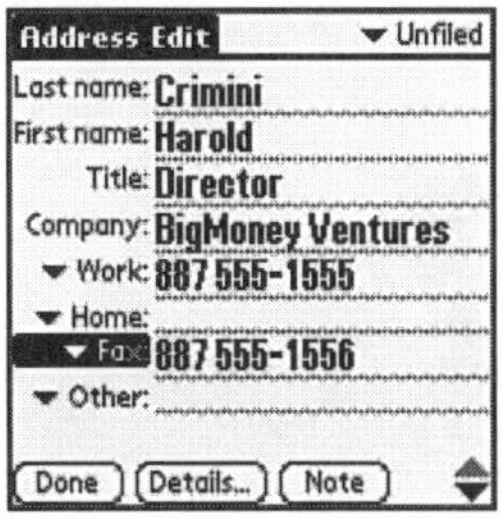

You fill out this form to add a new contact to your Address Book.

You can more easily enter contacts on your PC and HotSync them to your Address Book.

The PC has a full-fledged keyboard, which makes entering new contacts much easier than it is on the PalmPilot. When possible, enter new contacts on your PC and HotSync them over; you can save lots of time. And if you really want to save time—but spend some extra money—get a business-card scanner, such as the Corex CardScan, to scan in business cards.

When you're filling out the form, you might find it a little annoying that you have to keep lifting your stylus from the Graffiti area to tap on the next field on the form you need to fill out. For example, after you finish writing in someone's last name, you need to lift the stylus to be able to write in someone's first name. At least, *I* find it annoying.

Guess what? I know a shortcut. When you're done filling out one field in the form and need to go to the next, keep your stylus in the Graffiti area, and use the keystroke shown on the left in the following figure. To move to a previous field in the form, use the keystroke shown on the right. In both instances, make sure to pass the stylus back across the same line on the return stroke.

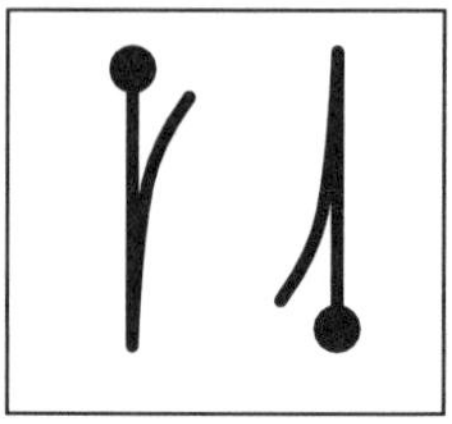

A quick way to move from field to field in the Address Book is to use the Graffiti stroke on the left to move to the next field and the one on the right to move to the previous field.

Save time by bulk-loading all your contacts into the Address Book.

If you already have your contacts in a program on your computer such as Outlook or ACT!, you don't need to add them by hand into the PalmPilot. Instead, you can use an add-in program such as Desktop to Go or IntelliSync to take all the names from your computer and do a HotSync to send them all to the Address Book on your PalmPilot. If you find it difficult to add names into the Address Book using the PalmPilot, you can instead add the names on the Palm Desktop Address Book and then use HotSync to send them into your PalmPilot Address Book.

You've no doubt noticed that all the various ways to contact people is getting totally out of hand. One person may have an email address, a regular phone, and a pager; another might have a cellular phone and a fax number; another might have two email addresses; another might have all that and more. At first glance, the PalmPilot is one-size-fits-all; it appears to offer no way to put in two email addresses for one person, for example, and a cellular phone and a pager for another.

Actually, you can enter multiple items, and you can do so easily. As you're entering information about someone, if you want to change the label (such as pager, email, and so on) for the contact information, you can. Simply tap on the triangle next to one of the labels, and you can change the label. The following figure shows you what I mean.

You can easily change the kind of contact information you track for anyone. Tap on the triangle next to a label, and then choose from this menu.

Adding Details in the Address Book

The Address Book can do a whole lot more for you than just let you simply add names. You also can keep some names private, you can categorize your contacts to make it easy to find the ones you want fast, and more. To do all that, you use what's inelegantly called the Address Entry Details screen. To get to that screen, which is shown in the following figure, tap on **Details** when you're adding a new name.

In the Address Entry Details screen, you can add all kinds of details to any of your contacts in the Address Book.

Get used to this screen. You're going to use it a whole lot as you go through the rest of this chapter to perform tasks such as keeping contacts private.

How to Edit Contacts in the Address Book

After you put a name into the Address Book, you can still change any of the information there, such as phone numbers, the name itself, or any details at all. To edit a record, first tap on someone's name from the Address List. When you see a record with all the information in it, tap on **Edit**. The same form that you used to create the record in the first place then pops up. Use it as you normally would, including using the Address Entry Details screen shown previously.

Keep Your Names to Yourself: How to Keep Contacts Private

So, you have Harold Crimini as a contact. Great. But you still have a problem. You don't want anyone else to be able to see his name or phone number, just in case friends or co-workers have competing business plans of their own that they want to pitch to him. You want to keep his record private.

To make a record private, tap on the **Details** screen, and from the screen that pops up, check the **Private** box. To make sure that the record doesn't show up, go to the

Security application by tapping on **Applications** and then **Security**. In that screen, make sure that you've chosen to hide private records.

Adding Notes to the Address Book

One of the more useful features of the Address Book is that you can add notes to the names you put there. Why bother to do that? A number of reasons. The first is that you can put in extra information about people—for example, information about your last contact with them or about their families. That way, when you call Harold Crimini with your business plan, you can ask him how his daughter Chantarelle is enjoying her riding lessons.

When you attach notes, you also make it easier to be able to find the name you want fast. In the note, put in any information that might help you later find the person's name, such as when and where you met the person, the person's interests, and so on. That way, when you use the PalmPilot's Find feature, you can easily find the person's name, even if all you remember about him or her is that he or she likes to eat sautéed puffball mushrooms. You're able to find the person with this limited information because the Find feature searches through attached notes.

To add a note, tap on the **Note** for the person, and then write in a note. Finito!

Categorizing Your Contacts

If you use your Address Book enough, pretty soon you're going to end up with a long list of contacts (right now I'm at 257 and counting…). It would be nice if you somehow could see smaller lists of contacts—for example, just friends or family or mushroom lovers.

Luckily, you *can* see these smaller lists. Use categories. (For all the ins and outs and in-betweens of using categories, refer to Chapter 9, "Using PalmPilot Categories to Organize Your Life.") Categories let you see lists of people by the categories you choose.

To have the name of a person show up in a particular category, tap on that person's **Details** screen, and then choose a category from the screen that pops up. When you want to see a list of people only in a particular category, when you're on the main screen of the Address Book, tap on the triangle in the upper-right corner of the screen, and choose the category you want to view.

Cycling through the categories in the Address Book is easy.

If you want to see lists of people in your Address Book by category, one category after another, just press the **Address Book** hard button on the PalmPilot (the one with the picture of the telephone on it). Each time you press it, it shows you all the contacts in a different category.

Customizing What Information Shows Up in Your Lists

When you look at your lists of contacts, you'll notice that phone numbers appear. (Hard to miss that one.) If a contact has only one phone number—for example, only a work number or only a home number—that number appears. But if someone has more than one phone number, the number that shows up, by default, is the work number.

However, what if you don't want things that way? What if you have a work and home number for a friend, but you rarely call the work number? You would rather see your friend's home number by default.

The PalmPilot again comes to the rescue. You can easily change the phone number displayed for any particular contact. To do so, tap on the **Details** button for a contact to get to the Address Entry Details screen. Then tap on the triangle next to **Show in List**. You then can choose what phone number to display, as you can see in the following screen.

Here, you can choose which phone number should show up in the Address List.

You can get more room to display names by hiding phone numbers in the Address List.

You can have a whole lot of room to show people's names by hiding phone numbers in the Address List. To hide names there, for each person, go to the Address Entry Details screen to change what phone number shows up in the Address List. Tap next to **Show in List**, and choose **Other** or some other label that has no information in it. Now, when you look in the Address List, no phone numbers appear—only a whole lot of room for names. By the way, you still can see each person's phone number by tapping on his or her name to see the full record.

Deleting Records from the Address Book

Mr. Crimini, the venture capitalist, has turned out to be a fraud. In fact, he was merely a lover of exotic mushrooms, looking to see how many wood ear, oyster, and Hen of the Woods (Maitaki) mushrooms he could eat for free. Begone! You never want to see his name again.

To delete a record from the Address Book, open the record, and then tap on **Edit**. Now tap on **Details**, and you see your old friend, the Address Entry Details screen. Tap on **Delete**. Farewell, Mr. Crimini.

If you would like, you can delete the record from your Address Book but still keep an archived copy of it on your computer. To keep the archived copy, when you delete a record, make sure the **Save Archive Copy on PC** box is checked. For information on how to get copies of records from archives, refer to Chapter 5, "Keeping Your Life in Sync: HotSyncing Your PC and PalmPilot."

Where Did I Put That Name? Finding Names in the Address Book

You can choose from the following two ways to find names, addresses, and other information in the Address Book:

➤ When you're in the Address List, go to the Graffiti area and write the first few letters of the *last name* of the person you're looking for. You then jump to the person whose name most closely matches those letters. The more letters you write, the more closely the match will be. This is the simplest and fastest way to find a person. You can use it if you know the last name of the person you want to find. Note that if you choose to sort by company name instead of last name, you instead write the first few letters of the company name.

- Tap on the **Find** icon, and type a word that you're looking for. This word can be a first name, last name, company name, or other words that might appear in a note you've attached to a contact—in short, almost anything. You get a list of all records that include the word you wrote. This method searches through your entire PalmPilot, by the way, not just the Address Book. It's a slower way of searching; however, it's very useful if you don't remember someone's name but do remember some piece of information about him or her. For more information on using Find, turn to Chapter 15, "Where Did I Put that Note? Finding Information on Your PalmPilot."

How to Use Custom Fields in the Address Book

The information you can track about people in the Address Book is fairly standard stuff: names, addresses, phone numbers, and the like. Useful. But what if you want to keep track of something else? Let's say you want to know not just people's names, addresses, and similar information, but also their Web pages or birthdays?

You can keep track of that information by using custom fields. You get four of them, and you can name them anything you like. When you name one of the custom fields, that field shows up in every record in the Address Book. For example, name a custom field **Web Page**, and every contact in your Address Book will have a field that says *Web Page*.

To set up a custom field, tap on **Menu** when you're in the Address Book. Now choose **Rename Custom Fields** from the **Options** menu. When you see a screen with a list of four custom fields, just type the name of the new field you want to use, as shown in the following figure. Then, when you look at any contact in your Address Book, you see the new field you can use.

Using this screen, you can create a new custom field in your Address Book.

Beam Yourself to Another PalmPilot

It's become as much a routine of business life as early mornings, late nights, and stale doughnuts at staff meetings: the ritual handing out of business cards when you meet someone.

Well, the PalmPilot may well change that ritual. Instead of handing over business cards, from now on people will be pointing their PalmPilots at each other with abandon. That's because one of the neatest features of the Palm III and higher is the ability to beam information to another Palm III. (Sorry, PalmPilot and lesser users, your digital plaything can't do this trick unless you buy an upgrade card.)

You can create a business card for yourself in your Palm III or higher. Then, when you meet someone with a Palm III, you can beam your business card to that person, and it'll show up right in his or her Address Book. And your new friend can do the same for you.

To beam your business card, first create a record in the Address Book with all the information you want to be made public about yourself, such as name, address, email address, and the like. Don't save it yet. If you've already created the record before, open it.

Now tap on the **Menu** button, and choose **Select Business Card** from **Record**. The resulting screen, shown in the following figure, asks whether you want to make this record your business card. Choose **Yes**. Then choose **Done** from the next screen that appears.

What's an infrared (IR) port?

The Palm III and higher contains a little gizmo that sends out an infrared beam that can carry information. If you look at the top edge of the Palm III, you'll see a small, dark, curved piece of plastic. The IR beam comes out of this area. As shipped, this IR port doesn't work with the IR port on your PC or with your TV set. But when it comes to technology, ingenuity rules. Amazingly enough, some add-on programs and hardware let you do a lot with your infrared port—for example, communicate with a special cellular phone and even control your TV like a remote control does.

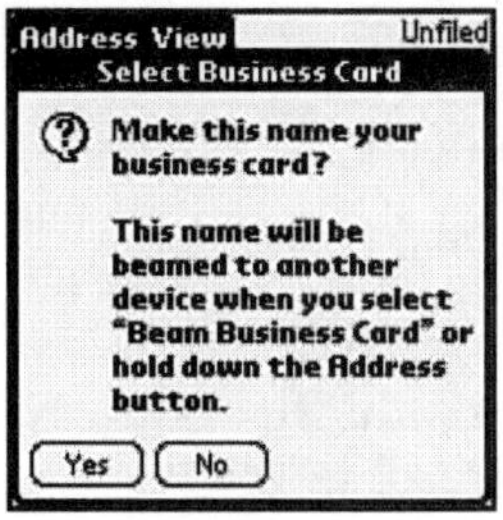

Using this screen, you can make a virtual business card that you can beam to others.

Now, whenever you encounter another Palm III user and want to send your business card, go to your Address Book, tap on the **Menu** button, and choose **Beam Business Card** from the **Record** menu. You also can receive business cards this way. For more information on beaming information between Palm IIIs, turn to Chapter 19, "Beam Me Up, Scotty! Using the Palm III's Infrared Port."

By the way, you can beam and receive more than just your own business card this way. To beam any other individual contact, open that contact, tap on the **Menu** button, and choose **Beam Address** from the Record menu. (Alternatively, you can use the Command stroke shortcut **/B**.) And to beam every single contact in an entire category, go to that category, tap on the **Menu** button, and choose **Beam Category** from the **Record** menu. (No Command stroke shortcuts are available for this one, unfortunately.)

Smart Strategies for Using the Address Book

Your Address Book can do more than just keep track of people and their contact information. It can also help you create mailing lists. Use the smart strategies I describe next for helping manage your life and getting the most out of the PalmPilot's Address Book.

Creating Form Letters, Mailing Labels, and Addressing Envelopes

Maybe you run a small business. Maybe you send out a newsletter for your local Parent Teacher Organization (PTO), your church, or some other organization. Maybe you send out holiday cards to many people every year. And maybe you just plain hate hand-addressing envelopes. You have to find a better way to do all this work than by hand, you think, as you're thoroughly buried in paperwork.

There *is* a better way. Believe it or not, the PalmPilot Address Book can create form letters, mailing labels, and can address envelopes for you. You use the Address Book in concert with the Palm Desktop and Microsoft Word to accomplish these feats.

The first stop is the PalmPilot Address Book. Let's assume that you want to create form letters and mailing labels for a fundraising effort for your local PTO. (Use these

Adding many names in a single category is easy.

If you're going to be adding several contacts to the same category, before creating any of them, switch to the category. Any contacts you create when you're there are automatically put into that category, so this trick speeds up adding new names to your Address Book.

general instructions, but customize them for your specific project.) Create a category titled PTO in your Address Book. Now put in the names and addresses of all the people who are going to receive the mailing, and put them all in the PTO category. If you already have people's names in the Address Book but not in that category, recategorize them so that they're all in the category.

Okay, you have the names and addresses of all the people who are going to receive your mailing, and you've put them into the PTO category. Now HotSync your PalmPilot with your PC. All those new names are then added to your Palm Desktop's Address Book.

Next, go to the Palm Desktop, and open the Address Book. At this point, open the PTO category. Now highlight all the names in the category, and drag them to the Microsoft Word icon in the lower-right portion of the screen. When you do so, you get a message asking what you want to do with the contacts. Choose either to create a form letter, create mailing labels, or address an envelope, depending on what you want to do. From this point on, follow the directions in Microsoft Word. By the way, in this instance, you drag all the names twice. The first time you drag them to create a form letter. The second time you drag them to create mailing labels. And then you're done.

Keep a Copy of Your Address Book on the Web and Share It

You can keep a copy of your Address Book on the Web so that it's accessible to you even when you don't have your PalmPilot. In fact, you can even use your Address Book when you don't have your own computer, but instead borrow someone else's to get on the Web.

When you keep a copy of your Address Book on the Web this way, you also can let people add their contact information to your Address Book. You then can decide whether you want to keep those contacts. You synchronize information back and forth between the Web and your PalmPilot. So, if you add a contact using the Web, it is added to your PalmPilot Address Book. And if someone adds contact information on the Web, you get to decide whether to keep it when you sync with your PalmPilot.

When you work this way, not only do you get access to your PalmPilot via the Web, but it's a great way to keep a backup of all your contacts in case your PalmPilot and computer crash.

Set up your Address Book for free at a site called PlanetAll at `www.planetall.com`. Head to the site for detailed instructions. And for more details, see Chapter 23, "Traveling with Your PalmPilot."

Track Your Private Passwords, PIN Numbers, and Similar Information

Your life is filled with passwords, PIN numbers like ones you use on your ATM machine, and other secret information. How to keep it all straight? If you're like me, you type your PIN password when trying to get into a registration-only Web site and your Web password when trying to get money out of the bank.

The PalmPilot is the perfect place to keep track of all this information and to keep it all safe from prying eyes.

To get started, create a category in the Address Book where you can keep all this information. Then, for each Web site or ATM account, create a separate contact, and put the password and PIN information there. Then make each of them private, following the instructions in this chapter. Now only you can see them. Even if someone steals your PalmPilot, he or she can't see this information because you'll have marked it as private, and only someone with the right password—namely you—can get at it.

The Least You Need to Know

- If you have a personal information manager on your PC, save time by bulk-loading names from it into your Address Book.
- Tap on **Details** when you want to categorize your contacts and keep some contacts private.
- Add notes to contacts as a way to track personal details about people and to make it easier to find names quickly using the **Find** function.
- Create custom fields so that you can include information about people such as their Web pages or birthdays.
- Create a business card in the Address Book that you can beam to others who have Palm IIIs or higher.
- Use the PalmPilot, the Palm Desktop, and Microsoft Word to create form letters and mailing labels and to address envelopes.

Chapter 13

Take Control of Your Life with the To-Do List

In This Chapter

- Creating new To-Do items
- Assigning priorities to To-Do items
- Using To-Do categories to make managing all your tasks easier
- Keeping your to-dos private and checking them off as done
- Customizing the way you view to-dos
- Discovering smart strategies for using the To-Do List to take control of your life

It's March 19. What do you have to get done today? You don't quite remember, but that's okay. So, you wing it, like you always do. Let's see…you remember something about some kind of report and about food of some kind, and you have some vague memory of maybe doing something with the kids. No problem. All that will come to you in due time.

The day flies by. You come home late to an empty house. You find a message from your boss on your answering machine telling you that today has been the last straw; you're fired, because for the seventh time in a row, you failed to turn in your monthly report on the effect that average monthly rainfall has on mushroom sales in Northeast Pennsylvania (your sales territory in your job at ManyMushrooms, Ltd.). You also find an angry note scribbled to you from your wife: It was your turn to cook dinner, and because you forgot yet again, she's having dinner with a friend—an old flame from high school in town just for the night. Don't bother to stay up waiting for her, the note says. She'll be late—*very* late. As for your kids, they stare at you accusingly because you forgot to bring home the Furby (that animated, stuffed animal) you promised them.

If you had used your PalmPilot to keep track of everything you had to do, you would still have a job, your wife wouldn't be out with an old flame until the wee hours of the morning, and your kids wouldn't be staring daggers at you.

In this chapter, you learn how to take control of your life with the To-Do List so that you never forget something important again.

How to Do Those Things You Do with To-Do

To start your To-Do List, press on the hard button that looks like a checklist (it's the second from the right) on the bottom of your PalmPilot, or tap on the **To-Do List** icon on the Applications screen. You then see the following screen.

With this list, you can keep track of all those things you need to do.

When should you use a To-Do item, and when should you use the Date Book?

When you need a reminder that something needs to be done, you can use either the To-Do List or the Date Book. So how do you decide which to use? When I have to get something done at a specific date and time—such as an appointment—I use the Date Book. When I need my PalmPilot to beep a reminder at me, I use the Date Book as well, because you can't set alarms in the To-Do List. However, for most other tasks—such as reminding me which projects need to be done, letters I need to write, and people I need to contact—I use the To-Do List. And I often include the same item in both the Date Book and To-Do List, such as a deadline for a project or a reminder to cook dinner.

Next to each item on the list is a check box and a number. The number indicates how important the item is (more details on this issue later). The check box indicates whether you've completed the item yet. (You can clear all the items from the list that have check boxes; stay tuned for more instructions later as well.) Scroll through your To-Do items if you have more than a screen's worth by pressing the hard scroll buttons at the bottom of your PalmPilot or by tapping on the up and down scroll triangles on the right side of the screen.

Creating a New To-Do Item

To create a new To-Do item, tap on the **New** button. Then write in what you want. Now tap on a blank part of the screen. That's all there is to it. You're done.

Well, you're done if you have so few things that need to be done in your life that you can see them all at a glance on a single screen. (And if your life is that simple, you probably don't need a PalmPilot anyway.) If you're like me, though, and have so much to do that it seems that not even a Cray supercomputer can keep track of them all, you can do a whole lot more with the To-Do List to get your life under control. You can add all kinds of information and details to each To-Do item to help you. You can do the following:

Use this shortcut to create a new To-Do item.

To create a new To-Do item, you don't even need to tap on the **New** button. When you're in the To-Do List, just start writing in the Graffiti area. A new To-Do item is created, containing whatever you write in Graffiti.

- Assign each To-Do item a priority on a scale of 1 to 5 so that you can easily see which tasks are most important and which are least important.
- Give your To-Do items deadlines so that you can track when they need to be done and can sort them by order of when they need to be done.
- Assign each To-Do item a category so that you can easily see at a glance all the things that need to be done in different parts of your life or on different projects.
- Mark To-Do items as private so that only you can see them.
- Attach notes to To-Do items so that you can include a great deal of detail about each item.

You can do even more, as you learn later in the chapter, but the preceding tasks are the main ones. Now let me tell you how to do each.

First Things First: Assigning a Priority to a Task

Which to do first, take your rabbit for a walk or finish your monthly sales report? (I would walk the rabbit first, but that's because I don't do sales reports.) You can give one task a higher priority than the other. Doing so is easy in the PalmPilot. The simplest way is to tap on the number next to the item, and choose a number from 1 to 5 from the box that pops up, as you can see in the following figure.

Pick a number, any number (as long as it's from 1 to 5). This way, you can choose which priority to assign to a task in the To-Do List.

You can assign a priority in another way, though. You use this other way when you want to do more than just assign a priority—for example, when you want to mark a To-Do item as private or set a due date for it. To use this other way, tap on an item in the To-Do List, and then tap on the **Details** button. When you see the following screen, tap on the priority you want to assign to the item. As you can see, you can do a whole lot more from this screen as well. Think of it as master control for the To-Do List. You'll be using this screen a whole lot more in the rest of the chapter.

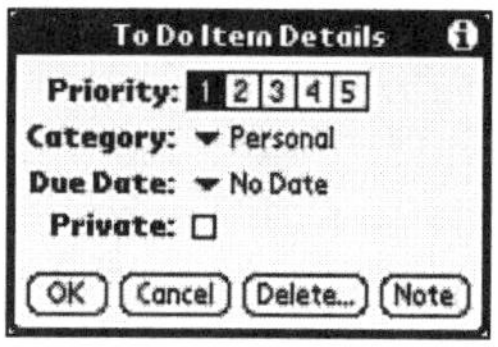

Master control for the To-Do List: the To Do Item Details screen.

You can easily create To-Do items that all have the same priority.

Let's say you want to create several items, and some of them have a priority of 3. Creating each item and then having to manually assign a priority to each one would be a pain. Let me tell you a simpler way: Tap on a To-Do item that has the priority of the items you want to create. Then tap on the **New** button. This new To-Do item automatically has the same priority as the item you tapped on. And every subsequent item will automatically have the same priority. In fact, each item will also have the same category and other details as well.

When you assign priorities to To-Do items, the items with the top priority (those with the number 1) show up first in your To-Do List, and those with lower priorities show up below. You can, in fact, change this sort order, as you see later in the chapter.

Hurry Up, Please, It's Time! Assigning Deadlines to a Task

Time is tyranny, but it's a tyranny that we all must obey. (Whew! Heavy stuff for a *Complete Idiot's Guide*, no?) So, to make best use of your To-Do List—and to escape tyranny to the greatest extent possible—use the To-Do List's capability to assign deadlines to tasks. This way, you can see the deadline for each of your To-Do items. You also can sort your to-dos by deadlines.

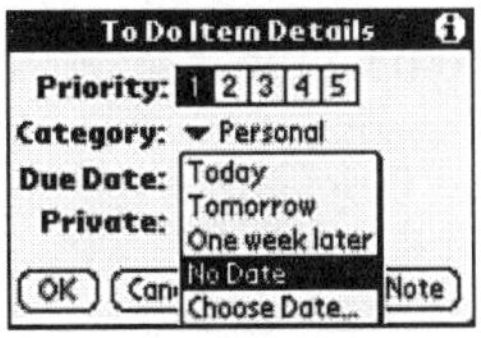

Time after time...assigning a deadline to a To-Do item.

To assign a deadline to a To-Do item, tap on the **Details** button to get to the To Do Item Details screen, shown previously. From there, choose a date to assign to the task by tapping on the triangle next to **Due Date**. The options are shown in the preceding figure. If you choose **Choose Date**, you are sent to a calendar where you can navigate to the specific date for which you want to set a deadline.

Change deadlines fast in the To-Do List.

If you've chosen to show your deadlines in the To-Do List, use this fast way to change any of those deadlines. Just tap on the date next to the task with the deadline you want to change, and you can change it lickety-split.

As you know by now, the To-Do List automatically sorts your tasks by priority. (You've been paying attention, haven't you?) But what if you have several items in the same category? How does it sort them then? If you assign due dates to your tasks, it sorts them by due date. In other words, the To-Do List puts all your "1" To-Do items at the top of the list; it puts the "1" To-Do item with the nearest due date first, the "1" To-Do item with the second due date second, and so on.

Fine, you're thinking. But why, after you've done all that work assigning deadlines to your tasks, do those deadlines not show up in the To-Do List? Why, oh why, do you have to tap on the **Details** button to see them?

Allow me to let you in on a little secret. You *can* show your deadlines in the To-Do List. Tap on the **Show** button, and then check **Show Due Dates**, as shown in the figure on the left. Your To-Do List then shows deadlines, as you can see in the figure on the right.

To make your due dates show up in the To-Do List, check **Show Due Dates** *after tapping on the* **Show** *button (left). After choosing this option, you see all your deadlines in the To-Do List (right).*

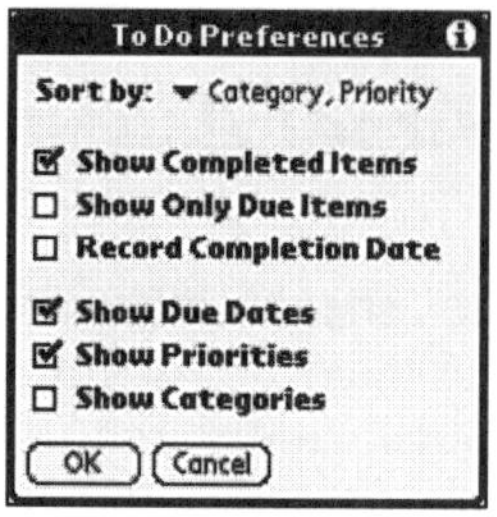

Grouping Your To-Do Items by Categorizing Them

Because you have so many tasks that need to be done, the odds are great that simply putting them all in one large list isn't going to help you a whole lot. You'll have so many screens' worth of To-Do items that you'll no doubt become quickly demoralized: "Surely, no one can do all those things," you'll think, "So why even bother trying?"

Create To-Do items fast in the same category.

Let's say you have a lot of To-Do items you want to create in the same category. To categorize them quickly, switch to the category where you want to create items, and then create them one by one. Each one you create is automatically put into that category.

Resist such sloth! You can put all your To-Do items into categories, such as Personal, Home, Budget Plans, and so on. When you group the items, you can see at a glance what needs to be done in any different aspect of your life. (For more information on how to use categories in general to organize your life, turn to Chapter 9, "Using PalmPilot Categories to Organize Your Life.")

To assign a task to a category, tap on the **Details** button to get to the trusty To Do Item Details screen. Then choose the category where you want to assign the task. You're done.

Now, when you want to see your tasks only in a particular category, tap on the triangle on the upper-right part of your screen, choose the category you want to see, and you see all the tasks in that category. By the way, when you look at all the tasks in a category, they are sorted in the usual way—first by priority, and then within each priority, by due date.

Keeping Your To-Dos Private

A business brainstorm hits again. You figure the quickest way to riches is to build a chain of combination supermarket/haircut outlets so that people can get their hair cut when they go to the grocery store. You'll call it Chop 'N Shop. How could it possibly miss?

To set your plan in motion, you enter a new to-do in your list: Create Chop 'N Shop business plan. But you don't want your boss seeing that to-do over your shoulder, or anyone else seeing it, either—even your spouse who has started belittling your business acumen every time you come up with a new can't-miss proposition (which, for some reason, your spouse refers to as a "hair-brained scheme").

To keep to-dos private, tap on the **Details** button to bring up the To Do Item Details screen, and check the **Private** box. To make sure that the item doesn't show up, go to the Security application by tapping on **Applications** and then on **Security**. In that screen, make sure that you've chosen to hide private records.

It's Duly Noted: Attaching Notes to To-Do Items

You want to jot down a few ideas about the Chop 'N Shop chain. For example, you figure you could have the chain offer special deals; when people get certain haircuts, they get deals on specific foods (a free carton of eggs when they get baldie cuts, for example). However, you don't want to have to create a memo about your ideas in one place and a To-Do item in another.

Edit any To-Do task by tapping on the Details button.

If you've created a To-Do item already and want to edit its details— such as whether to mark it private, to change the category, or to edit a note—tap on the **Details** button. You then can edit the details using the To Do Item Details screen. If all you want to do is edit the description of the To-Do item and add no details, simply tap on it and edit it.

No problem. You can add a note to a To-Do item. Tap on the **Details** button to bring up the To Do Item Details screen, and then tap on the **Note** button. You then can add a note.

Cross It Off the List: Marking Your To-Do Tasks as Done

Take it from me: You'll do fewer, more satisfying things on your PalmPilot than marking a To-Do task as done; that means you'll have one less thing to think about.

Let's say you've finished the business plan for the Chop 'N Shop chain. Time to cross that To-Do item off the list.

You have two ways of marking off items. One is to delete the To-Do item entirely. To delete it, tap on the item, tap on the **Details** button to bring up the To Do Item Details screen, and then tap on the **Delete** button. It's gone.

When you use this approach, though, that To-Do item vanishes forever. Maybe you want to keep it around for a time, or maybe you want a permanent record of what you've done. In that case, you do things differently.

To mark an item as done, tap on the check box next to it. A check appears next to it, as you can see in the following figure.

The check marks tell you've done a To-Do item.

That To-Do item still shows up on your To-Do List, but it shows up with a check mark next to it.

At some point, your screen may start to get cluttered with many To-Do items, and you might want to get rid of the ones that you've marked as done. To purge them all at once, tap on the **Menu** button, and then choose **Purge** from the **Record** menu. (You can also use the Command stroke shortcut **/E**.)

Keep archived records of all your to-dos on your computer.

Even after you delete or purge your to-dos, you might like to have a permanent record of all your to-dos stored somewhere. You can keep an archive of them all on your PC and then call them up when you want them. To do so, when you delete or purge records, make sure that the box next to **Save Archive Copy on PC** is checked. When you check this option, the records are saved in a special place on your PC, and you can get copies of them using the Palm Desktop. Turn to Chapter 6, "Oh, Yeah...You Have a Computer, Too. Using the Palm Desktop," for details.

To-Dos with a View: Changing the Way To-Dos Are Sorted and Displayed

We're all different. Some of us like ballet, whereas others like baseball. Some prefer pizza, whereas others prefer panini. Some like Barry Manilow, whereas others...hold on a minute, scratch that. There *are* limits to what people will endure.

The point is, though, that everyone works and lives differently. The To-Do List was built with that in mind. It has a myriad of different ways it can show you all the stuff you need to get done. You can change what kind of information shows up in the To-Do List, and you also can change the order that To-Do items show up in the list.

To customize your information, when you're in the To-Do List, tap on the **Show** button. You then see the To Do Preferences screen, as shown in the following figure. From here, you can change the way your tasks are sorted and displayed.

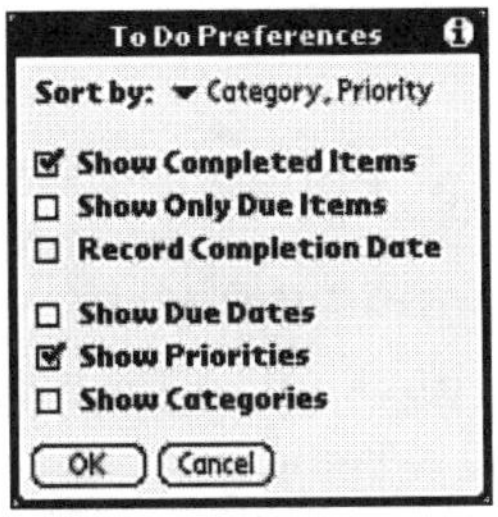

Bend the To-Do List to your will. In this screen, you can change the way it sorts and displays your tasks.

Changing the Way That To-Dos Are Sorted

You can use the Preferences screen to change the ways that to-dos are sorted. To do so, tap on the **Sort By** triangle to see the options shown in the following figure.

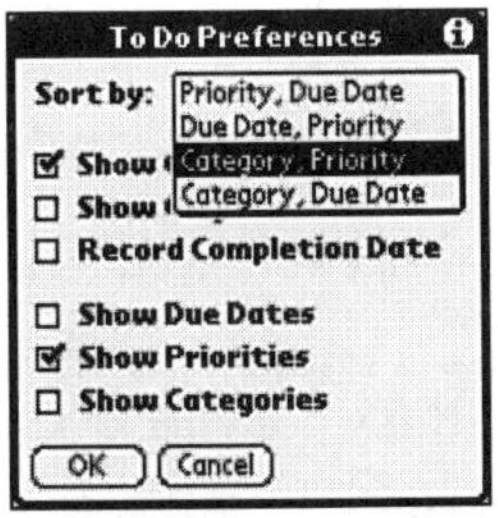

Changing the way you sort your to-dos.

You need to know the following information about these options:

- **Priority, Due Date** This is the PalmPilot's default sorting order. It puts the top priority items first. Within each level of priority, it puts those with the nearest due date first. Most people use this sorting order.
- **Due Date, Priority** If you're a deadline-driven person, you should use this sorting order. It sorts your items first by their due date, and then for items with the same due dates, by priority.

- **Category, Priority** This view makes sense only when you look at your To-Do items in the All category. In that category, every one of your to-dos shows up, regardless of what category it's in. (When you view items in any one particular category, only items in that category show up.) When you choose this option, to-dos are listed by category in alphabetical order, so to-dos in the Business category show up before those in the Classwork category, and so on. If you're going to use this way of sorting your to-dos, make sure to have your categories displayed right next to each To-Do item (see the next figure in the chapter to see what I mean).
- **Category, Due Date** This view is a whole lot like the preceding one. The only difference is that items in the same category are listed in order of due date, not priority.

Add people's names and phone numbers to a To-Do item.

Often, the tasks you need to do involve contacting other people. You can easily add someone's name and phone number to a To-Do item. When you're in the item, tap on the **Menu** button and then choose **Phone Lookup** from **Options**. (Alternatively, you can use the Command stroke shortcut **/L**.) You then can add the name and phone number of anyone in your Address Book to the To-Do item.

Changing What Details Show Up on the To-Do List

You can change not only what order you see to-dos, but you also can change what information shows up about each item, such as the due date, category, and so on. You use the Preferences screen to make these changes. Just check the box next to the option you want to display. Let me tell you what you need to know about each:

- **Show Completed Items** If this box is checked, items that you've marked as complete show up in your To-Do List. If it's not checked, they don't show up.
- **Show Only Due Items** When you check this box, any item that has a due date different from today's date doesn't show up. In other words, when you check this option, you see all items that have a due date of today or that don't have a due date at all.

- **Record Completion Dates** Want to know when you've completed your tasks? Just check this box. Then, whenever you mark a task complete by checking it as done, your PalmPilot records that date. If you initially put a due date for the task, the completion date replaces it. If you want to see the completion date as part of the list view, check the **Show Completion Dates** box, as described next. Even if you don't show them in the list view, they still show up when you look at the details of any To-Do item.
- **Show Completion Dates** If you check this box, the completion dates show up in the list view. Even if you don't show them in the list view, they still show up when you look at the details of any To-Do item.
- **Show Priorities** If you want the priorities for each to-do to show up in the list view, check this box. Even if you don't show them in the list view, they still show up when you look at the details of any To-Do item.
- **Show Categories** If you want the categories for each item to show up in the list view, check this box. Even if you don't show them in the list view, they still show up when you look at the details of any To-Do item.

If you check a whole lot of these boxes, your To-Do List shows you much details about all your tasks. It also gets a bit crowded. The following figure shows the list view with several display options turned on.

Everything you wanted to know about your tasks: the To-Do List with many of the display options turned on.

Smart Strategies for Using the To-Do List to Manage Your Life

If you're like me, you have far too many tasks to keep track of. So if you want to help the To-Do List best manage your life, use these smart strategies, tips, and techniques:

- **Every morning, go through every single item in every category on your To-Do List, and every evening go through them again.** When you go through them in the morning, change the due dates and priorities of any that need changing. Also, add new to-dos, and change the categories of any that need changing. This way, you start the day knowing what needs to be done in the day ahead. At night, check off all those to-dos that you've done, and also change the due dates and priorities of any that need changing. And spend your time in the evening adding new to-dos that need to be done.

Cycle through your categories fast.

You can view all the to-dos in each of your categories, one after another, by pressing the **To-Do List** hard button. Each time you press it, you go to a different To-Do category.

- **Create a Today category, and use it to organize all the tasks that need to be done today.** If, like me, you have many different categories on your PalmPilot, cycling through them all each day and seeing what needs to be done can be difficult. So do what I do: Create a Today category. Then each day, move all those things that need to be done into that category. That way, you have one central place where you can go to see what needs to be done every day.
- **When you're working on a project with others who have a Palm III or higher, use the Beam feature to send to-dos back and forth to each other.** You can beam individual to-dos or entire categories of to-dos. For example, if you have a list of to-dos that you want one of your employees to complete, create a category for him or her, and beam the entire category. To beam an item, tap on it, tap on the **Menu** button, and then choose **Beam** from the **Record** menu. (Alternatively, you can use the Command stroke shortcut **/B**.) To beam an entire category, go to the category you want to beam, tap on the **Menu** button, and choose **Beam Category** from the **Options** menu.
- **Use the Show Only Due Items feature to keep your To-Do List uncluttered and to schedule to-dos months in advance.** Let's say you need a reminder to set a doctor's appointment or get your car tuned up, but you don't need a reminder to do those things for another six months or even a year. If you put them in your To-Do List, they just clutter up your lists. Instead, do the following: Put due dates on them. Then enable the **Show Only Due Items** feature of your PalmPilot. (See "Changing What Details Show Up on the To-Do List" earlier in this chapter for details.) That way, you can see any To-Do items that are due today, that are past, or that have no due date, but you don't have your To-Do List cluttered with less-timely to-dos.

The Least You Need to Know

- Assign priorities to to-dos by tapping on the number next to the to-do and choosing a priority number from 1 to 5.
- Give deadlines to tasks to make sure that you get them done on time.
- Using categories in your To-Do List makes it easier to track all your to-dos.
- Edit any existing task by tapping on the **Details** button.
- Change the way that to-dos are sorted and displayed to better help you keep track of your tasks.
- Go through your to-dos at least twice a day—once in the morning and once at the end of the day—to mark off what's been done, reorganize them, and add new to-dos.

Chapter 14

Time Is Money: Tracking Your Expenses with the PalmPilot

In This Chapter

- How to record your expenses
- How to categorize your receipts
- How to record details about each of your receipts, such as the city, who attended the meeting, and more
- How to create expense reports with Excel and print them

Money may make the world go 'round, but if you're like me, trying to keep track of it can make your head spin.

Good news for those whose heads gyrate uncontrollably when it comes to tracking their expenses: The PalmPilot comes to the rescue. It has a built-in Expense program that allows you to keep track of your expenses. It's absolutely ideal if you travel on business and need to track what you spend so that you can get reimbursed from your company expense reports. But it's equally useful if you have a small business and need to keep track of expenses for tax purposes or other reasons as well. And you can even track your household expenses with it.

So whether you're a budgetary pro or the kind of person who throws your receipts into a basket and then forgets about them, the PalmPilot helps you track your expenses. Read on for details.

A Look at How Expense Works

Before you start using Expense, take some time to understand what it can do for you and what it can't do for you. It *can* keep track of your expenses—when you go on a business trip, for example, or for a particular project that you're involved in. It *can't* work as a personal finance program. So you cannot balance your checkbook with it, keep track of your investments, plan for retirement, or figure out what to do with that $7 million that your Aunt Tillie left you in her will. (If she did leave you that money, let me give you this one piece of financial advice to follow: Send me a spare million. Don't worry; I promise I'll spend it wisely.)

What's a spreadsheet?

A *spreadsheet* is a kind of electronic ledger that lets you perform many different kinds of calculations on numbers, from simple functions such as adding and averaging to very sophisticated statistical functions. It's mainly used for budgeting and number crunching of all kinds.

You track your expenses with Expense, and when you want to print them, you HotSync with your PC. After you HotSync, you can open your expenses in an Excel spreadsheet. (It has to be Excel version 5.0 or higher.) You can then print that spreadsheet and file it with your company for your expense account, or simply keep a paper record of it somewhere. When your expenses are in a spreadsheet, you can do all kinds of fancy calculations with those numbers as well. By the way, Excel doesn't come as part of your PalmPilot. You have to buy it separately.

How to Record Your Expenses

Okay. Let's get ready to spend some money. Let's say that the company you work for, ManyMushrooms, Ltd., is looking to expand the types of mushrooms it sells, so it's sending you to France on a fact-finding mission. (Hey, it's a tough job, but someone has to do it.) All your expenses are going to be out-of-pocket, so you want to keep track of them all, down to the last centime, so that you get reimbursed from the company as soon as possible. Otherwise, those expenses will be out of mind, and the expenses really *will* be out of your pocket.

You've just bought your airline ticket. Now you should record the expense. Tap on the **Expense** icon. From the screen that appears, tap on the **New** button. When you do that, a blank expense line appears, as shown in the following figure. Each expense has three pieces of information associated with it: a date, an expense type, and the amount of the expense.

*Tap on the **New** button, and you can create a new expense item, which is just itching to be filled in.*

When you create a new expense item, the date is automatically today's. If you want to change that date, tap on the date to open a calendar. Choose the date on the calendar that you want to appear, and the date is put in.

Now you have to say what kind of expense it is. Tap on the words **Expense Type**, and you see a long list of all the kinds of expenses the PalmPilot recognizes (and no, wine, women [or men] and song is not among them, so be careful what kinds of expenses you rack up). When you see the list in the following figure, choose the type of expense.

You can track many types of expenses in your PalmPilot, but wine, women (or men), and song aren't among them.

Make absolutely sure that you put in an expense type. If you don't, you're asking for trouble. If you put in a date and the amount you've spent (I tell you how to do that next), but you don't put in an expense type, the PalmPilot simply deletes the expense item. So make sure to put in an expense type for every one of your expenses.

After you choose the expense type, write in the amount of the expense using Graffiti. Congratulations, you've just tracked your first expense.

What if the PalmPilot doesn't include your expense type?

When you tap on the expense type, you can choose from many different kinds of expenses. But what happens if your expense type isn't there? Unfortunately, you can't add a new type of expense. To create a workaround, attach a note to the expense, describing what the expense was for. That way, you always have a record of it. If you use the PalmPilot's Find function, you can find the expense easily because Find searches through attached notes. Later in this chapter, you learn how to attach notes to expense items.

Take the Express Lane: How to Enter Your Expenses Fast

When you're traveling, you're usually on double-time: You move double-fast, you eat double-quickly, and you may even chew Doublemint gum. The faster you enter your expenses, the better; otherwise, you might forget to put them in.

Let me share the fast way to enter an expense item: Don't bother tapping on the **New** button. Instead, start writing either the expense type or the amount of the expense. When you do so, Expense automatically creates a new expense item for you and automatically starts filling it in, based on what you wrote.

For example, if you write the letter **a**, Expense automatically creates a new expense item for you with the expense type of Airfare. If more than one type of expense starts with that letter, write the second letter of the expense type, and Expense creates a new item with that correct expense type filled in. For example, to create a new expense item for a toll you just paid, you type **to**, and the expense type is Tolls.

Details, Details, Details...Recording the Details About Your Expenses

Just tracking the date, type, and amount of an expense isn't really enough for you. If you file expense reports, or if you're tracking your expenses for your small business or for home, you want to know a lot more about each expense. Your boss certainly wants to know more details about each expense, so if you want to get reimbursed for your expenses, make sure to keep detailed records of them.

Expense performs that task for you. For every expense, you can record these details:

- **The Category**, which can be anything you want, such as the name of a city or a specific project or trip. Categories shouldn't be used for the type of expense, such as lunch, because you record that information in the expense type.
- **The Expense Type**, which we covered previously in the chapter.
- **The Payment**, in other words, how you paid for the expense, such as with a specific credit card, cash, or check.
- **The Currency**, which lets you choose what kind of currency you're using, such as dollars or pounds.
- **The Vendor**, which is a fancy way of saying where you spent the money, such as at a particular restaurant or hotel.
- **The City**, which, of course, means the city where the expense was incurred.
- **The Attendees**, which means the people who were at the lunch or the meeting or in some other way were involved with the expense.

To record these details, tap on the **Details** button on the bottom of the Expense screen. You then see the Receipt Details screen, as shown in the following figure.

Here, you record all the details about each of your expenses.

Get used to seeing this screen. I keep referring back to it throughout the chapter.

Categorizing Your Receipts

As a way to help you track your expenses, you can put your receipts into different categories. Remember, these categories are different from expense types; categories should help you group your expenses into trips, projects, or even weeks and months as a way to track expenses for time periods, projects, or specific trips. The PalmPilot comes with two categories: New York and Paris. Nice places to visit, certainly, but not a very good use of the Categories feature, because as you already know, the Receipt Details screen lets you put down the city where you incurred an expense. I suggest deleting these two categories.

Your best bet is to create much more specific categories for a time or specific business trip or project, such as April '99, Texas Trip, or Buyout Project. For more information on how to use categories, turn to Chapter 9, "Using PalmPilot Categories to Organize Your Life."

Changing the Expense Type

You've already learned how to set your expense type for any particular expense. You choose the expense type in the Receipt Details screen the same way you normally do. You can choose from a long pull-down list.

Detailing the Payment

Under Payment in the Receipt Details screen, you record the way you paid your expense—for example, by a specific credit card such as Visa, by check, or by cash. You can also choose **Prepaid**. You use this option if, for example, your company has prepaid the expense, such as buying your airline ticket. If you have a prepaid expense, marking it as prepaid is very important; otherwise, you get errors when Excel creates your expense report.

You can record mileage in Expense.

You may be reimbursed by your company for each mile you drive in your car. If so, you need to record your mileage. To do so, choose the Mileage expense type. With all other expenses, you record the dollar value of the expense. In Mileage, though, you record only the total number of miles traveled.

Choosing the Currency

If you do all your travel in the U.S. (poor you), you don't need to worry about choosing the currency. Just don't touch this option in the Receipt Details screen. By default, all your expenses are measured in dollars. (Anyway, these days the dollar seems to be becoming the international currency.) If you're traveling to jolly olde England, you can record your expenses in pounds, for example. Just choose the currency for the country you're traveling in.

If the currency of the country you're traveling to isn't listed, you might still be able to find it.

By default, the only currencies listed are dollars, the English pound, and the German Deutsche mark. However, you can also choose currencies from many other countries. To do so, choose **Edit Currencies** from the **Currency** pull-down list. Then follow the prompts to choose the other kind of currency you want to use.

Picking the Vendor

The Vendor, on the Receipt Details screen, is a fancy way of saying where you spent the money. Had lunch at Joe's Greasy Spoon? Then tap that in. Stayed the night at the Plaza? (Good choice of hotel. Hope your company doesn't mind paying the freight.) Tap that in.

Picking the City

You know the drill: In the Receipt Details screen, type the name of the city where you spent the money. Enough said.

Detailing the Attendees

If the expense involves other people, such as a business lunch, you put their names in the Attendees line of the Receipt Details screen. (Just make sure that if your lunch meeting is important, you don't take them to Joe's Greasy Spoon.) Tap on the **Who** button, and then write in people's names here.

If the names of the people at the meeting are in your Address Book, you can use a neat shortcut. After you tap on the **Who** button, you go to a screen where you type the names of the people attending the meeting. At the bottom of the screen is a button labeled **Lookup**. Tap on it, and you can look up a name or names and add them as attendees. Their names and companies are included.

By the way, you might notice that the space where you put in people's names is freeform. In other words, you don't need to just put people's names in there. You can type anything you want about the meeting as well.

You can attach a note to an expense item.

Sometimes you need more information attached to an expense item than can be put into the Receipt Details screen. For example, some companies require that you detail the purpose of a luncheon meeting if you want to get reimbursed. To attach a note to an expense item, tap on **Note** on the Receipt Details screen.

Creating Expense Reports with Excel and Printing Them

Tracking your expenses on the PalmPilot is well and good. But what if you need to print them—for example, to file an expense report or for tax reasons?

Printing is easy. After entering your expenses, you HotSync with your PalmPilot, run the Palm Desktop, and then use Excel to create an expense report and print it from there. You get a choice of using any one of several slick-looking expense reports.

(By the way, if you don't have a copy of Excel 5.0 or higher, you're out of luck; you can't do any of this. If you have a Pilot instead of a PalmPilot or a Palm III, you can't print either.)

To start, HotSync your PalmPilot with your PC. (For help, turn to Chapter 5, "Keeping Your Life in Sync: HotSyncing Your PC and PalmPilot.")

Add-on programs can help you with your personal finances.

Expense doesn't help you manage your personal finances, but you can get other programs for your PalmPilot to help you manage your money. Pocket Quicken, for example, is a PalmPilot program designed as a companion to the best-selling Quicken personal finance software. You can find other personal finance software as well; head to `www.palmpilotsoftware.com` for others. Turn to Chapter 20, "Installing New Software on Your PalmPilot," to learn how to install new software. Also, check the CD at the back of this book for money-management software.

Now that your expense information is on your PC, you're ready to roll. Start the Palm Desktop, and click the **Expense** icon to fire up Excel.

Depending on how you've installed Excel, you might get a weird, not-very comprehensible error message at this point. (Of course, *every* error message from a computer is a weird, incomprehensible error message, so why should this one be any different?) It may tell you that the file you're opening contains something called *macros* and that the macros might contain a virus. Then Excel asks you what to do. Ignore the message. Tell the program to enable macros.

When Excel launches, it shows you the dialog box you see in the following figure. A whole lot is going on in this little box. The most important thing right now, though, is to tell it what categories of expenses you want to create a report for. Select one, some, or all of them.

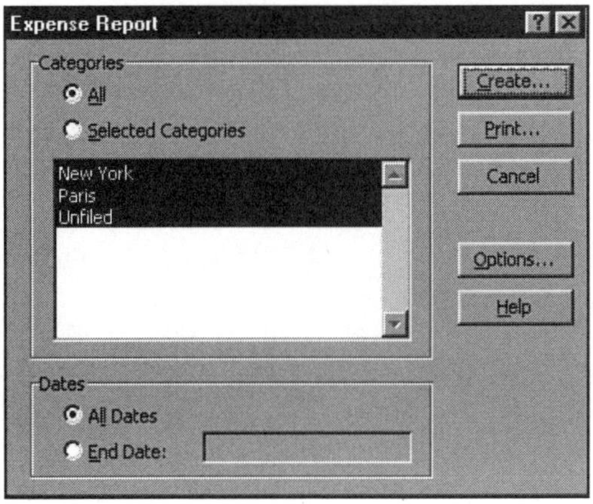

You use this Excel dialog box to create Expense reports.

If you like, you can specify an ending date for the report. You add this date if, for example, you're filing a monthly expense report. Let's say that it's July 25, and you're filing your June expense (a little late, aren't you?). You then put in an end date of June 30.

I know you're eager to create that report (need the expense money, am I right?), but hold on a minute, you should know a few more facts. You can customize your expense report before creating it. Click the **Options** button to do so. When you click this button, you see the dialog box on the following page.

Put in your identifying information. When you put the information here, it shows up later in your expense report, as you see later.

Now, you can do just one more thing. Choose which expense report template you want to use. A *template* is a kind of master form; it determines what information appears on the report and how the report looks. You can choose from four templates. To choose one, click the **Template** drop-down arrow. If you want to use the main one, don't do anything. Just leave it be. By the way, the main one is my favorite. To see what they all look like, you can check out Appendix A of the *Applications Handbook* that comes with your PalmPilot.

Here, you can type information about yourself and choose a specific style for your expense report.

Finally, the moment you've been waiting for has arrived. All the options have been chosen. Click **Create** in the Expense Report dialog box, and sit back a minute while Excel does its magic. You then should see a spreadsheet like the one in the following figure.

All you need to do now is print this baby and turn it in to your boss. Then you can figure out how you want to spend your money.

Finally! Your expense report is done. Now file it fast with your boss so that you can get your moolah.

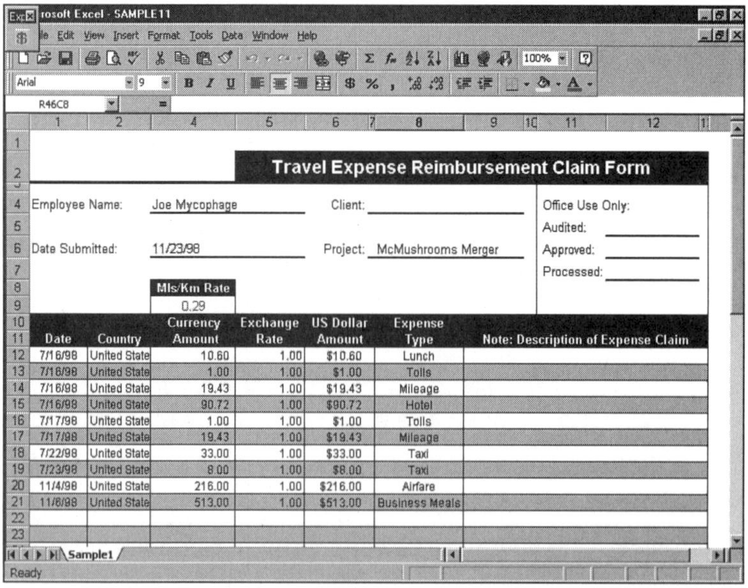

You can create your own customized expense reports.

You might not like the forms for expense reports that come with the PalmPilot. Or maybe your company has a specific spreadsheet that you have to use when you file your expenses. What to do? You can create a customized expense report. That way, your report takes all your expense information and puts it into the exact expense report that you want. Be forewarned, though; creating customized reports is not for the weak of heart. You had better be a pretty serious spreadsheet jockey if you want to attempt it. If you do, head over to Appendix B of the *Palm III Applications Handbook* or Appendix C of the *Pilot Handbook*. Good luck. You'll need it!

The Least You Need to Know

- To create a new expense item, start writing the name of the type of expense or the amount of expense, and the item is automatically created.
- Use the Receipt Details screen to record details of each receipt, such as the city or the business where the expense was incurred.
- Attach a note to an expense item to record details about any expense.
- To create expense reports and print them, HotSync your PalmPilot with your computer, and then use the Palm Desktop Expense program.

Chapter 15

Where Did I Put That Note? Finding Information on Your PalmPilot

In This Chapter

- How the Find command works
- How to find anything on the PalmPilot
- How to use the Phone Lookup command to paste names and phone numbers into memos, To-Do items, and appointments
- How to find information on the PalmPilot using smart strategies and tips

If you have a Palm III with 2MB of memory, it can hold about 20,000 names and addresses, memos, To-Do items, appointments, expense items, and other sundry stuff. Great news, isn't it? Just *think* of all the information you can track.

Sure, that's great. Good luck trying to find any of it. It's 3 p.m. on Thursday afternoon, and you need to find the name of someone you met eight months ago at someone's cocktail party. You couldn't care less about 20,000 items; you need just one vital piece of information. And now you can't find it.

What you've discovered is that information is no good unless you can find it. Entering contacts, meetings, and to-dos in your PalmPilot is great, but if you can't find what you need when you need it, this information doesn't do you a whit of good.

Up until now, you've learned mainly how to put information into your PalmPilot. In this chapter, you look at how to find that information, no matter how hard it tries to evade your gaze, and no matter how deep it's burrowed in the depths of your little device's memory banks.

You learn the basics of searching using the PalmPilot and then learn great techniques and tips for making sure that information will always be at your fingertips when you want it.

Finders, Keepers: How Find Works on the PalmPilot

Some time this year—and you can't remember exactly when—you met someone who may well hold the key to your future in her hands. Your latest business brainstorm is to turn abandoned toxic waste dumps into combination theme parks/factory outlets/educational centers. (Heck, *one* of your ideas has to hit, why not this one? Well? Why not?) You figure you can get the land dirt cheap, and this woman was a realtor who specialized in selling lots that no one in his right mind would want to buy (her words, not yours).

The problem is that you can't remember her name, her company, when or where you met her, or any other kind of information about her.

You've been a good student of my book, so you know that you recorded information about this woman in the PalmPilot. You whip out your digital companion, tap on the **Find** button, search for the word **toxic**, and sure enough, you find her—not just her name, address, and phone number, but also a memo you wrote about her, the exact date and time of your meeting with her, and even her favorite ice cream (Ben & Jerry's Rocky Road or Phish Food.) Toxic waste dumps, here you come!

Use FindHack for more powerful searches.

The PalmPilot does a pretty good job of searching for information. However, a powerful add-in called FindHack turbocharges the kind of searching you can do on the PalmPilot. You can get it at many sites on the Internet, including `www.palmpilotsoftware.com`.

The Find feature is one of the most useful features of your PalmPilot. It lets you search for information anywhere on your PalmPilot. Although some individual programs, such as the Address Book, let you look up information only in them, the Find feature lets you find information everywhere that information lives in your PalmPilot. It looks through the five major programs—the To-Do List, the Address Book, the Date Book, the Memo Pad, and Expense. It also searches through all the notes attached to all those items in those programs as well.

If you know how Find works, you can use it more effectively. Let me tell you how it works its magic. Find searches through every one of the PalmPilot programs, one by one, for the text you write in. Then it shows you the results; and to see the information, just tap on it. It's that simple.

Enough about how Find works. Let's check out how to use it and then learn some smart strategies for how to find any information fast.

Discovering the Needle in the Haystack: Using Find on Your PalmPilot

To use Find, tap on the **Find** button. The Find screen appears, as shown in the following figure. Write in the word you're looking for, and tap on **OK**.

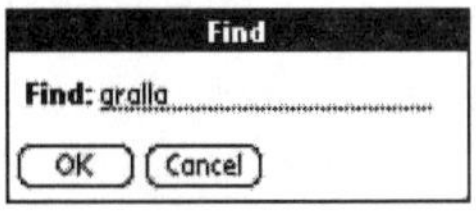

Using Find, you can find any piece of information, anywhere, anytime, anyhow, on your PalmPilot.

The PalmPilot now churns away (actually, it doesn't really churn because it searches quite quickly; maybe it really zips) and then shows you a list of all the items that contain the word you're looking for. The following figure shows you what the results look like.

The PalmPilot displays this type of screen when it finds what you're looking for.

As you can see, the PalmPilot lists what it finds program by program. So, if it finds seven items in the Memo Pad, two in Expense, and one in the Address Book, it groups them accordingly.

To view any of the items, just tap on it. When you do so, you open the item and can work with it as you would normally. Find does have one major drawback, however: You can't open one item, go back to the screen that has your Find results, and then open another item, and so on. After you open a single item, the PalmPilot promptly forgets the results of your search. You have to start all over again. So, tap on **Find** again, and do your search again. Find does, however, at least remember the last thing you searched. After you do a search and then look at an item, when you head back to Find, your search term is already in there.

By the way, keep in mind that you don't need to write in an *entire* word when you're searching; you can write in just the first part of the word. For example, if you're searching for the word *rainfall*, you can just type **rain**, and it finds the word *rainfall*. It finds every other word beginning with *rain* as well. And you don't even have to type complete words. In this instance, you can type the letters **rai**, and it finds every instance of the word *rainfall*—and also of *rain* and *raise* because both of these words start with the letters *rai*.

The PalmPilot searches for text only at the beginning of words.

When you write in a word or letters to search for using Find, the PalmPilot checks to see whether any items have words in them that start with that word or those letters. However, it doesn't search the *end* of words. So, for example, if you search for the word *work*, it doesn't find any items with the word *homework* in it but does find items with the word *workplace* in it.

When you search, the PalmPilot doesn't pay attention to capitalization. Uppercase, lowercase—it's all the same as far as your PalmPilot is concerned. It doesn't matter whether you use capitals or lowercase letters. Because writing a lowercase letter takes fewer strokes than a capital, you might want to search using lowercase letters.

Using the Phone Lookup Command

One of the more useful searching features of the PalmPilot is its Phone Lookup command. (You can use it only if you have Palm OS 2 or higher, by the way.) This helpful command lets you look up people's names and phone numbers from the Address Book and then automatically pastes that information into the Memo Pad, To-Do List, or Date Book.

Using this command is simple. If you're writing a memo, jotting down a to-do, or creating an appointment, tap on the **Menu** button, and choose **Phone Lookup** from the **Options** menu. (A shorter method is to use the **/L** Command stroke shortcut.) When you choose this option, you see the following screen.

Looking up a name and phone number to paste into a memo, To-Do item, or appointment.

This screen looks a whole lot like your Address Book—probably because in essence it *is* your Address Book. Find the name you're looking for, tap on the **Add** button, and the name is pasted into your memo, To-Do item, or appointment, as you can see here.

After you look up the name and tap on **Add***, the name and phone number are automatically pasted into the program from the spot where you looked up the name.*

You can highlight a name or part of a name and search for the full name using Phone Lookup.

Another way to use Phone Lookup can save you time if you've already written a name into a memo, To-Do item, or appointment. Let's say you wrote in only part of someone's name, or else you don't know the phone number. First, highlight the name by dragging the stylus across it. Then use the **Phone Lookup** command. You are sent to the screen you saw before, but with the person's full name already highlighted. Tap on **Add**, and the person's entire name and phone number are pasted into whatever program you were in.

Smart Strategies and Tips for Finding Information in Your PalmPilot

So now you know how to tap all the buttons to help you find information. But that's only part of the battle. You also need smart strategies for finding information; otherwise, no matter how well you know how to use the Find function, you'll still be drowning in a sea of data. So follow these tips and strategies for smarter, faster, more effective searching:

- **Always attach detailed notes to memos, to-dos, and appointments.** The Find function searches through notes attached to all items you create. If you attach detailed notes to all your items, you can easily find the information you want. For example, if you meet someone at a cocktail party at your friend Hank Snow's house on July 19, write that tidbit in a note attached to that person's entry in your Address Book. Then, eight months later, when all you remember about him is that you met him at cocktail party, search for the word *cocktail,* and you can find the contact.

When you find what you're looking for, tell your PalmPilot to stop.

If, like me, you have hundreds or thousands of items in your PalmPilot, doing a search can take awhile. So when you do a search, as soon as the PalmPilot finds the information you're looking for, tap on the Stop button. This way, you can stop the PalmPilot from searching anymore.

- **Devise your own shorthand keywords that describe important information to you, and then put those keywords into every relevant item.** For example, you might create the keyword *acquisition,* which you include in any item related to the planned buyout of a rival company. You can put that keyword directly into the item—for example, in a memo or a To-Do item—or instead put the keyword in a note attached to the item. No matter which way you do it, when you search for the keyword *acquisition*, you can find everything you've ever done related to the buyout—whether it be a meeting, a memo, a To-Do item, or even an expense.
- **Speed up searches by running Find from the application where you're looking for information.** Let's say you know that you're looking for a memo. First, go to the Memo Pad, and then run Find from there. Find first looks for information in whatever program you're in, so it looks in the Memo Pad first. Whatever it finds there appears at the top of the list.
- **To do a Find fast, highlight a word, and then launch the search.** Highlight a word by dragging your stylus across it. When you launch a Find after highlighting a word, Find automatically searches for the word you highlighted—saving you the effort of having to write in the word using Graffiti.

The Least You Need to Know

- When you use the Find function, it searches through every item and all attached notes on your PalmPilot.
- You can search for the first part of a word, and the PalmPilot finds any items that have the entire word in them.
- You can use the Phone Lookup command to paste the name and address of anyone into a memo, To-Do item, or appointment.
- You can attach detailed notes to all your memos, To-Do items, appointments, and expenses. Doing so makes it easier to find information when you need it because Find searches through notes as well as the items themselves.
- If you know the application in which the information you're looking for is stored, start your search there. Find first looks through the current application, so this method speeds up your searches.

Part 3

Using Email, Internet, and Infrared Communications To Keep You in Touch

There's a big world out there. And you want some way for your little PalmPilot to communicate with that big world. Because if you don't, you'll be out of touch, and if you're out of touch, you're out of mind—not to mention, out of a job.

In this section, we cover how you can use your PalmPilot to stay connected to the world. You learn how to use email on your PalmPilot, see how to use it with a modem and dial into Internet service providers, and find out how you can hop onto the Web and browse the Internet for any reason you want. And most amazingly, you see how you can use the Palm III's (and later models) infrared port to send and receive information—any kind of information, whether it be a business card, a memo, an appointment, or even an entire program.

So, remember: no man, woman, or PalmPilot is an island. Check here to see how to stay connected.

Chapter 16

YOU'VE GOT MAIL!

How to Stay in Touch with Email

In This Chapter

- Understanding how the PalmPilot's Mail program works
- Sending and receiving messages using Mail
- Customizing your email messages so that Mail works the way you want
- Using Folders to manage your email
- Discovering strategies and tips for taking control of your email to make your life easier and more productive

You've got mail!

No, you may never hear those words on your PalmPilot because its speaker is too small, but you can certainly use the PalmPilot for email. You can compose and read email on your PalmPilot, but you can't directly send or receive email. You HotSync your PalmPilot to your computer's email program, and that email program sends and receives the email.

You'll find it a great help to be able to read and compose your email when you're not near your computer. In this chapter, you learn how to use the PalmPilot's built-in email program. If you want to be able to send and receive email directly from your PalmPilot, you have to buy extra software and hook your little digital companion to a modem. I'll cover all that information later in the book. For now, though, it's time to check your mail.

How the PalmPilot's Mail System Works

The first time I heard about the PalmPilot's email program I practically did a double-take. "Let me get this straight," I thought. "It's an email program, but it can't send or receive email by itself. Do I have that right?"

Yes, it turns out. I did have that right.

The PalmPilot's email program isn't designed to work on its own. Instead, it works with whatever email program you have installed on your PC, such as Eudora or Outlook. Let me explain how it works. You start by HotSyncing your PalmPilot with your PC's email program. Any email you've received on your PC is then sent to Mail on your PalmPilot. Now you can read your email using Mail on your PalmPilot. You can respond to any email or compose new email messages. After you've done that, HotSync again, and this new email you've written is sent to your PC's email program. The next time you connect to the Internet, it dutifully sends the email.

Only the PalmPilot Professional and Palm III and higher feature built-in email.

Previous versions of the PalmPilot don't have the email software built in. You still can use them for email, though. But to do so, you have to buy an extra add-on program. You can test many of these programs at a download site such as `www.palmpilotsoftware.com`. Check to see whether they work with your version of the PalmPilot, though.

By the way, you can send and receive email directly from your PalmPilot. To do so, you need to use a modem and an email program such as One-Touch Communicator or MultiMail. To learn how to use these features, turn to Chapter 17, "How to Use a Modem with Your PalmPilot," and Chapter 18, "Connecting to the World: Getting onto the Internet with Your PalmPilot."

The PalmPilot's Mail program is simple and convenient, but power-packed it's not. You can't read files attached to messages or attach files to messages, for example. Still, that's a small price to pay for portability.

First, Set Up the PalmPilot for Email

Before you can use Mail, you have to set up your PalmPilot properly to use it. When you first install the Palm Desktop, you're given the option of whether to set up your

PalmPilot for email. If, like me, you were a bit leery of doing that, and you said you didn't want to, don't worry. You can still set it up later. If you're running Windows 95 or Windows 98, just choose **Programs** from the **Start** menu; then choose **Palm Mail Setup** from the **Palm Desktop** entry.

PalmPilot Professional's Mail setup is more complicated than the Palm III's.

Setting up the PalmPilot Professional's Mail program is more difficult than setting up the Palm III's. The PalmPilot Professional doesn't have a separate setup program for Mail. You instead have to do some fancy configuring using the HotSync program. The best advice I can give you is to check the manual and cross your fingers for good luck.

The Mail setup program for the Palm III is about as simple as it gets: Choose the email program you use from a drop-down list from the Mail Setup program, as you can see in the following figure, and then click **Finish**. That's all there is to it.

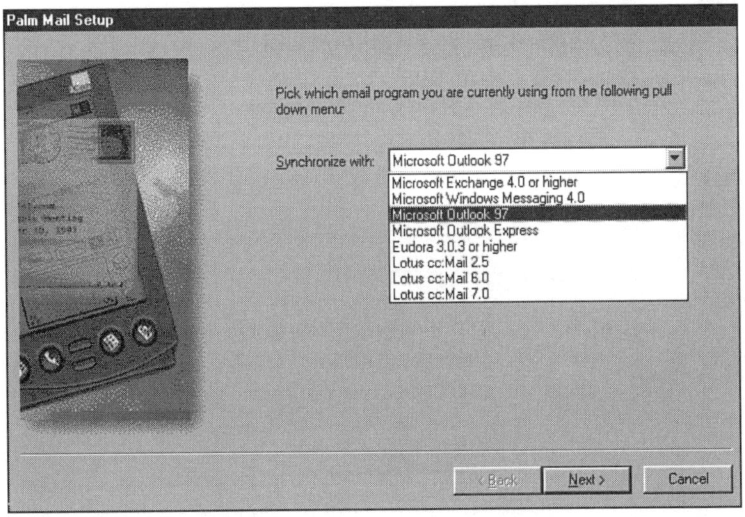

Click, go, and email: Choose your email program from the list in Mail Setup, and you're ready to use Mail on your Palm III.

Now, each time you do a HotSync, any email you've received on your PC is sent to your Palm III, and any email you've composed on your Palm III is sent to your PC's email program for delivery.

Okay, I'm All Set Up. Now Let's Start Mail

After you've set up Mail properly, HotSync your PalmPilot. You're then ready to start sending email. To begin, tap on the **Mail** icon. When the Mail program starts, you see a list of all the email that you've received and that's been sent to your PalmPilot. The following figure shows Mail's main screen.

This Palm III owner won't win any popularity contests; his mailbox is just about empty.

From this main screen, you do most everything you do with Mail—send and recieve email, manage your mailboxes—just about everything except lick the stamps, which thankfully you don't have to do.

By the way, let me share one interesting note about the mail list you see. Sometimes you see the real name of the person sending you the email. Other times, you see only the email address. Why is that? If the name of the person sending you email appears in your Address Book, the PalmPilot very nicely substitutes that person's real name for his or her email address. If the name of the person isn't in your Address Book, it doesn't.

Those check marks and that bold-faced type you see in the Mail list mean something.

When you go into, your Mail program, notice that some email messages have checks next to them, and some are bold-faced. What do these characteristics mean? A check next to an email message means you've already read it. A bold-faced message means that it's been sent to you as high priority.

How to Create an Email Message

Creating a new email message is a breeze. Tap on the **New** button, and you see the form for creating an email message, shown here.

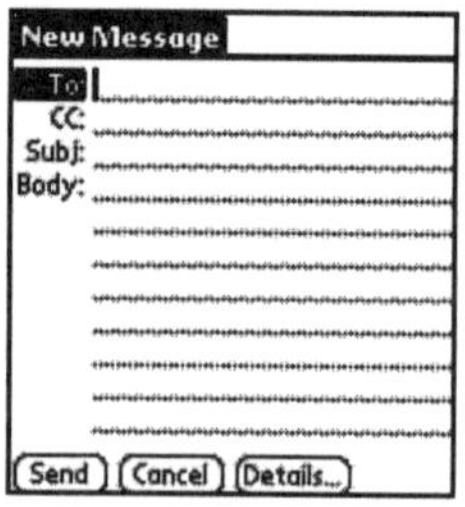

Getting ready to compose an email message using Mail.

Write in the email address of the person on the To line. If the name of the person appears in your Address Book (or you think it might), instead tap on the **To** button, and then from the screen that pops up, tap on **Lookup**. You then see the following screen.

You can add an email address using the Lookup feature.

Now simply tap on the name of the person to whom you want to send the message, and then tap on **Add**. That email address is automatically put into the To field.

Why don't the names of everyone in the Address Book show up when you tap on the Lookup button?

When you tap on the Lookup button to add an email address to a message, notice that not everyone in your Address Book shows up. You don't see all the names because the PalmPilot is pretty smart: When you tap on Lookup here, it shows you only the names of people who have email addresses to make things easier for you.

If you want to send a copy of the email message to someone, fill in that person's name in the CC field in the same way as you did in the To field. You can, by the way, have multiple addresses in each field. After you have the names in, write in the subject of your message and the message itself. Then tap on the **Send** button. That's all there is to it. The next time you do a HotSync, your email message will be transferred to your PC's email program and will be sent on its merry way.

Reply to Sender: How to Read and Answer Your Email

If you're more popular than the poor soul whose email Inbox you looked at a few pages back, you'll be spending a good amount of time reading your email. Reading email is easy: Simply tap on the message you want to read. When you're done reading, and you don't want to do anything with the message, tap on **Done** If you want to delete the message, tap on the **Delete** button.

You can recover messages that you've deleted.

When you delete an email message, it isn't really deleted. Instead, it's moved to the Deleted folder. That means you can easily recover messages you've deleted. To do so, after you've deleted a message, go to the Deleted folder by tapping on the triangle in the upper-right portion of the screen and choosing **Deleted** Then tap on the message you want to recover, and tap on the **Undelete** button. Your message then appears back in the folder where it was before you deleted it. After you do a HotSync, though, the email in your Deleted folder is truly deleted. So remember to recover and delete email before you do a HotSync.

Of course, your Deleted folder can get pretty full if all the messages you ever deleted end up there. As a result, it uses up precious memory on your PalmPilot. So what to do? Tap on the **Menu** button, and choose **Purge Deleted** from the **Message** menu. (Alternatively, you can use the Command stroke shortcut /E) This action permanently, absolutely, truly deletes any email in the Deleted folder. Beware, though, because after you purge your email, it truly is gone forever.

Replying is simple. Tap on **Reply** when you're reading a message, and you see the following screen. As you can see, you can choose from a bunch of options here.

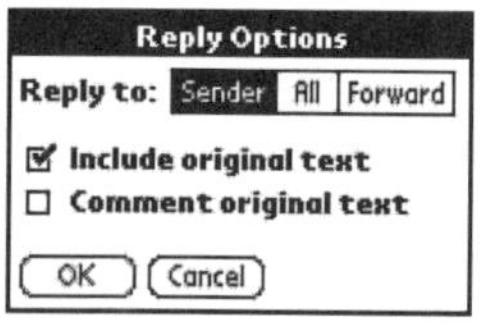

Reply to sender: Using this screen, you can answer your email messages.

Let me explain what all these options mean:

- **Reply to Sender** Means your message goes only to the person who sent you the message.
- **Reply to All** Means your message goes to every single person who received the email—in other words, not just the sender, but anyone the sender sent the message to in addition to you.

- **Forward** Lets you forward a copy of the message to someone who didn't originally receive it.
- **Include Original Text** Means that the entire text of the message that you're responding to is pasted onto the top of your response. Including all the text is pretty common in email etiquette, especially responding to other people's comments or questions.
- **Comment Original Text** Meansthat the original text is pasted in, and a kind of bracket symbol like this > is put in front of the text. The addition of this character makes it easy for people to see what the original message was and what your response is.

Customizing Your Email Messages

Every email message you send out is different. Some are sent to friends, some to family, others to strangers (and the stranger, the better...), some to coworkers, and others to potential clients. You can easily customize the messages you send out with Mail.

To customize your messages, tap on the **Details**button when you're composing the message. When you do so, you see the following screen.

Make your email your own: Here, you can customize the email messages you send out.

Tap on how you want to customize your email, and then tap on **OK**to customize it. You can do the following from this screen:

- **Set a priority for the message.**Set it to High, Medium, or Low. That way, the recipient knows whether the message is urgent. By the way, this option works only if your PC's email program and the recipient's email program can handle and display priorities. Not all do. If your email program doesn't handle priorities, don't bother using this field. Otherwise, give it a shot. It can't hurt.
- **Send "blind copies" of your messages.**This option sends a copy of your message, but no one else who gets the message will know that another person has been sent a copy. So the main recipient of the message and those in the CC field don't know you're sending a blind copy to another person. When you check this option, a new field labeled BCC (meaning blind carbon copy) shows up in your email message. Use it to send email in the same way that you use the To and CC fields.

Sending blind copies is often considered bad form.

Some people (me among them) believe that sending blind copies is bad form, that people have the right to know other people are reading the messages they send and receive. In fact, some companies believe this issue so strongly that they have outlawed the sending of blind copies on internal email systems.

- **Add a signature to the bottom of the message.** This signature isn't handwritten; rather, it's a message that appears at the bottom of your message, such as your title and contact information. Later in this chapter, I clue you in on more information about how to add a signature.
- **Confirm that someone has received your message.** If you check this box, you get email confirming that the person you've sent email to has received your message.
- **Confirm that someone has read your message.** If you check this box, you get email confirming that the person you've sent email to has read your message.

Be careful asking for email confirmations.

You might think it's really cool to be able to get confirmations that people have received your email and that they've read your email. Be aware that when you choose these options, your email box will soon get clogged with many dozens of these confirmations. For example, if you ask for both of these confirmations on an email message that you've sent to four people, you get eight confirmation messages from that one message. Multiply that number by the scores of email messages you send out, and you'll see that you can soon become overwhelmed by these messages. My advice: Don't check these boxes unless absolutely necessary.

Creating Your Signature

A signature is text that appears at the bottom of your email messages to identify who you are or add some personal information about yourself. Many people like to put famous quotations in their email or add some kind of personalized twist (and I've seen more than my share of very twisted signatures, I must say). Most popular email programs let you add signatures, by the way.

The first step to creating a signature is to check the **Signature** box in the Message Details screen. But doing that by itself doesn't append a signature to your email. You also have to create the signature. To create a signature, when you're in Mail, tap on the **Menu** button, and then choose **Preferences** from the **Options** menu. (Alternatively, you can use the Command stroke shortcut **/R**.) You then see the following screen.

You can customize your signature with any text you want.

After you've created your signature and told the Message Details screen to use it, you're done.

Managing Your Email with Mail Folders

Managing your email is tough when you have dozens or hundreds of email messages you've sent and read. They can quickly overwhelm you so that you'll never be able to find what you've sent or what you've received.

To help you manage all your messages, Mail lets you use five folders: Inbox, Outbox, Deleted, Filed, and Draft. The folder system on Mail isn't nearly as sophisticated as the kinds of folders you might be used to using on a computer's email program, but still, it can help manage your email. Next, I describe what you need to know about each folder to get control of your email.

Using the Inbox

When you read email, it shows up in your Inbox automatically. I covered how to read email and respond to it earlier in this chapter, so no need to go into those details again.

Soon, you'll notice that your Inbox is getting pretty full, and you might like some way to move email out of there so that it contains only the newest messages. You can delete the email, or else you can file it, which means you move it to the Filed folder. To move email from the Inbox to the Filed folder, when you're reading the email you want to move, tap on the **Menu** button and choose **File** from the **Message** menu. (Alternatively, you can use the Command stroke shortcut **/I**.) It is then moved to the Filed folder. By the way, after you move a piece of email to the Filed folder, it stays there; you can't move it back into the Inbox.

You can sort your email by date, sender, or subject.

The PalmPilot sorts email in your folders by date. You can sort your email by sender or subject as well. To sort your email this way, tap on the **Show** button when you're in any folder. Then choose whether you want to sort by date, sender, or subject. You can also choose whether to show the date of the message from the Show screen.

Using the Drafts Folder

You're in the middle of composing an email message when you get interrupted and need to move to another task. What to do? You don't want to send the email but don't want to lose what you've written so far either.

You can use the Drafts folder to keep all the email messages that you're in the middle of writing but don't yet want to send. You can also use it to keep email messages you've written but want to read again before sending—such as that letter of resignation to your boss you wrote after deciding it was time to head to Tibet and become a Buddhist monk.

To move a message to the Drafts folder, when you're composing a message, tap on the **Menu** button and then choose **Save Draft** from the **Message** menu. (Alternatively, you can use the Command stroke shortcut **/W**). Another, sneakier way to move it is to tap on the **Cancel** button when you're composing, and then tap on **Yes** when asked whether you want to save the email message in your Drafts folder. I don't suggest using this latter method, though; you can easily tap the wrong button and lose your email entirely.

To get to email in your Drafts folder, tap on the triangle at the top right of the screen, and choose **Drafts**. Next, tap on the message you want to work with, and then tap on **Edit**. This way, you can edit the message or send it. When you're done editing, tap on **Send** to send the message, or save it again in your Drafts folder in the ways outlined previously.

Using the Outbox

Whenever you compose an email message and decide to send it, the email gets moved to the Outbox. The email sits there, waiting for you to HotSync. When you HotSync, the email is sent to your computer's email program, which then sends it on its merry way.

Having email sit in your Outbox folder like this is a nice fail-safe mechanism. That means that even after you tap on **Send** and choose to send email, you still have a chance to edit it, delete it, or move it to another folder. So, if you've sent your letter of resignation because you were going to become a Tibetan monk but suddenly realized that you can't become a monk because you have a hard time being silent for more than 15 seconds at a time, all isn't lost. You can still delete the email before it gets sent.

To see what's in your Outbox and edit messages there, tap on the triangle in the upper-right corner of your screen, and choose **Outbox**. You can work with messages there just like in any other folder: You can delete them (in which case, they aren't sent; they are moved to the Deleted folder). You can move them to yourDrafts folder or even to your Filed folder, and in both cases, the messages are not sent. You also can edit them and send them by tapping on **Send** after you've finished your editing.

Using the Filed Folder

The Filed folder is the place where you put email that you've already read or that for some other reason you want to keep in a single, filed place. You can move email into the Filed folder from the other folders. Keep in mind that email in the Filed folder isn't sent to a folder on your computer's email program, so you can't read it in your email software on your computer.

You read, edit, and use messages in the Filed folder in the same way that you work with messages in your other folders.

Using the Deleted Folder

Whenever you delete a message, it ends up in the Deleted folder. Earlier in the chapter, I explained how you can recover email from this folder. Keep one thing in mind, though: After you do a HotSync, the messages in your Deleted folder are deleted; they don't stay there permanently. And when you do a purge, as described earlier, they vanish forever as well.

A Lean, Mean Mail Machine: Smart Strategies for Managing Your Email

In a lot of ways, email reminds me of that old 1950s movie *The Blob*. It's a constantly growing, amorphous mess that consumes anything in its path. If you're not careful, you could spend all your time reading and responding to email and managing your messages, all the while getting absolutely no work done. Follow the tips and strategies I present next, though, and that'll never happen: Instead, your PalmPilot will become a lean, mean mail machine, and you'll lead an easier, more productive life.

Customize HotSync to Save Time, Memory, and to Manage Messages

If, like me, you live and die by email, your PalmPilot will very soon get thoroughly clogged with email messages you've sent and received. It'll get so bad that you'll soon run out of memory, not just on your PalmPilot but inside your brain as well.

A simple solution is at hand. You can customize the way Mail HotSyncs with your desktop computer. To customize it, when you're in Mail, tap on the **Menu** button, and choose **HotSync Options** from the **Options** menu. (Alternatively, you can use the Command stroke shortcut **/H**.) You then see the HotSync Options screen, as shown in the following figure.

Save time and memory by customizing how HotSync works with email. Use this screen to make these changes.

You can use this screen to decide which messages are sent to your PalmPilot from your email program. That way, you get only email on your PalmPilot that you haven't already read on your PC's email program. You can even set filters so that messages from certain people and email addresses aren't sent to your PalmPilot. You can also decide to truncate very large messages so that they don't consume too much memory on your PalmPilot. Let me describe the various options on the screen and how to use them:

- **All** When you choose this option, all the email you've received on your computer's email is sent to your PalmPilot, and all the email you've composed is sent to your computer. Choose this option only if you don't send or receive a whole lot of email.
- **Send Only** Choose this option to send email from your Outbox to your computer's email program so that it can be sent. But you don't receive any email. Use this option if you're in a hurry or if you know you're going to read email on your computer's email program. That way, you don't clog up your PalmPilot's Mail program.
- **Filter** Filtering is the most powerful way you can customize how you HotSync with your PC's Mail program. With this option, you can choose to receive only certain messages. Tap on **Filter**, and you see the following screen. As you can see, you can tell HotSync to ignore messages sent from a specific address, sent to a specific address, or that contain a specific subject. And you can tell HotSync to retrieve messages only from a specific address, to a specific address, or that contain a specific subject. You can also tell HotSync to retrieve only High Priority

messages. With all these Filter options, you can get only the messages you want. You are able to filter out junk mail or mail that's not important to you.

You can filter out messages in a variety of ways using the Filter option.

Why filter on the To field in email?

It may seem odd to you that you can choose not to receive email sent to a specific email address. I mean, doesn't every piece of email you get have your address in it? Actually, the answer is no. If you subscribe to mailing lists, and if you get junk mail, for example, the To address in the email you get might not be yours. If you want only email specifically addressed to you, tell the Filter to send only those messages that contain your precise email address.

- ➤ **Unread** Choose this option to get only email that you haven't yet read on your computer's email system. This option is a big time-saver; if you use it, your Inbox isn't clogged up with email you've already read.
- ➤ **Truncate** Email messages can get pretty big. If a few whoppers are sent to your Inbox, they can all by themselves eat up a whole lot of your PalmPilot's memory. So you can choose to truncate messages—that is, receive only the first part of them. With this option, you get to choose how much to truncate the message and can choose to receive somewhere from 250 characters to 8,000 characters. Tap on **Truncate**, and you see the following screen.

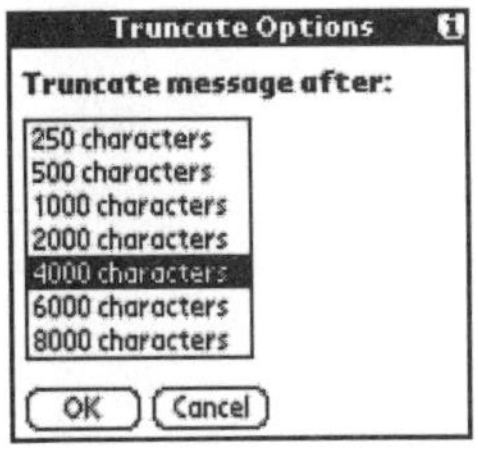

Too much of a good thing: Here, you can make sure that email messages don't eat up all your PalmPilot's memory by truncating the larger ones.

Turn Off HotSync If You Don't Want to Receive Email

Sometimes when you HotSync, you might not want to receive email at all. Maybe you're in a hurry and know that if you HotSync email, it'll take a long time to do the HotSync. Or you have no email to send, and you don't want to read any either. For whatever reason, you can choose to send and receive no email when doing a HotSync.

To choose this option, run the Palm Desktop on your computer. Then choose **Custom** from the **HotSync** menu. On the screen that appears, choose the **Mail** conduit. You then see a screen like the one in the following figure. Choose **Do Nothing** Now, the next time you HotSync, your email won't be HotSynced.

Here, you can turn off your Mail HotSync.

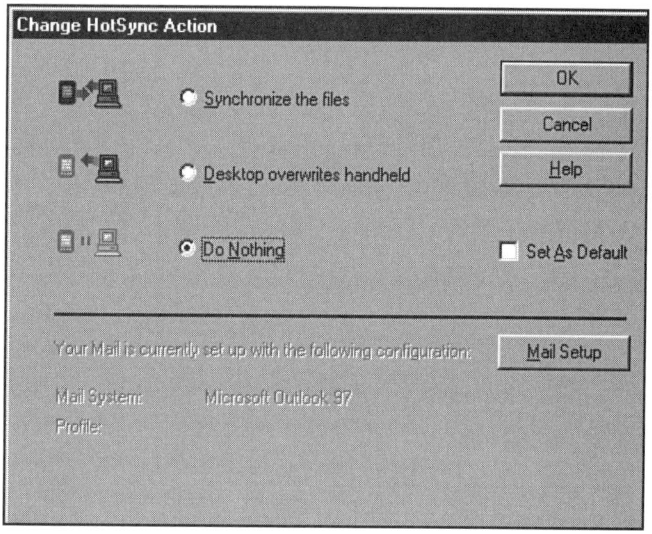

Travel Light: Catch Up on Email When You're on an Airplane

Travel time, especially on long airplane flights, is a great time to catch up on email. Maybe you don't own a laptop, though. Or perhaps you don't want to lug around a multi-pound behemoth when that mean little machine in your pocket will do.

Use your PalmPilot to catch up on email on plane trips. Follow these tips before you go:

- Before you travel, HotSync your PalmPilot so that you get all the email that you need to read and respond to.
- Make sure you put all the email addresses you need into your Address Book so that you have all the addresses close at hand.
- Use the To-Do List to put together a list of all the email messages you need to send.

➤ Now all you needto do is read your incoming email, respond to it, and create any new email messages while you're in flight. If you want, when you get to your destination, you can even HotSync with your desktop PC by using a modem, and it can then send and receive email for you. For more information on how to send messages this way and on traveling with your PalmPilot, turn to Chapter 23, "Traveling with Your PalmPilot."

Sort Your Email to Find Messages Fast

When you have a lot of email, finding the message you want is often very difficult. The Find command helps, but only if you know an exact word that appeared in a message. Perhaps you vaguely remember the name of the person who sent you the message or who you sent it to, or you may somewhat recall the subject. As a way to find messages fast, sort your email by person and by subject matter instead of by date. I often find the quickest way to locate the message is to sort my mailbox several ways: by person and by subject. That way, when I scroll through my messages, I can usually find what I want.

Use Distribution Lists to Send Email to Many People

What if you have a group of people you need to send the same email to regularly—perhaps a group of people at work, a group of friends who meet regularly, or perhaps a PTA or church list? Having to find everyone's name in your Address Book and paste it in can be a very tedious process, and you always run the risk of leaving off someone's name.

A faster and foolproof way is to create an email distribution list. When you create such a list, you need to add only a single contact to an email message, and that contact has all the email information in it. Let me explain how to do it.

Let's say that you're creating an email distribution list for a group of friends who meet once a week for dinner. You're always sending email to the group to see where to meet for dinner in the coming month. First, create a single entry titled Thursday Group in your Address Book. Put the words **Thursday Group**in the Last Name field, and leave the First Name field blank. Next, in the Email field, put in everyone's email address, with a comma and space between each one. Now tap on **Done**

When you're composing an email message, all you need to do is put the entry Thursday Group into the To field, and all the email addresses in the Thursday Group are automatically filled in.

You can make as many email distribution lists as you would like this way. Making this feature even more powerful is the fact that you can put multiple lists into a single To field, so you can easily enter several lists and send a single email message to many people simultaneously.

The Least You Need to Know

- You don't send or receive email directly with Mail; instead, it HotSyncs with your PC's email program that does the sending and receiving.
- If you want to send and receive email directly, you need a modem and an add-on email program.
- You can recover email you've deleted by going into the Deleted folder and undeleting individual messages, but only if you haven't HotSynced recently.
- After you've read a message, you can move it into the Filed folder so that you can more easily manage your email.
- You can customize the way HotSync works to keep your email down to a manageable size on your PalmPilot.
- If you often send email to the same group of people, you can create an email distribution list to save yourself time and to make sure you don't forget to send the email to someone important.

Chapter 17

How to Use a Modem with Your PalmPilot

In This Chapter

- How to set up the PalmPilot modem
- How to use other modems with the PalmPilot
- How to set up your desktop computer to do a HotSync using a modem
- How to set up the PalmPilot to do a HotSync using a modem
- How to do a HotSync with a modem

Take out your PalmPilot. Kind of amazing how much computing power you can hold in one hand, isn't it?

Well, that's nothing. You can literally hold the entire world in the palm of your hand. (Please, no choruses of "He's Got the Whole World in His Hands." It'll cause me distressing flashbacks.) You can use your PalmPilot to browse the Web, send and receive email, chat with others, send faxes, and even HotSync with your computer from long distances (distances that far exceed the length of your cradle's cord, by about 3,000 miles or so).

To perform any of these tasks, you need to use a modem with your PalmPilot. Don't get the shakes thinking that setting up a modem with your PalmPilot is difficult. As you see in this chapter, setting it up is a cinch. In this chapter, I cover how to set up a modem with your PalmPilot and also how to do a HotSync via modem. In the next chapter, "Connecting to the World: Getting onto the Internet with Your PalmPilot," you'll see how you can use the Internet after you get your modem set up.

What Kind of Modem Can You Use with a PalmPilot?

Let me share this odd fact: You can use any kind of modem you want with your PalmPilot. Your best bet, though, is to use the PalmPilot modem that 3COM sells. It's tiny, snaps right onto the bottom of your PalmPilot, and you'll find it a breeze to set it up. The only drawback is that it's a pretty pokey modem; it lets you connect only at 14,400 bps. Considering that the newest modems connect at 57,600 bps, this modem works at kind of a snail's pace. Still, you generally won't be sending or receiving a whole lot of information, so that slow speed is a small price to pay for portability and ease of setup.

You can use a cellular modem with your PalmPilot.

Several companies sell cellular modems and cellular services that work with PalmPilots. As a result, wherever you travel, whether or not you're near a telephone line, you can hook up to the Internet, to your email, or to HotSync to your computer. Your best bet for finding such services is to head to the `www.palm.com site` and look for information about them there. The Palm VII announced by 3COM includes a cellular connection as well.

You can use other modems with your PalmPilot, though. You need a special cable and might have to do some additional setup, but you'll find that they work. I tell you how later in the chapter.

How to Set Up Your PalmPilot Modem

The PalmPilot modem you buy from 3COM has been specifically designed to work with your PalmPilot, so you can easily set it up. It comes with two batteries, a telephone cable, and a handbook for setting up the modem. Put that handbook away because you don't need it. Instead, follow these directions, and you'll soon be sending and receiving data faster than you can say "World Wide Web."

The first thing you need to do is snap your modem onto the bottom of the PalmPilot. When you hear a little "snap" sound, you know that it's ready to go. (Don't wait for the "crackle" and the "pop" because you won't hear them; after all, your modem isn't a breakfast cereal.)

After you've attached the modem to your PalmPilot, put one end of the phone cable into the jack located at the bottom of your PalmPilot modem and the other end into a telephone jack or a data port of a telephone. If the modem doesn't have any batteries, put in two AAA alkaline batteries. On the bottom front of your modem is a battery door. Slide it toward you by gripping on the outside ridges; then put in the batteries, and close it back up.

Make sure that your modem's batteries don't run out of juice.

Your PalmPilot's modem is powered by batteries, which means that at some point they're going to run out. The modem doesn't have a battery gauge like your PalmPilot does, so you can't check the battery level. However, when you have about four minutes of battery time left in your modem, it beeps at you, and the beeps repeat every minute until your batteries are dead. If you often use your modem, consider buying an AC adapter. It costs about $20.

Good. You've got the easiest part done. Now it's time to fiddle around with your PalmPilot to get it to work with the modem.

Configuring Your PalmPilot to Work with the Modem

To get your PalmPilot to work with the modem, you're going to have to change your modem preferences. To start off, tap on the **Applications** button and then on the **Prefs** icon. When you do that, you see the Preferences screen. Now tap on the little triangle in the upper-right corner of the screen, and choose **Modem** from the drop-down menu. You then see the following screen.

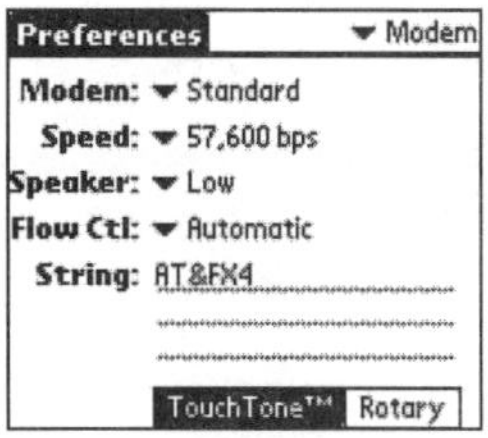

On this screen, you can set up your PalmPilot to work with your modem.

The first thing to do is choose your modem type. Tap on the triangle next to the word **Modem**, and choose **Palm US/Canada**. If you're in the United Kingdom, instead choose **Palm UK** because the UK uses a different phone system. (Those Brits—always have to be different, don't they? And when will they start speaking proper English, for heaven's sake?)

If you own a Pilot 1000 or Pilot 5000, choose Megahertz from the drop-down list.

If you own a Pilot 1000 or Pilot 5000, notice that no Palm US/Canada or Palm UK choices appear in your drop-down list. You don't see these choices because the PalmPilot modem wasn't yet shipping when those Pilots were built. Instead, choose **Megahertz** from the drop-down list, and you should be fine.

Now tap on the triangle next to **Speed**, and choose **57,600**. Yes, I know; this is confusing, isn't it? The speed of the modem is only 14,400, but you're supposed to choose 57,600. You do so because when you choose the higher speed, the modem uses compression magic to try to speed up sending and receiving information.

Next, tap on the triangle next to **Speaker**, and choose **Low**, **Medium**, **High**, or **Off**. If you can't stand the whining and screeching of a modem, you might like to turn off the sound. The truth is, though, the modem speaker is so tiny that it hardly makes any sound at all. I leave mine on Medium—and believe it or not, I actually *like* the sound of a modem. Makes me feel as though I'm doing something high-tech and productive.

Tap on the triangle next to **Flow Ctl**, and choose **Automatic**. Don't even bother to *ask* what this means. Take my word for it; you don't want to know. Simply choose Automatic, and let it do automatically what it's supposed to do automatically.

Next step, leave the gobbledygook next to the word **String** alone. These strange, arcane commands use a bizarre language called the *AT command*, which your PalmPilot sends to the modem to get the thing working.

Now choose the dialing method you're going to use—either touch tone or rotary. That's it; your PalmPilot modem is all set up and raring to go.

Well…sort of. Depending on what you want to do next, you're going to have to do a little more setup. If you want to do a HotSync, turn to the section later in this chapter on how to HotSync via modem for more details. If you want to get onto the Web or use the Internet for another reason, turn to the next chapter, "Connecting to the World: Getting onto the Internet with Your PalmPilot."

If you're a hard-core techie, you can change the AT commands.

Hard-core techies and communications wizards can change the strings sent to the modem by the PalmPilot by entering those commands next to the word **String**. Appendix A of the handbook that comes with your PalmPilot modem contains a complete set of these commands. Beware, though: Only experienced modem geniuses should try changing the commands.

Make sure to use an analog phone line with your PalmPilot modem.

A typical household phone line is called an *analog line*, and it's the same kind of phone line that's used most places. It's the kind of line your PalmPilot modem works with. However, you might run across another kind of phone line, called a *digital line*, that your PalmPilot modem doesn't work with—and that could even damage your modem. You might come across these lines in some hotels or offices. If you're not sure what kind of line it is, first check. If you do plug your PalmPilot modem into a digital line, it makes three beeps. When you hear that sound, immediately disconnect the modem from the line.

Setting Up a Regular Modem to Work with Your PalmPilot

You follow almost the exact same steps when you use a regular modem with your PalmPilot as when you use the 3COM modem specifically built for the PalmPilot. However, a few things are different when you're setting up another modem:

- **You need to buy a special modem cable.** Notice that you cannot plug a normal modem into your PalmPilot. To use your PalmPilot with a normal modem, you have to buy a special modem cable that costs about $20.
- **You have to choose a modem type from the drop-down list next to Modem.** When you set up your PalmPilot modem, you chose **Palm US/Canada** from the drop-down list. When you're setting up a different modem, you have to choose a different modem type. Only a few modem names appear in the drop-down list. If yours isn't listed, try **Hayes Smartmodem** or **Standard**. One or the other should work.

Far, Far Away: Using a Modem to Do a HotSync

Now that your modem is set up properly, you can surf the Web, send and receive email, and do HotSyncs when you're away from your computer. For details on how to use a modem to connect to the Internet, turn to the next chapter, "Connecting to the World: Getting onto the Internet with Your PalmPilot." In this chapter, I cover HotSyncs.

Why would you want to do a HotSync using a modem when you're away from your computer? You might want to do so for a few different reasons. One big reason is that, this way, you can always have a backup of all your information when you're traveling. If, while you're in a city away from home, for example, you're putting contact information, travel expenses, To-Do items, and so on into your PalmPilot, you don't want to lose that valuable information. If something goes wrong with your PalmPilot, you could lose all that information because you don't have a copy of it on your desktop computer. If you do a HotSync via modem, however, you have a backup of all that info on your computer at home.

Use your To-Do List to remind you to turn on your computer and modem before you leave on a trip.

If you want to HotSync via modem from the road, your computer and modem have to be turned on. To make sure that you turn them on before leaving, create a To-Do item that reminds you to prepare your computer for a HotSync before you go on your trip.

If you happen to have an assistant who handles your schedule, the assistant can put in new scheduling information. When you do a HotSync, you can get all that information, and your assistant can see the schedule information you put in as well.

To do a HotSync by modem, you need to set up your desktop computer, set up your PalmPilot, and then dial in and HotSync, as I describe next.

First, Set Up Your Desktop Computer

To do a HotSync via modem, you have to set up your desktop computer for a HotSync. Keep this point in mind: To do a HotSync this way, your computer needs to be running, your modem has to be attached to a phone jack and turned on, and your HotSync software has to be set up and running properly.

First, make sure that the HotSync software is running. (Turn to Chapter 5, "Keeping Your Life in Sync: HotSyncing Your PC and PalmPilot," for details on how to run HotSync.) If it's not running, you can't continue with the setup.

When you know the HotSync software is running, run the Palm Desktop software. Then choose **Setup** from the **HotSync** menu. From the screen that appears, click the **Modem** tab to see a screen like the one shown in the following figure.

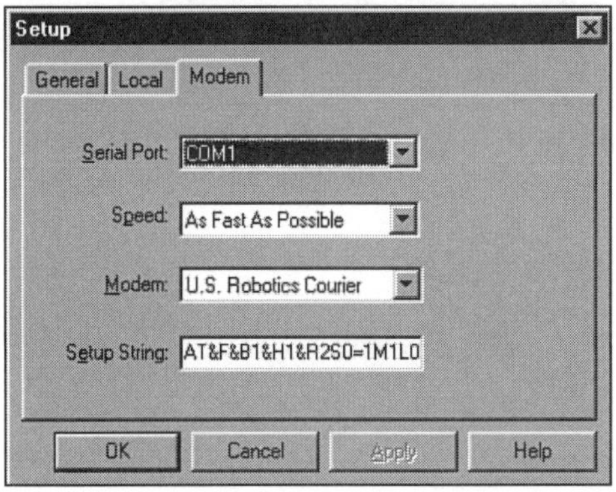

You use the Modem tab in your HotSync setup to configure your computer to be able to accept HotSyncs via modem.

First, you have to tell the software what serial port your modem uses. The serial port is what connects your modem to your computer. If you're not sure what serial port to use, you can find out easily enough. Click the Windows 95 or Windows 98 **Start** menu, choose **Settings**, and then choose **Control Panel**. Now double-click the **Modems** icon. In the resulting dialog box, click **Properties** to find the serial port your modem uses.

Next, you need to choose the speed of your modem on the Modem tab. Choose **As Fast As Possible**. You might think it very odd that anyone would choose any other speed. (There is no As Slow As Possible, so luckily you can't pick that option—although if you have a lot of data to HotSync, it'll certainly *feel* as if you've chosen As Slow As Possible.) You would choose another speed only if you've found by personal experience that you can't connect your PalmPilot to your computer via modem using this setting. Setting it at a slower speed could solve connection problems.

Now choose your modem type. Only a few are listed. If yours isn't listed, **Hayes Smartmodem** or **Hayes Basic** should work. When you choose your modem type, a setup string is automatically put into the Setup String box (good place for it to appear, don't you think?).

After you've filled in the Modem tab, click **OK**.

Now right-click the **HotSync** icon in your Windows 95 or Windows 98 taskbar. Then choose **Modem**, as shown in the following figure.

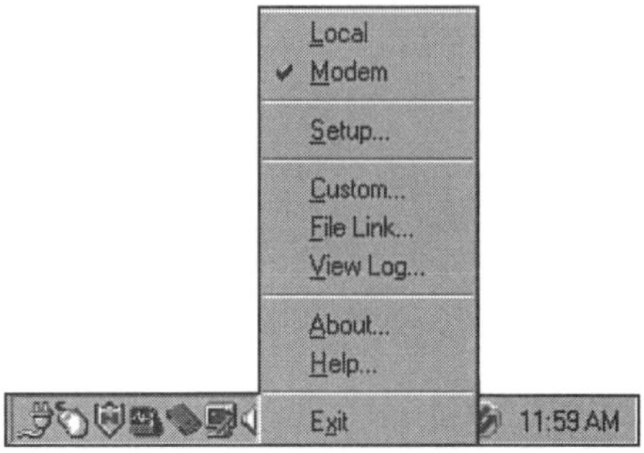

You've done it! Your computer is set up and ready to do a HotSync via modem.

That's it; your computer is now ready to accept a HotSync from your PalmPilot when you dial in from the road.

Nothing else can use the phone line you use for your HotSync.

When you turn on your computer and modem, configure them for a HotSync, and leave them running, that phone line cannot be used for anything else. If someone makes a phone call to it, for example, HotSync answers. So make sure a phone line is dedicated to HotSync and nothing else. Also, keep in mind that you shouldn't leave any other communications software, such as fax answering software, running on your PC at the same time as HotSync.

Next, Configure Your PalmPilot for a Modem HotSync

When your computer is set up to do a modem HotSync, turn your attention to the PalmPilot. (Anyway, it's been getting lonely lately because of all the attention you've paid to your PC.) It's time to set up your PalmPilot to do a HotSync.

Start by tapping on the **Applications** button and then on the **HotSync** icon. Tap on the **Enter Phone #** box. If you instead tap on the **Modem Synch** button, you get an annoying error message telling you to first put in a phone number. (By the way, is there such a thing as an error message that isn't annoying? I don't think so.)

When you tap on the **Enter Phone # box**, you see the following screen.

The Phone Setup screen lets you tell your PalmPilot what phone number to dial to do a HotSync.

Next to the Phone # area, write in the number that you dial to do a HotSync—in other words, the telephone number where your modem and computer are plugged in. If you're going to be dialing into your computer from a different area code, make sure to put in the area code as well.

Next, choose whether to dial a prefix before calling the number. Most hotels require that you dial a 9 or an 8 before making a call, so check this box and put in the specific dial prefix you need.

What are all those commas in the Phone Setup screen?

Notice that commas appear after some numbers, and four commas appear at the beginning of the Use Calling Card entry. A comma is a command that tells the modem to pause for a moment before dialing the next set of numbers. This pause makes it easier for the phone system to understand modem commands, so keep them in.

Now you have to decide whether to disable call waiting. Some telephone lines have a call-waiting service that beeps at you if you're on the line and someone else is trying to call you. If you're connected and doing a HotSync, this beep can trash your HotSync and bump you off the line. Hotels generally don't offer call waiting, but some personal lines do. If you're dialing from a line with call waiting, check this box.

Finally, if you plan to use a calling card, check the **Use Calling Card** box, and enter your calling card number.

You might notice a problem with the calling card entry; it might not be big enough to accommodate all the calling card numbers you have to dial. For example, some calling cards require that you dial an access code, then the phone number, and then your calling card number. So what to do?

To solve the problem, first tap on the **Dial Prefix** box. If you need to dial a 9 or an 8, put that number in there. After that, write in your access code. Then check the **Use Calling Card** box, and write in your calling card number. When you use this workaround, your modem first dials your access code, then the normal phone number that you've put in the Phone # box, and finally your calling card. Mission accomplished!

Now that you have all the information entered, tap on **OK**. You're ready to do a HotSync.

Test a modem HotSync before you hit the road.

All kinds of things can go wrong when you do a HotSync via modem. Maybe you made an error choosing the modem type or serial port on your PC, for example. So before you go on the road, do a HotSync via modem from your office or house to make sure that everything is configured right. That way, you won't be stuck in a city 3,000 miles from home unable to do a HotSync.

If you want, though, you can do one more thing to make your HotSync go more smoothly. You can tell your PalmPilot to HotSync only some data. For example, you might not want to HotSync your email when you're away, or maybe you don't use your Memo Pad and don't need to HotSync it. The fewer things you HotSync via modem, the faster your HotSync will go, and the more likely you will avoid running into any problems.

You can easily tell your PalmPilot which information shouldn't be included in a HotSync. First, tap on the **Applications** button and then on the **HotSync** icon. Now tap on the **Menu** button, and choose **Conduit Setup**. (Alternatively, you can use the Command stroke shortcut **/M**.) When you see the following screen, uncheck any information you don't want to HotSync, and tap on **OK**.

You don't need to HotSync everything on your PalmPilot; just uncheck what you don't want to HotSync, and everything will go faster.

Now Do a HotSync via Modem

You've got everything set up. Now comes the simple part. When you're away from your computer and want to do a HotSync, attach your modem to your PalmPilot, and plug the modem into a phone jack using phone wire. Now tap on **Applications** and then on the **HotSync** icon. Finally, tap on the **Modem HotSync** button. Your modem then dials, makes the usual horrifying screeches and wailing sounds, and then gives you a message telling you that you've connected. It then does a HotSync, like any other. For more information about how to HotSync, turn to Chapter 5, "Keeping Your Life in Sync: HotSyncing Your PC and PalmPilot."

The Least You Need To Know

- The PalmPilot modem from 3COM has been designed for use with the PalmPilot, so setting it up is easy.
- To use a modem other than the PalmPilot modem, you have to buy a modem cable for about $20.
- When you're setting up your desktop software to use a modem, if that modem isn't listed, choose **Hayes Basic** or **Hayes Smartmodem**.
- To do a HotSync via a modem, you have to make sure that your computer is set up right and that the computer and modem are turned on and connected to a phone line.

Chapter 18

Connecting to the World: Getting onto the Internet with Your PalmPilot

In This Chapter

- How to set up your PalmPilot to dial into the Internet
- How to send and receive email over the Internet using the PalmPilot
- How to browse the World Wide Web with your PalmPilot
- Where to find the best PalmPilot-related sites on the Internet
- How to use your PalmPilot like a fax machine and a pager

How big is your PalmPilot? Just about the size of the world, I'd say, considering that you can browse the Web, chat with others on the Internet, directly send and receive email with it, and even send faxes and use it as a paging device.

I cover all these tasks in this chapter. You find out how to set up your PalmPilot to hop onto the Internet and then see all the neat stuff you can do when you're there. You also see how you can send faxes using your PalmPilot as a pager. So, when you use your PalmPilot from now on, you'll be lonely no more.

How Can the PalmPilot Get Me onto the Internet?

To get onto the Internet using your PalmPilot, you need a modem, an account with an Internet Service Provider (ISP), the willingness to spend a bit of time fiddling around with your PalmPilot settings, and some extra software. (For information on how to set up a modem with your PalmPilot, turn to Chapter 17, "How to Use a Modem with Your PalmPilot.")

When you connect to the Internet, you first connect to an ISP using your modem. After the connection is made, you then launch software to send and receive email, browse the Web, chat, or do other cool Internet stuff. You can perform all these tasks because the PalmPilot Professional and the Palm III include, hidden deep inside them, something called *TCP/IP*. Think of TCP/IP as the secret handshake of the Internet. If you know the handshake (which your PalmPilot or Palm III does), you can get onto the Internet. If you don't know the handshake, you're out of luck. (Shameless plug alert: If you want to know how TCP/IP or any other part of the Internet works, check out my book *How the Internet Works*, by Que. I tell you everything you ever wanted to know about it. Nice pictures, too.)

What does TCP/IP stand for?

TCP/IP, the underlying language of the Internet, stands for *Transmission Control Protocol/Internet Protocol.* These protocols are essentially a set of complex rules that govern how computers send and receive information to each other and all over the world.

That's enough background for now. Let's get moving. It's time to get you online.

First, Set Up Your Internet Connection

As I said before, to get onto the Internet, you need an Internet Service Provider (ISP), such as AT&T WorldNet, CompuServe, or many others. Their prices vary, but you can figure they'll cost you about $20 or so a month.

When you have an account with an ISP, you can set up your PalmPilot to dial into it. I have some good news and some bad news about setting up your PalmPilot for your ISP. Here's the good news: Maybe you'll be lucky, and setting it up will be easy. Here's the bad news: You might not be lucky. If that's the case, be prepared: Setting up your PalmPilot could take some fiddling and diddling.

To set up your PalmPilot for connecting to the Internet, tap on the **Applications** button and then on the **Prefs** icon. Now tap on the triangle at the upper right of the screen, and choose **Network**. The following Network Preferences screen then appears.

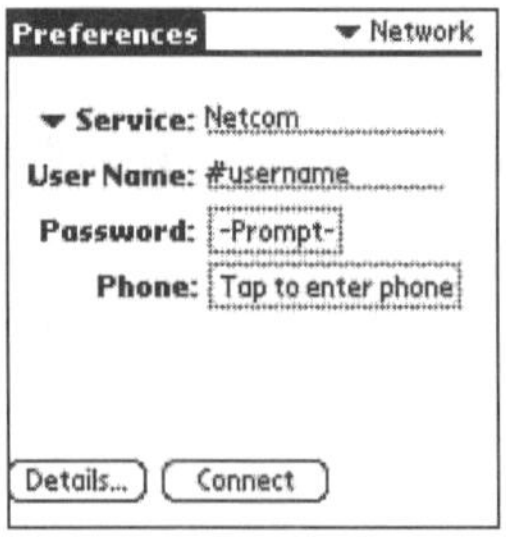

In the Network Preferences screen, you can set up your PalmPilot to dial into your ISP.

Next, tap on the triangle next to the word **Service**, and choose your ISP from the drop-down list, as shown in the following figure.

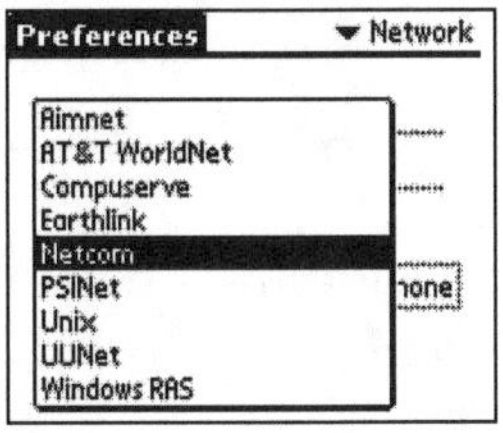

Pick a peck of ISPs. You can choose one from this list.

If your ISP is in the list, you're in luck; setting up your PalmPilot to dial in will probably be easy. To do so, tap on its name. You then see the Network Preferences screen shown earlier in this chapter, but with the name of your ISP listed.

Now enter your username in the place indicated on the Network Preferences screen. Your username is the one that you use to log in to your ISP. For example, if your name is Ali Baba, your username might be `alib`. Don't, however, use your entire email address, such as `alib@nights.net`. That doesn't work.

Call your ISP's tech support number and have them walk you through setting up your PalmPilot.

Your ISP's tech support people know a whole lot more than you do about arcane things like DNS entries, IP addresses, and login scripting. Therefore, if you're having trouble setting up your PalmPilot to connect to your ISP, call the tech support number. Be prepared to wait on hold for a long time; most ISPs get a lot of calls and don't have a whole lot of people working on tech support. Still, their tech support people may be able to easily solve your problem.

Next, tap on the box next to **Password**. When the following screen appears, write in your password, and then tap on **OK**. Notice that after you do so, when you get back to the main screen, next to Password, the box now says *Assigned*. The PalmPilot adds this word so that no one can look over your shoulder and steal your password.

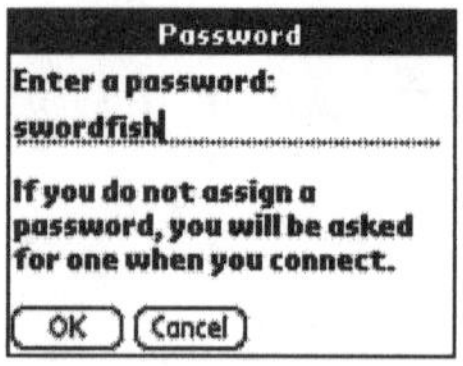

Here, you can type your super-secret password.

Now tap on the box that says **Tap to Enter Phone**. When you see the following screen, you can put in the phone number of your ISP.

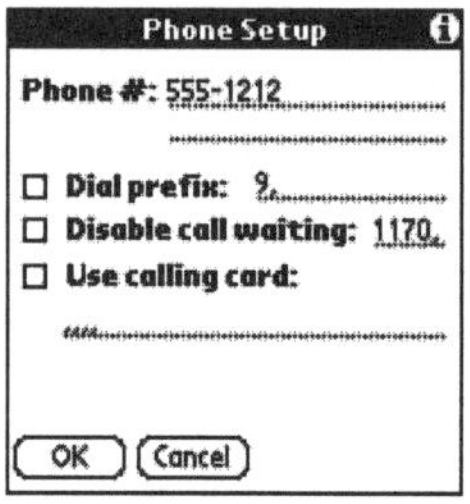

Enter the phone number of your ISP here. You can also disable call waiting from this screen, for example.

Fill in the phone number and tap on **OK**. This screen also lets you set other options, such as disabling call waiting or dialing a prefix before dialing the ISP's number. For information about all these options and how to use them, turn to the preceding chapter, "How to Use a Modem with Your PalmPilot."

That's all there is to it. You should be all set and ready to dial into the Internet. All you have to do now is make sure your modem is connected to a phone line and then tap on the **Connect** button in the Network Preferences screen. Your modem then dials into your ISP and logs you onto the Internet. If you have trouble, call your ISP's tech support line.

Ah, but here's a rub. What if your ISP *isn't* listed? (Mine wasn't, by the way.) What do you do then? One option, of course, is to sit on the floor and weep. Another is to tear your hair out and throw ashes into the air. If neither of these options seems like a good one to you (although, I have to say, they worked pretty well for me), then you should try to set up an ISP account without the PalmPilot's help.

To set up an account, after you get to the Network Preferences screen, tap on the **Menu** button, and then choose **New** from the **Service** menu. (Alternatively, you can use the Command stroke shortcut **/N**.) You see the familiar Network Preferences screen, but next to Service, it says *Untitled*. Write in the name of your ISP there. Now fill out the form the same way as I just explained to you. Then make sure your modem is connected to a phone line, tap on **Connect**, and hold your breath. If you're lucky, you can log on.

Don't try dialing into America Online.

America Online isn't a normal ISP (but if you use America Online, you kind of knew that already, didn't you?). Because it works differently than other ISPs, you can't dial into it with your PalmPilot. You might want to check with America Online to see whether it has solved the problem, though. It probably hasn't, but the call is worthwhile, just in case.

If you're not lucky, you could try troubleshooting by tapping on the **Details** button to get to the Details screen, as shown in the figure on the left. You could also try something mind-boggling like writing a script to log you onto your ISP, by tapping on the **Script** button and using all kinds of weird languages and commands, as you can see in the Log-In Script screen shown in the figure on the right. But take it from one who's tried: Don't bother. Instead, call your ISP's tech support line, and have the tech support people walk you through the entire setup. They're more prepared for this kind of thing than you are.

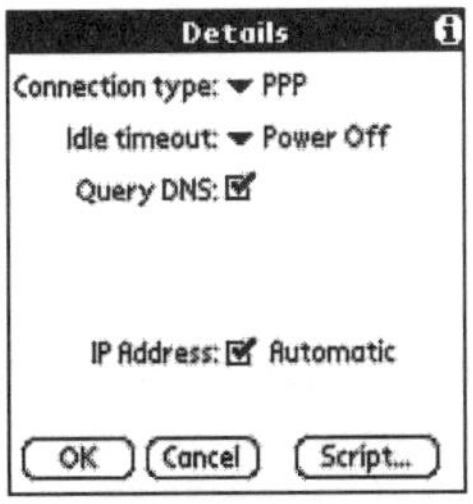

Not for the weak of heart: You can wrestle with these two screens if you want to troubleshoot your ISP login. Don't bother, though; call your ISP instead.

Use the Duplicate command if your ISP has more than one phone number.

Often, ISPs have more than one phone number you can use to dial into them. They might have different phone numbers for different cities, or several phone numbers in the same city you can call in case one is busy. Instead of filling out an entire new form each time you want to add a phone number, use the Duplicate command. With the ISP you want to copy displayed, tap on the Menu button, and then choose Duplicate from the Service menu. (Alternatively, you can use the Command stroke shortcut /L.) When you use this command, you make a new copy of the entry, exactly the same as the original in every way except that it's titled *(ISP name) Copy*. Rename it if you want—for example, to Earthlink Boston. Then enter a different phone number. You can now choose to dial a different phone number into your ISP whenever you want.

PalmPilot email software usually doesn't sync with your desktop PC's email software.

One drawback to most PalmPilot email software is that most don't HotSync with your desktop PC's email software. You're therefore going to have your email in two different places. One program, MultiMail, does HotSync with some desktop email programs, but not all of them.

How to Send and Receive Email Using the Internet

As you've discovered by now, and as I mentioned in Chapter 16, "How to Stay in Touch with Email," the Mail program that comes with your PalmPilot doesn't let you directly send and receive email over the Internet. Instead, you use HotSync and your PC to send and receive email. Many people, myself included, find that approach a less-than-stellar idea. The Mail program on the PalmPilot is a bit awkward, for a start. And if you're traveling, you can't send and receive email with your PalmPilot unless you continually do long-distance HotSyncs via modem.

What you really want to do is send and receive email, straight from your little digital friend. If you've set up your PalmPilot to dial into the Internet, as I just described, you can send and receive email directly on your PalmPilot. All you need to do is get a PalmPilot email program.

Several of the email programs I've used are quite good. I recommend HandMAIL, MultiMail, and One-Touch Communicator. My current favorite is One-Touch Communicator, which has the most features and options of them all.

Any email program you choose will be worthwhile. You can try all of them before deciding which one to buy. To test them first, head to `www.palmpilotsoftware.com`; you can find them all there. Just download and install. (For information on how to download and install programs from the Internet, turn to Chapter 20, "Installing New Software on Your PalmPilot.") You should also check out the CD in the back of this book for email software as well.

These programs all work very much like a desktop computer's email program. You can send and receive email, put email into folders, and generally do almost anything you can do in a normal email program. One big difference is that you cannot receive very large messages or attachments. Another difference is that none of them can read HTML email as can an email program such as Outlook or Eudora.

How to Configure Email Software

Every email program you use is different, and all require different kinds of setups. But all of them require some very specific information about your email setup. For example, they need your username and password, so you can log on and get your mail. They also need information about your ISP's mail *servers*—the computers that your ISP uses to let you send and receive email.

If you're using an email program on your PC, you might already have the information about the servers. Then again, the information is so easy to forget that you probably don't know it anymore. The best bet is to call your ISP's tech support people and ask them for the information. Here's what you need to know:

- **The POP3 server** This is the ISP's mail server that lets you receive mail. It is probably something like `mail.bignet.net` or `pop3.bignet.net`, assuming that the name of your ISP is Bignet. Again, though, ask your ISP's tech support people for the exact name.
- **The SMTP server** This is the ISP's mail server that lets you send mail. It is probably something like `smtp.bignet.net`, assuming that the name of your ISP is Bignet. But ask your ISP's tech support people for its exact name.

When you're armed with this information, you can set up your mail program and email with abandon (or with anyone else you want, for that matter).

Get the World Wide Web in the Palm of Your Hand

Amazingly enough, you can browse the Web using your PalmPilot. Tone down your expectations of what you can do, though. Don't expect videos or sound or fancy-looking pages. However, you are able to browse the Web, including getting graphics as well.

To browse the Web, you first dial into your ISP, as outlined previously. Then you launch a Web program specifically designed for the PalmPilot.

HandWeb and ProxiWeb are two good ones. I like ProxiWeb better than HandWeb. It uses some pretty smart and sophisticated technology, using what are called *proxy servers*, to deliver Web pages to you. They aren't perfect, but as much as possible, they have been streamlined for viewing on your PalmPilot, and they include graphics as well. (Pitch alert: If you want to know all about proxy servers, check out my book *How the Internet Works*.)

AvantGo delivers information from the Web by way of your PC.

A great piece of software called AvantGo takes a different approach to Web browsing. It uses your PC to grab pages from the Web and then sends them to your PalmPilot via HotSync. When the pages are on your PalmPilot, you can view them whenever you want, without being connected to the Internet. Many sites have built special sections specifically designed for AvantGo so that they look great on the PalmPilot. I recommend this software highly. Get it at `www.palmpilotsoftware.com` or `www.avantgo.com`.

You can get ProxiWeb and other Web browsers at `www.palmpilotsoftware.com`, by the way. (For information on how to download and install programs from the Internet, turn to Chapter 20, "Installing New Software on Your PalmPilot.")

You Can Do Other Stuff on the Internet as Well

When you connect to the Internet, you can do even more than send and receive email and surf the Web. You can also *chat* with other people, which means that you communicate live with them, one-on-one, by writing on your PalmPilot. Whatever they write, you can read, and whatever you write, they can read. A great program called ICQ lets you communicate this way. You can find a version of ICQ for the PalmPilot as well as for the PC and the Mac.

You can also participate in *newsgroups*, which are, in essence, global-spanning bulletin boards where you can send and receive public messages about any interest you have, whether it be about sports, computers, clothing, entertainment, or even about the PalmPilot itself.

You can find a lot of other things like this to do on the Internet. To do any of it, though, you have to get software. You can get it all at—yes, you guessed it—`www.palmpilotsoftware.com`.

Best PalmPilot Sites on the Internet

A wealth of information about PalmPilots is available on the Internet, more sites than you can possibly visit. More are popping up all the time. Check out this short list of some of my favorites:

- PalmPilotSoftware at `www.palmpilotsoftware.com` Great site for finding and downloading any kind of software. It reviews and rates the programs, so you know which are the best, and it offers advice on which software to use. It's also the place where I write the monthly column *Preston's PalmPilot Picks,* in which I choose the best PalmPilot software. Information required by the Gralla Truth in Publishing Act: I'm in charge of this site, as Executive Editor for the ZDNet Web site.
- PalmPower magazine. at `www.palmpower.com` Very good site for getting news about the PalmPilot, reviews, and for hints, tips, and tricks.
- Palmzone at `www.palmzone.com` Very nice site with reviews, news, and hints, tips, and tricks.
- 3COM's official PalmPilot .site at `www.palm.com` If you want the official word and news straight from 3COM about the PalmPilot and anything to do with it, check here. This site also has operating system upgrades, cool things to buy, and help if something goes wrong with your PalmPilot.

Paging and Faxing Using Your PalmPilot

When it comes to communicating, the Internet isn't the only game in town. You can communicate in a lot of other ways as well—and you can do them with your PalmPilot.

You can fax from your PalmPilot, although you can't receive faxes. To fax, use a program called HandFax. Just compose a fax, hook up to a modem and telephone, and fax away. You even can use its graphics tools to create a company logo that appears on a cover sheet to your faxes. Get the program at `www.palmpilotsoftware.com`.

You can also turn your PalmPilot into a pager that can send and receive pages, in addition to the normal PalmPilot tricks it does. To do so, you buy a $170 Synapse Pager card and install it into your PalmPilot. As I write this chapter, the pager card doesn't work with the Palm III. Don't worry; someone will build one that works. For details, head to 3COM's PalmPilot site at `www.palm.com`.

The Least You Need to Know

- Before you can connect to the Internet, you have to configure the Network Preferences screen. Choose your ISP from the drop-down list, and fill in information about it.
- If you have any trouble setting up the Network Preferences, call your ISP's technical support line for help.
- If you want to browse the Web or send and receive email directly from the Internet, you have to buy email and browser software. You can try them out for free at `www.palmpilotsoftware.com`.
- To configure email software for the PalmPilot, you need to know your ISP's POP3 and SMTP servers. Call the ISP's technical support line to find out what they are.
- If you use America Online as your way to get onto the Internet, you cannot directly dial into it to use your PalmPilot.

Chapter 19

Beam Me Up, Scotty! Using the Palm III's Infrared Port

In This Chapter

- How infrared beaming works
- What kind of information you can beam to other Palms
- How to beam and receive information using the Palm
- Smart tips and strategies when using beaming to make your life more productive

One of the more amazing features of the Palm III is its capability to send and receive information to other Palm IIIs via its beaming port. You can send and receive items such as memos and to-dos, entire categories of information, programs, and even business cards. Beaming is great when you need to share information with others about projects, plans, and contacts.

When you beam information to someone, you're copying it to that person's Palm via the beaming port. The information that you beam over stays on your Palm; only a copy of it is sent.

What's an Infrared Beam, Anyway?

The Palm III does its bit of magic using an *infrared (IR) beam,* which is a beam of light that's invisible to the human eye because its rays are in the part of the electromagnetic spectrum that's beyond the limits of what we can see. (Whew! How's that for complicated, high-tech talk?) Data travels along the beam from the beaming port on the top of one Palm III to the beaming port on the top of the other. The Palms' beaming ports have to be pointed at one another, and nothing can be in between them to break the beam. (The beam can't go through walls like Superman's x-ray vision, for example.) They should be anywhere from about 2 inches to about 40 inches apart for best performance. (For those of you who think metric, think between 5 centimeters and 1 meter.)

What does IrDA stand for?

You may have seen the acronym *IrDA* used when referring to infrared technology on computers and printers. IrDA stands for the *Infrared Data Association,* a group of hardware makers that developed a standard for sending data via infrared light. Many computers—especially laptops—come with IrDA ports, and increasingly, printers come with them as well. Computers and printers equipped with IrDA ports can communicate with one another—for example, a computer can print without using a printer cable; it prints using an infrared beam. The infrared port on the Palm III isn't an IrDA port, so the Palm III can't communicate with IrDA-equipped hardware. The WorkPad, however, can communicate with the IrDA-equipped ThinkPad laptop computer.

Some computers have infrared ports called IrDA ports. The infrared beam of your PalmPilot can't communicate with them, however, because different technology is used for each.

Your TV remote control and other kinds of remote controls, such as remote controls for CD players, also use infrared beams. Don't try pointing your Palm III at them, however, because it unfortunately doesn't work.

Amazingly enough, though, you can buy special software and hardware that let you turn your Palm III's infrared beam into a universal remote-control device. With this software and hardware, you can control your TV, your CD player, and other items in your home that can be controlled by an infrared remote control. You can find several of these devices and software, including one called the Wedge and another called OmniRemote.

You also can buy a program called PalmPrint from Stevens Creek Software that allows you to use your beaming port to print with IrDA-equipped printers.

What Kind of Stuff Can You Beam?

You can beam almost anything on your Palm III to another Palm III. Here's the low-down on what you can send and receive:

- **Any single entry in the Address Book, Date Book, To-Do List, or Memo Pad** You therefore can beam (or receive) appointments, to-dos, memos, and contact information to another Palm III.
- **Entire categories in the Address Book, Date Book, To-Do List, or Memo Pad** If you have a category of contacts called Prospects you want to send (or receive), for example, you can do so by using the infrared beam. You can beam any category in any of these applications.
- **Entire programs that you've installed on your Palm III** Let's say you've installed a neat game or other kind of program, and you want someone else to try it. No problem. Beam it over. Before you beam or receive a program, though, make sure that you're not violating the program's copyright by doing so. Check the program's documentation; when you weed through the lawyer-ese, you should find a statement telling you whether this kind of thing is kosher.

Non-Palm III models can be upgraded to beam as well.

If you don't have a Palm III and are jealous of your friends who beam with abandon, don't despair; there's hope for you. You can buy a 2MB upgrade card (that also has beaming capabilities) from 3COM for about $130 and can plug it into your existing PalmPilot. Then you can start beaming with the best of them.

- **Your own personal "business card"** You can put contact information such as your name, phone number, and email address (and even your favorite color, if you like) into the Address Book and then designate that entry as your business card. You can then send that business card to someone else with a Palm III, and you can receive business cards from others as well.

Be aware that your infrared beam doesn't let you transfer absolutely anything you want from Palm III to Palm III. You can't beam over any information from the Mail or Expense programs. You also can't beam the built-in programs that come with your PalmPilot, such as the Date Book and Memo Pad. You can beam information from those programs, as I explained before, but not the programs themselves.

So Let's Get Beaming Already: How to Beam Stuff to Others

Beaming information from Palm III to Palm III sounds awfully sci-fi and high-tech. The truth is, though, it's very easy to do. You can beam individual items, entire categories, whole programs, and business cards.

The first thing you need to do before beaming is make sure that a Palm III is nearby, ready to receive. After you've found a willing victim—I mean someone who wants to receive your information—point your beaming port at that person's beaming port, and make sure you're from within about 2 to 40 inches from each other. Then you're ready to go.

In the following sections, you learn how to beam each different kind of item to another Palm III.

How to Beam an Individual Item to Another Palm III

After you've pointed your Palm IIIs at each other, select the individual item you want to beam to another Palm III, such as a memo in the Memo Pad. Then tap on the **Menu** button. When you see a screen like the one in the following figure, choose **Beam**. (Instead of using the Menu button, you can use the Command stroke shortcut **/B**.)

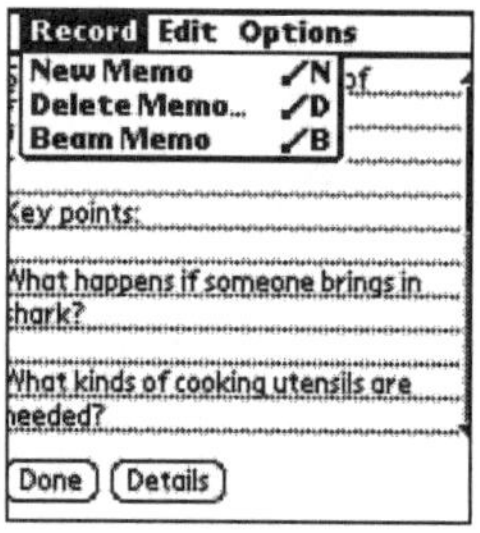

On your mark, get set, beam…Here, you can choose to beam an individual item to another Palm III.

After you choose this option, you see a very brief message telling you that the item is being prepared for beaming. Another brief message tells you that your Palm III is searching for another Palm to transfer information to. When it transfers the information, a screen tells you that you're sending the information. Congratulations! You've just beamed your first piece of information to someone else. The whole process shouldn't take longer than a few seconds.

How to Beam an Entire Category to Another Palm III

Beaming an entire category of information to another Palm III is just as easy as beaming a single piece of information. To beam an entire category to another Palm III, just switch to the category you want to beam by tapping on the **Category** triangle in the upper-right corner of your screen. Then tap on the **Menu** button. When you see a screen like the one shown in the following figure, choose **Beam Category**. (There's no Command stroke shortcut for beaming an entire category, by the way.) The same things happen as happened when you beamed an individual item. The only difference is that transferring the category might take a bit longer because a category is made up of many items, not just a single one.

You can just as easily beam an entire category as you can beam an individual item.

How to Beam a Program to Another Palm III

Beaming an entire application to another Palm III is quite easy. First, tap on the **Applications** button. The Applications screen then appears, showing you all the programs on your PalmPilot. Now tap on the **Menu** button, and choose **Beam**, or use the Command stroke shortcut **/B**. When you choose this command, you see the following screen. Notice that some of the programs have a little picture of a lock next to them; the lock means that they can't be beamed.

When you see a lock next to a program name on this screen, it means that program can't be beamed.

Tap on the name of the program you want to beam. Then tap on the **Beam** button. Your Palm III then goes through the now-familiar beaming routine. Beaming an entire application usually takes even longer than sending a category because most applications are larger than categories. However, even the largest program shouldn't take more than several minutes to beam.

You can't beam just any application from one Palm III to another.

I mentioned before that you can't beam the Palm's built-in applications from one device to another. Neither can you beam some other programs. You cannot beam some add-on software to another Palm III. You cannot do so because the software company worries that if you had this capability, everyone would be beaming the software to each other, and very few people would bother to buy it. You can tell which software can't be beamed by looking for the little lock icon.

Beaming Your Business Card to Another Palm III

Beaming your business card to another Palm III is a breeze. It's a two-step process. First, you designate an entry in your Address Book as your business card. Then you beam away.

To designate an entry as your business card, either create a new one, or open an existing one. With it open, tap on the **Menu** button, and then choose **Select Business Card** from the **Record** menu. You then see the following screen.

On this screen, you can designate an entry as your business card.

Just tap on **Yes**. That's all it takes; you're ready to beam your card to someone else. When an entry is your business card, it gets extra-special treatment from your PalmPilot: A little icon that looks like a rolodex card appears at the top of the entry, as you can see in the following figure.

To beam the business card, go to the Address Book. (You don't have to open your business card itself.) Then tap on the **Menu** button, and choose **Beam Business Card** from the **Record** menu. It is beamed then, just like any other item on your Palm III.

When you see the little icon that looks like a rolodex card at the top of an entry, it means that entry is your business card.

Receiving Information on Your Palm III via the Infrared Beam

Receiving information on your Palm III is a bit different than sending it. You get to say whether you would like to receive the information; therefore, a few different steps are required.

When someone tries to beam you something, you get a brief message saying "Preparing," which flashes by quickly. Then comes another brief message saying "Waiting for Sender," and another screen tells you it's receiving the data being sent. At this point, even though the data is being sent to you, note that it's not yet stored permanently on your Palm III. After all the information is sent, you get a message asking whether you want to accept what's being beamed to you. You are told specifically what's being sent. If you don't want to accept it, tap **No**. (Your motto must be "Beware of geeks bearing gifts.") To accept it, tap **Yes**. (Your motto clearly is "Don't look a gift horse in the mouth.")

If you choose to accept the item, you get a note telling you it's being accepted. Then the item (or category, or whatever is being beamed) opens. You can edit it at that point if you want, or you can simply store it. That's all there is to this process.

When you're sent a category of items, you receive the items, but they are uncategorized.

One of the oddest things about receiving information via infrared beam is how the Palm III handles receiving entire categories. When you receive a category, every single item in that category is sent to you. Oddly enough, though, each item in that category is listed as Unfiled; in other words, the items aren't linked to a specific category. So, for example, if someone sends you the To-Do List category of Football, which has 13 To-Do items in it, you get all the To-Do items, but they aren't listed under Football. The Football category doesn't show up anywhere on your Palm III. The items are all Unfiled. You have to create the Football category yourself and then manually categorize them if you want them to be associated with the Football category.

How Beaming Can Make Your Life More Productive

Want to make your life more organized and more productive? Follow these tips and strategies for how to beam, and you can make it so:

- **Create several Address Book entries that you can use as your business card.** Like many people, you probably wear many hats in your life (no silly ones, I hope). You may have a job and also a small home-based business. You may spend time volunteering for a good cause. And even in your job, you may perform a variety of different functions. Having customized business cards for everything you do would be nice. Creating the cards is easy with the Palm III. Just create separate entries for each business card. Then, when you want to use a particular one for beaming, designate that one as your current business card.
- **Stop the madness: Turn off beaming.** Beaming is a very neat thing to do. It can be annoying as well. You don't want to always be bombarded with beams that interrupt your work and thoughts. You can easily turn off beaming so that you don't receive beams and so that you aren't even notified when someone tries beaming something to you. To do so, tap on the **Applications** button and then on **Prefs**. From the triangle in the upper-right portion of your screen, choose **General**. Then tap on the triangle next to **Beam Receive** and choose **Off**, as shown in the following figure. To turn it back on again, get back to this screen and choose **On**.

On this screen, you can turn off beaming.

- **Create To-Do categories that you can beam to others who work for you as a way of assigning tasks and coordinating projects.** Let's say you're working on a complex project, and as part of it, you need to assign tasks to one or more people. For each person on the project, create a To-Do category. Then, after you have a meeting with members of the team and want to more make sure they have the full list of what you need them to do, beam their categories to them. They then have an accurate list of what needs to be done.

The Least You Need to Know

- To beam or receive information using the infrared beam, your Palm III must be within from 2 to 40 inches of the other Palm III, with nothing blocking the beam.
- You can't beam or receive information using your Palm III and a computer's IrDA infrared port.
- You can beam individual items, entire categories, and whole applications, but you can't beam anything from the Mail or Expense programs.
- To make it easier to give people your contact information, create a business card and then beam it to them.
- If you don't want to be bothered by people beaming information to you, you can turn off the beaming option.

Part 4

Supercharging Your Life with the PalmPilot

Sure, organizing your life is fine. But let's face it; that's just the beginning. You don't want to settle for a merely organized life, do you? No, of course not. You want more than that. You want fame, fortune, widespread acclaim, you want to rule the world, the solar system, the cosmos…

Sorry, got carried away there. The point is, though, that you want to get more out of your life, not merely have a well-organized existence. In this section, you see how you can get more out of life, and master your PalmPilot as well. You see how you can install new software on your PalmPilot—software that will help you get more out of life. You learn how to bend the PalmPilot to your will so that it helps you get more out of life. You find out how you can use your PalmPilot to get all kinds of reference material. And, you learn how the PalmPilot can be your best travel companion by helping you with whatever problems you have when you're on the road.

Chapter 20

Installing New Software on Your PalmPilot

In This Chapter

- How to use the Palm Install Tool to install software on your PalmPilot
- How to delete programs from your PalmPilot
- How to find programs on the Internet and how to download and install them
- Great programs you can install on your PalmPilot

Gralla Rule #1 for using a computer of any kind: It needs more software. No matter how good your computer is, it can be improved by putting new programs on it.

That rule of thumb is certainly true of the PalmPilot. Although what comes on it is great, you can find software out there to make you more productive, help organize your life, make using the PalmPilot much easier—in fact, do everything including make the little thing jump through hoops. Oh, yeah; games are available, too, so you can have fun as well.

You can get programs to put on your PalmPilot from a number of places. Many came on the CD that you got when you bought your PalmPilot. Others you can buy from stores. Others you can download or buy on the Internet. For a great batch of software, turn to the CD at the back of this book; you can find all kinds of software to help you organize your life, get the most out of your PalmPilot, and have fun as well.

In this chapter, I cover how to install programs, as well as how to find programs on the Internet, and then how to download and install them. I cover deleting programs as well. Finally, I describe a baker's dozen of some of my favorite PalmPilot programs.

How to Install Software on Your PalmPilot

So you want to take advantage of the thousands of programs out there? No sweat. You'll see as you go through this chapter that it's easy to do.

> **What do .prc and .pdb stand for?**
>
> For those who like to know the English equivalents of computer speak: .prc stands for *Pilot resource,* and .pdb stands for *Pilot database.*

First, let's get some techie stuff out of the way. PalmPilot programs are different from programs that run on your PC or Mac. On a PC, for example, the names of files that run programs end with .exe or .com, such as winword.exe, which is the Microsoft Word program.

On a PalmPilot, the names of files that run programs instead end in .prc, such as Giraffe.prc. This file is the Giraffe game that teaches Graffiti; you can install it from the CD that came with your PalmPilot.

Some PalmPilot files you can install end in .pdb instead. They aren't actual programs. They're often information files that accompany a program—for example, a list of popular Web sites to accompany a PalmPilot Web browser. And some. pdb files can be installed by themselves—for example, a listing of PalmPilot tips and tricks.

Okay, are you all teched out? Then it's time to start installing programs.

Using the Palm Install Tool to Install Programs in Windows

Anyone who's ever installed a piece of software on a PC knows how confusing it can be. Sometimes you feel as if you need a Ph.D. in computer science to do it; even then, it's probably pretty tough.

Here's some good news: Installing software is easy on a Palm III. You can even use a special program called the Palm Install Tool.

Before you install a program, copy its files to your hard disk somewhere. I suggest copying the files to the C:/Palm/Add-On folder, which was created for you when you installed the Palm Desktop software. Copy them there because that's the first place the Palm Install Tool looks when you launch it. Also, if you copy them there, all the programs you might install are in one place and therefore harder to lose. If you decide to instead copy the files to a different spot on your hard disk, remember that place so that you can get there from the Palm Install Tool.

After you've copied the files, run the Palm Desktop. Then click the **Install** button in the lower-left portion of the screen. When you do that, you launch the Palm Install Tool, shown in the following figure.

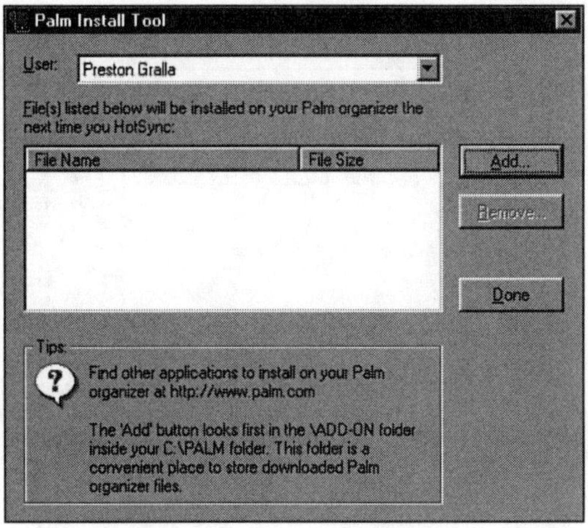

The first step to installing software: Run the Palm Install Tool.

Click the **Add** button. When you click this button, the Palm Install Tool looks in the C:\Palm\Add-On folder and lists any .prc or .pdb files it finds. As you can see from the following figure, I install a whole lot of software; my directory is chock full of software to install.

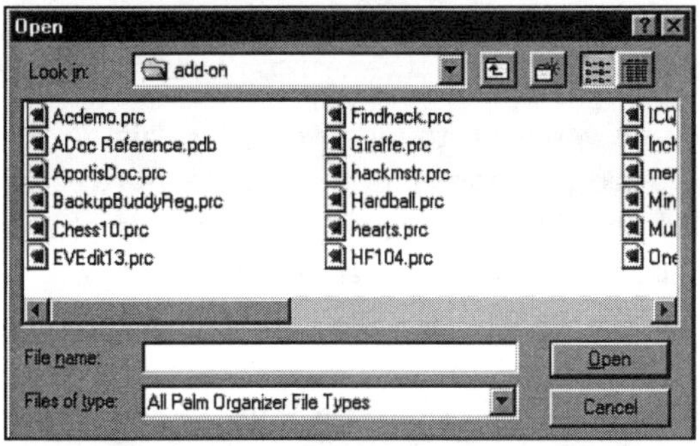

A whole lot of installing going on…Here, you can see a list of files that can be installed from my \Palm\Add-On folder.

Click the name of the file you want to install, and then click the **Open** button. When you do that, you are returned to the Palm Install Tool screen, and the file is listed there. If you want to install another program, click **Add** again, and repeat the process. When you're done, you see a screen like the following, listing all the programs you want to install.

The Palm Install Tool lists all the programs you've chosen to install.

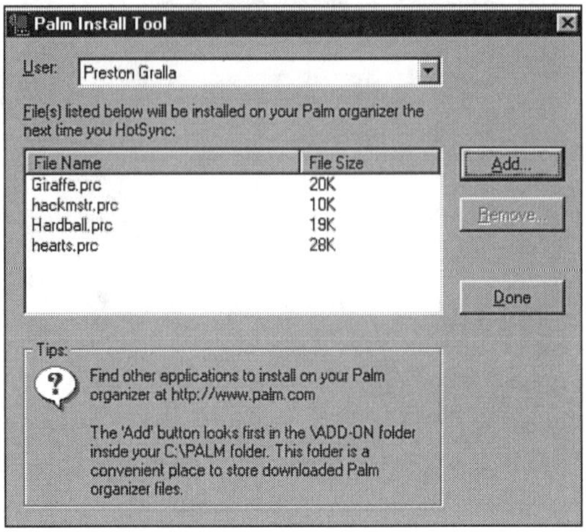

Use this shortcut for installing multiple programs in Windows.

Let's say you have several programs you want to install on your Palm III. Choosing them one by one can become a tedious process. Instead, use a shortcut to choose several at a time. After you click the **Add** button, click the name of the first file you want to install. Then hold down the **Ctrl** key, and click the name of every other one you want to install. Every file you click this way is highlighted, and when you click **Open**, they all are added to the Palm Install Tool screen.

If you decide at this point you don't want to install one or more programs that you've just chosen, click them and then click **Remove**. That program is removed from the screen and is not installed.

After you've chosen all the programs you want to install, click **Done**. You then get a screen telling you that the next time you do a HotSync, the programs you've chosen will be installed. The next time you do a HotSync, you'll get a message that programs are being installed. A button for each program then shows up on your PalmPilot. You can run them just as you would any other program, by tapping on their buttons.

Installing programs on the PalmPilot is more difficult than on the Palm III.

PalmPilot users will find it a bit more difficult to install software than do Palm III users. You're going to have to use the Instapp program if you're a Windows user or the InstallApp if you're a Macintosh user. They both work similarly: Run them, browse to the folder or directory where the programs are installed, and choose the program to install. As with the Palm III, when you next do a HotSync, whatever programs you chose to install will be installed onto your PalmPilot.

Installing Programs on the Macintosh

Installing programs on the Mac is similar to installing them on a PC. First, open the Pilot Desktop 1.0 folder. Then locate and run the InstallApp program. Click **Select**, and then navigate to the program you want to install. Click **Open**, and then click **Install**. To install more programs, click **Install Another File**, and then repeat these steps. The next time you do a HotSync, the programs you've chosen will be installed.

Get Outta Here! How to Delete Programs from Your PalmPilot

All good things must come to an end. Romance fades. A time will come when that beautiful new program you installed won't seem quite so appealing any more. It's time to bid it adieu.

Deleting a PalmPilot program is much easier than ending a romance; in fact, it's easier to do than almost anything. You don't need to use the Palm Desktop either. Instead, you can delete programs by using the PalmPilot itself.

To delete a program, tap on the **Applications** button. Now tap on the **Menu** button, and choose **Delete** from the **App** menu. (Alternatively, you can use the Command stroke shortcut **/D**.) The following screen appears, listing all the programs that you can delete from your PalmPilot. Note that it doesn't list the programs built into your PalmPilot, such as Memo Pad or the To-Do List. They aren't listed because you can't delete them; they're with you permanently, through thick and thin.

The thrill is gone: From this screen, you can delete programs you don't want on your PalmPilot anymore.

Tap on the name of the program you want to delete. You then see the following screen, asking whether you really, truly, absolutely want to delete the program. If you do, tap on **Yes**. If not, tap on **No**. After you've deleted all the programs you want, tap on **Done**. Now you've gotten rid of all the old stuff you don't want around anymore.

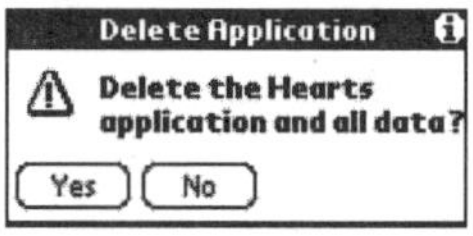

Last chance: Tap on ***Yes*** *to delete the program;* ***No*** *if you change your mind and want to keep it.*

Where to Find Programs on the Internet

I picked a whole lot of programs for you on the CD accompanying this book, so it's a good place to start when you're looking for software. If you're looking for a choice of thousands of programs—that's right, I said *thousands* of programs—then you should immediately head to the World Wide Web. You can find sites jam-packed with software you can download and try out.

Some of these programs are shareware, trial versions, or demos, which means that you can try them for a certain amount of time or number of uses, but if you continue to use them, you're supposed to pay the author for them. How do you pay the author? You can do that at some places on the Internet. The best thing to do, though, is read the documentation for the program. It has complete information on how to buy.

Many programs are free. That's right, free. I don't mean free to try; I mean free to use forever. And free, as we all know, is a good thing.

So where to find all this software? You can go to a lot of sites out there, but let me blow my own horn here for a minute. I think the best one is PalmPilotSoftware at `www.palmpilotsoftware.com`, which I run as Executive Editor for the ZDNet Web site. It rates and reviews the programs, so you'll know ahead of time whether you want to download something. It tells you any requirements needed to run a file. And it includes a lot of helpful advice, articles, and columns, including a monthly one written by yours truly, called *Preston's PalmPilot Picks*. (Have you noticed that I love alliteration?) You can even subscribe to a free email newsletter that will clue you in on the latest and greatest new software every week. The PalmPilotSoftware site is shown in the following figure.

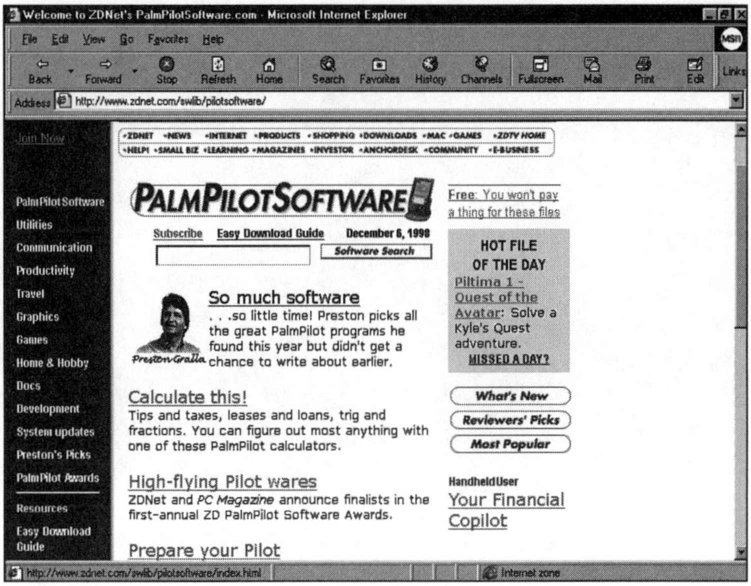

The best download site on the Internet includes a column written by yours truly.

How to Download and Install Programs from the World Wide Web

Thousands of programs may be available on the Internet, but what good are they to you? How can you get them from the big Internet into your tiny PalmPilot? You do so by downloading the programs to your computer and then installing them from there. *Downloading* means transferring the software from the Internet to your computer. Let me explain how to download. I use the example of downloading a file onto a PC, but the process works similarly on the Macintosh.

When you go to a site like PalmPilotSoftware, browse around until you find something you want to run on your PalmPilot. When you find it, click a Download link. The process varies site by site, but usually when you do that, your browser pops up a message like the one you see in the following figure, asking whether you want to open the file or store it to disk. Tell your browser to store it to disk, and then choose a location to store it.

You get this message when you start to download a file to your computer.

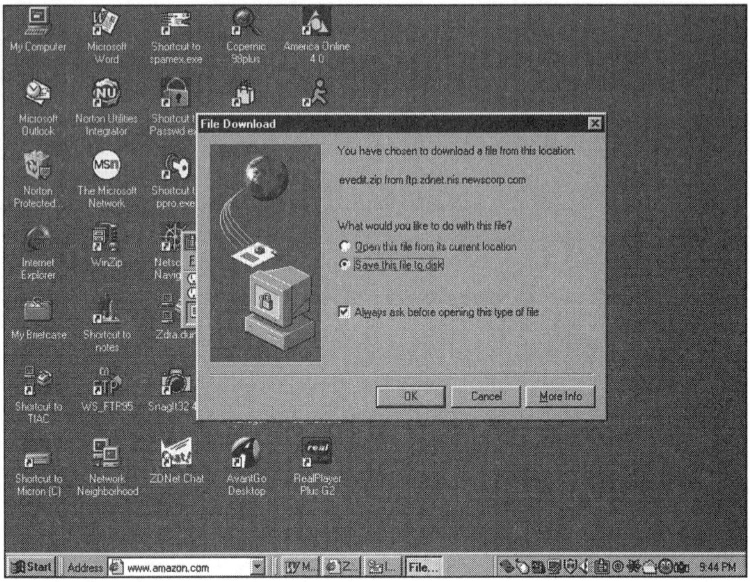

After you choose a location, the program downloads to your computer. Usually, the program has been compressed with a special piece of software so that it transfers more quickly to your computer. You need to decompress it. Almost all programs are in a format called *ZIP*. So you need a program that can decompress files in a ZIP format. Many are available, but the best one is called WinZip, and it's the one I recommend you use. (To get a copy of it, go to the ZDNet Software Library at `www.hotfiles.com`.)

What if you want to get help downloading and installing software?

Downloading and installing software can be confusing. If you're looking for a great primer on how to do it, head to `www.palmpilotsoftware.com` and click the **Easy Download Guide** link. You get a comprehensive, step-by-step walkthrough on how to download and install programs.

Run WinZip, and then open the file you just downloaded. Next, follow the WinZip instructions to decompress the file. Put the files into the C:\Palm\Add-On folder (or another folder of your choice), and then install them from there as you would any other PalmPilot program. That's all there is to it.

A Baker's Dozen of the Best PalmPilot Software

A whole lot of great software is available for the PalmPilot. Let me share with you a baker's dozen of my favorites, all of which you can find either on the CD at the back of this book or on the `www.palmpilotsoftware.com` site. And you can read my column every month at `www.palmpilotsoftware.com` for even more favorites.

Actioneer

What's the hardest thing you do on your PalmPilot? Organize information. The Actioneer program makes it much easier to get information into your PalmPilot and get it organized after it's there. Using this program, you can do things like write "Call Rob Thompson this afternoon," and the appropriate information will be put into your To-Do List and Address Book—complete with the contact information grabbed from your Phone Book. Great for busy people with lots to do—which pretty much means all of us, doesn't it?

Backup Buddy

One day your PalmPilot is going to crash, and then all the software you've put on it, all the customization information, and a whole lot more will go kaput! Here's the way to make sure it won't go kaput. Use the Backup Buddy program, and a complete backup is created on your PC, which you can use to restore everything to your PalmPilot. I've crashed and used this program to restore everything; it's saved my behind on more than one occasion. Try it, and make sure it'll save yours.

AvantGo

Combine the power of the Web with the convenience of your PalmPilot. The AvantGo program uses the PC to grab information from the Internet, reformats it for best viewing on your PalmPilot, and then sends it to your PalmPilot when it HotSyncs. A must-have for information junkies. Oh, yes, and it's free, so you never need pay for it.

HackMaster

No, the HackMaster program doesn't turn you into a super-hacker, master of the Internet and all it contains. Instead, it lets your PalmPilot do all kinds of neat tricks. You can find a whole lot of programs called *hacks* that make your PalmPilot more productive and easier to use. To use any of those programs, you need HackMaster.

EVEdit

EVEdit is a great program that powers up the editing function of your PalmPilot. Want to move text around by simply dragging it? This program lets you do it. It also saves multiple text items to your Clipboard and does a lot of other great stuff as well. Anyone who uses the Memo Pad or attaches many notes to items will want this program. It requires HackMaster to work.

AportisDoc Viewer

All kinds of great books, reference works, travel information, sports schedules, and similar stuff are available on the Internet. To read it, though, you need a special viewer. AportisDoc Viewer lets you read all this information. It's free, but if you want a more powerful reader, try the AportisDoc Mobile Edition. You can try this version for free, but then if you like it, you're supposed to buy it.

ProxiWeb

Amazingly enough, you can browse the Web from your little digital companion. You need a modem and Web-browsing software. ProxiWeb does it for you. And it's free.

HandFax

Hold a fax machine in the palm of your hand. All you need is the HandFax program and a modem, and you can send faxes. You can't receive them, but you can create customized logos on your cover sheets.

Pocket Chess

Who said the PalmPilot had to be all work? Load this Pocket Chess game, and have some fun. It's a surprisingly tenacious opponent. At the lowest level, you can probably beat it, but get to the higher levels, and you're in for some trouble.

TealPaint

Believe it or not, you can draw with your PalmPilot—and the TealPaint program lets you do that. It's a surprisingly sophisticated drawing program.

StreetSigns

Going on a trip and don't want to get lost? Then check out StreetSigns. You can get maps of many major cities and navigate your way through them. It helps you find directions and even helps you find landmarks, restaurants, and more. Great for the harried traveler.

Desktop To Go

I use Outlook as a personal information manager on my PC—which I thought was going to be a problem when I got my first PalmPilot. Then I found the Desktop To Go program—and no problema. It uses HotSync to synchronize all the information in Outlook and my PalmPilot, so I can use my favorite personal information manager along with my favorite digital companion.

Datebk3

If you have a very busy schedule and need something more powerful than the PalmPilot's Date Book, check out Datebk3. You get new views of your schedule, better links to your To-Do List and Phone Book, and much more as well.

The Least You Need to Know

- Use the Palm Install Tool to install programs on your PalmPilot.
- Filenames of programs that you install on your PalmPilot end in .prc.
- It's best if you put programs you're going to install into the \Palm\Add-On folder.
- Check out the accompanying CD for programs you can install on your PalmPilot.
- A great place to find programs on the Internet is `www.palmpilotsoftware.com`.

Chapter 21

Customizing Your PalmPilot for the Way You Live and Work

In This Chapter

- Remapping your PalmPilot's buttons
- Using and customizing the full-screen pen stroke
- Creating ShortCuts to make entering text easier
- Using several PalmPilots to work with a single PC

You can't paint hot-rod flames on your PalmPilot, tattoo it, put your monogram on it, or brand it with your ranch brand. (Too bad—I would kind of like to see a Ponderosa flaming brand on its side.)

You *can* customize it, however, in a whole lot of other ways. You can master your PalmPilot instead of having it master you. You'll find that customizing your PalmPilot for the way you live and work is easy. In this chapter, you find out how to change the way its buttons work, how to create ShortCuts to put in text for you automatically, and much more as well.

Cute as a Button: Remapping Your PalmPilot's Buttons

Don't like the programs that the buttons across the bottom of the PalmPilot run? No problem. You can make them run anything you want. Maybe you use the Calculator all the time, but never the Memo Pad. Or you always use a particular email program, but you never use the To-Do List. What a pain. Why should you be stuck with what some engineer has decided your PalmPilot buttons should do?

You're not stuck. You can easily change what programs the four PalmPilot hard buttons do when you push them. You can also change what the Calc button does when you tap it. In fact, you can even change what happens when you press the HotSync button on the PalmPilot cradle or modem. Let me tell you how.

First, tap on the **Applications** button, and then choose **Prefs**. Tap on the triangle in the upper-right corner of your screen, and choose **Buttons**. When you do so, you see the following screen.

Make your buttons run any program you want by using the Buttons Preferences screen.

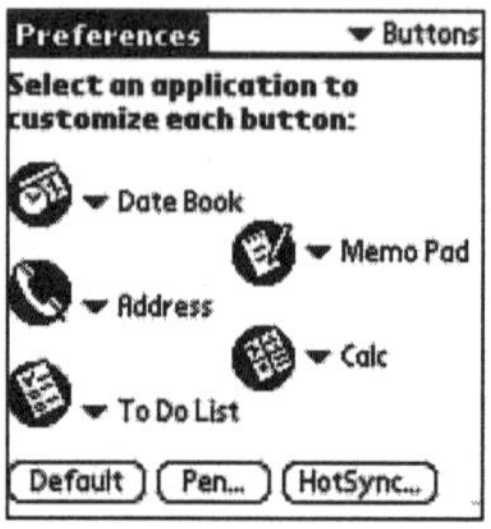

The five buttons listed on this screen are the Date Book, Memo Pad, Address Book, To-Do List, and Calc. Now, you might have noticed that you have only four physical buttons on your PalmPilot, but five buttons are listed here. The odd button out is Calculator, which doesn't have a physical button; instead, it's silkscreened on the PalmPilot glass. Don't worry; you can still remap any of them, including the silkscreened Calculator button. To remap one, decide for which button you want to run a different program than the one listed, and then tap on the triangle next to it.

After you tap on the triangle, you get a list of all the programs on your PalmPilot, as shown in the following figure. Choose the one you want to run when you tap on the chosen button. Now, whenever you tap that button, the program you chose, not the original program, runs.

Tap on the triangle next to the button you want to change, and from this list, choose the program you want that button to run.

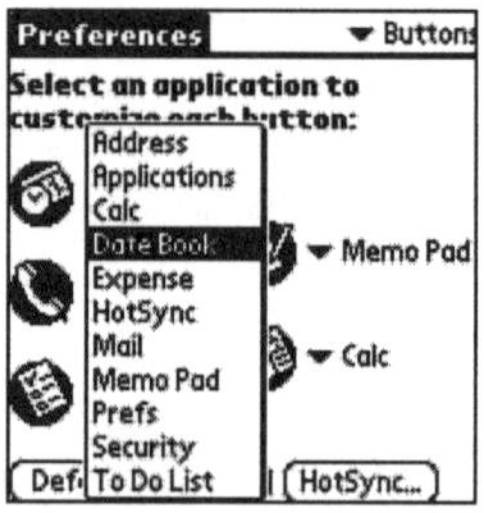

You can easily make all the buttons work the way they did when you bought your PalmPilot.

Let's say you've fiddled and diddled with all the buttons on your PalmPilot and changed them all, but you then decide that you liked them the way they were when you bought it. You don't have to manually change every button. Instead, tap on **Default** on the Buttons Preferences screen, and all the buttons work the same way they did the moment your PalmPilot came out of the box.

When Is HotSync Not a HotSync? When You Remap Its Button

Amazingly enough, you can also change what happens when you press the HotSync button on your PalmPilot cradle or modem. I must admit that I'm not exactly sure *why* you would want to change it, other than the fact that you *can* do it. (Why climb Mt. Everest? Because it's there. Of course, remapping your HotSync button is much easier than climbing a mountain.)

To remap your HotSync button, get to the Buttons Preferences screen as outlined previously. Then tap on the **HotSync** button. You then can remap both the HotSync button on your cradle and on your PalmPilot modem, in the same way you remap your other buttons, as outlined in the preceding section.

Use the Power of the Pen: Customizing the Full-Screen Pen Stroke

Let me share a secret you might not know about your PalmPilot: You can use a special pen stroke to do some pretty neat things. Doing the stroke is easy; it's not like you need to know how to dance the bugaloo or anything. To use the stroke, place the pen somewhere around the middle of the Graffiti writing area, and then draw it quickly straight along the face of the screen toward the top of the PalmPilot, as shown in the following figure. That's all there is to it.

This special pen stroke brings up the Graffiti Help screen.

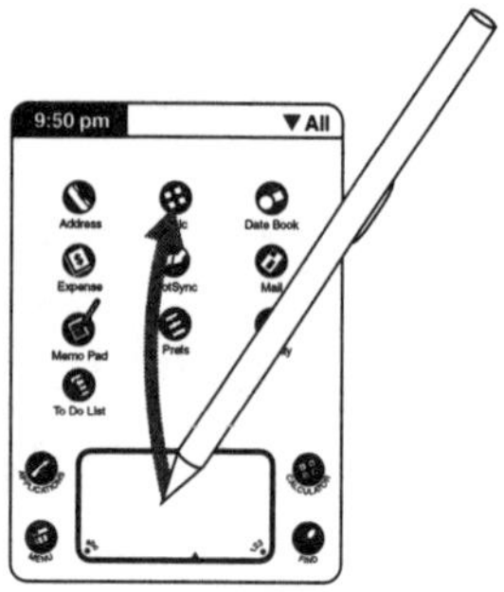

When you use this keystroke, it normally brings up the keyboard, which lets you tap to enter text into your PalmPilot. Ah, but let's say that you don't want this pen stroke to bring up the Help screen? Can you do anything about it? You certainly can. You can customize the stroke to do any of the following:

- **Turn on and off the backlight** Normally, to turn on the backlight, you have to press the PalmPilot's power button for two seconds. To turn it back off, you hold the button down for two seconds again. Instead, you can use this stroke. If the backlight's turned off and you use this stroke, it turns on the backlight. If the backlight's turned on and you use this stroke, it turns off the backlight. By the way, I use the stroke like this.
- **Call up the keyboard** This stroke normally opens the keyboard. You can tap away on the keyboard instead of using Graffiti strokes.
- **Get Graffiti Help** Having trouble remembering the Graffiti keystroke for a letter or number? You can pop up a Graffiti Help screen that shows you how to write each letter and number.
- **Turn off and lock** You're a secrecy freak. You worry about your phone being tapped. You use all kinds of encryption when you use the Internet. And you want to keep people and their prying eyes away from your PalmPilot. If so, then this feature's for you. It turns off your PalmPilot and then locks it so that only someone who knows the password can turn it back on again. Before you can use this feature, you have to turn on the password feature. For information on how to do that, turn to Chapter 4, "Organization 101: Touring the PalmPilot's Main Screen."
- **Beam data** Want a quick way to beam data to another Palm III? Just redefine the keystroke to beam away. Then whatever item you've been looking at is beamed to a nearby Palm III.

As I mentioned before, by default, this keystroke brings up the keyboard. To have it instead do any of the tasks in the preceding list, get to the Buttons Preferences screen as you would normally. Then tap on **Pen** to open the following screen. Now just choose what you want the pen stroke to do by tapping on the triangle.

Here, you can redefine the secret pen stroke.

Take the Express Lane: Using PalmPilot ShortCuts

Writing with Graffiti is no fun. It's slow. It's tedious. It's easy to make mistakes.

Using ShortCuts is a great way to make entering commonly used text and phrases into your PalmPilot faster. With them, you'll never make a mistake. They let you enter a short abbreviation and then have the PalmPilot do some PalmPilot magic and expand that abbreviation into a longer phrase. For example, let's say that you often write the phrase "These are the times that try men's souls." (If you do use that phrase a lot, by the way, then I think it's time for a vacation. Or a new job. Or maybe a new life.) Instead of entering that phrase each time, you can instead write the ShortCut **tti**, for example, and the PalmPilot writes out the longer phrase for you.

ShortCuts can be a maximum of 45 characters and spaces.

You are limited on how many characters you can expand a ShortCut into: 45 characters and spaces. Anything longer than that, and you're out of luck.

To use a ShortCut, you first write the Graffiti ShortCut character, shown in the following figure, and then write the ShortCut text. (Think of the ShortCut character as a lowercase cursive *L*; that should help you remember how to write it.) When you do, the PalmPilot takes over and automatically writes the text that you want.

You write the ShortCuts character like this.

The PalmPilot comes with a number of ShortCuts already built in. Table 21.1 shows what they are and what they do.

Table 21.1 PalmPilot Built-In ShortCuts

ShortCut	Turns Into
br	Breakfast
di	Dinner
ds	Today's date
dts	The current date and time
lu	Lunch
me	Meeting
ts	The current time

Creating ShortCuts of Your Own

No doubt, you'll want ShortCuts for more things than breakfast, lunch, dinner, and some date and time stamps. You can easily create your own by tapping on the **Applications** button and then choosing **Prefs**. From the screen that appears, choose **ShortCuts**. You then see the following screen.

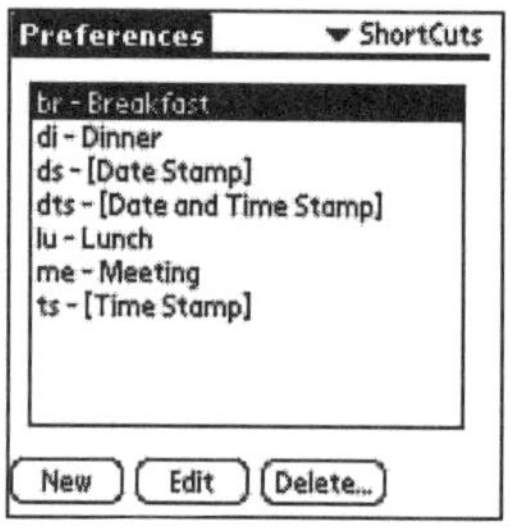

On this screen, you can get to be master of the ShortCuts universe.

To create a new ShortCut, tap on **New**. When you see the following screen, put in the name of the ShortCut at the top of the screen; in other words, enter the abbreviation that you want to write. At the bottom of the screen, write in the ShortCut text; in other words, enter what you want the ShortCut to expand to.

You create a ShortCut by entering text here.

When you're done, tap on **OK**. Now, whenever you enter the ShortCut character and the abbreviation you just entered, the abbreviation is automatically expanded into the full ShortCut text.

Editing Existing ShortCuts

Sometimes you might want to change a ShortCut after you've created it. You can easily edit a ShortCut that you've created. To do so, go to the ShortCut Preferences screen, tap on the ShortCut you want to edit, and then tap on **Edit**. At this point, you can edit the ShortCut. If you instead want to delete the ShortCut, tap on **Delete**.

Make sure to put a space at the end of your ShortCut text.

If you don't put a space at the end of your ShortCut text, you often have to put the space in manually after the ShortCut is entered. So, when you're defining a new ShortCut, make sure to put that space at the end.

Put Your Stamp on Your PalmPilot: Putting in Your Name

Let me cast my vote for the most useless PalmPilot feature ever created: You can write in your name as the owner. I don't know why this feature is here. I guess the thinking is that if you lose your PalmPilot and someone finds it, that someone will be enough of a Palm devotee and will know to look for the screen that defines who owns the PalmPilot. And then, of course, this devotee will immediately track you down and send you the PalmPilot. The thought would never cross the person's mind that all he or she needs to do is change your name to his or hers, and he or she will have just gotten a free many-hundred dollar device.

Well, let's take a vote for honesty, and assume that someone may well find your PalmPilot and return it to you. Just in case, let me tell you how to put your name in. Tap on the **Applications** button and then on **Prefs**. From the resulting screen, choose **Owner**. Then write in your contact information, as shown here. By the way, if you find this PalmPilot, make sure to return it to me.

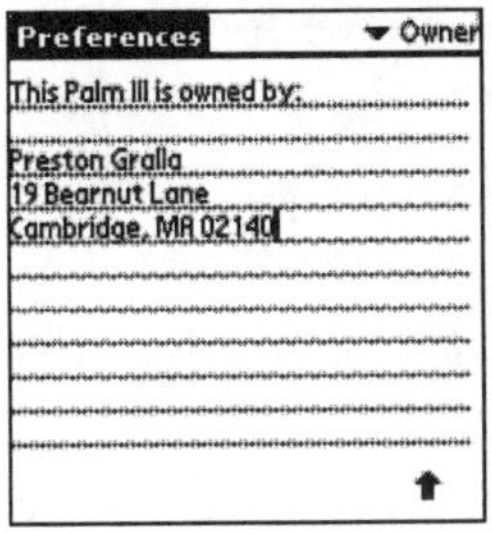

On this screen, you enter your name and contact information. If you find this PalmPilot on the street somewhere, please return it.

Setting Up Your PC for Multiple Users

Little-known fact: Several people can use their PalmPilots on the same PC. Several different people therefore can HotSync their PalmPilot data with data stored on the PC. The PalmPilot and the Palm Desktop program are smart enough to keep everyone's information straight.

Here's how it works. When you first set up your PalmPilot to HotSync with your PC, you're asked for your username. From that point on, the PC always recognizes that username and does the proper HotSync. So, just make sure that everyone picks a different username for their PalmPilot.

HackMaster can help you customize your PalmPilot.

A widely available program called HackMaster can help you customize the PalmPilot in about a zillion different ways—everything from customizing its sounds, its alarms, how you use Graffiti, and much more as well. You don't actually use HackMaster to make any of these changes. Instead, you install HackMaster, which allows you to install other system *hacks* that customize your PalmPilot. Turn to Chapter 20, "Installing New Software on Your PalmPilot," for information on where to get HackMaster and system hacks.

The Least You Need to Know

- To remap your PalmPilot's buttons, you use the Buttons Preferences screen.
- You can remap the HotSync cradle button and modem button so that it runs any program you want, not just HotSync.
- You can customize the full-screen pen stroke for the PalmPilot feature you use most.
- ShortCuts can save you a great deal of time; you can use abbreviations that automatically input up to 45 characters and spaces.

Chapter 22

Using Reference Files with Your PalmPilot

In This Chapter

- What kinds of reference files you can get for your PalmPilot
- Where you can get reference files
- How to get reference files from the Internet and put them into your PalmPilot
- What you need to read reference files
- The best sites on the Internet for finding reference files

How would you like to be able to look up a zip code in an instant on your PalmPilot? Get a list of the best hotels in San Francisco? Get medical and nutritional information and sports schedules?

You can do all that, and a lot more, using the wealth of reference material available for your PalmPilot. Pretty much all of it is available for free. And you can find material to make your life easier, more productive, and often more fun as well.

In this chapter, you look at how to get all this reference material and more into your PalmPilot. You can find it on the Internet, download it to your computer, and then HotSync it over to your PalmPilot from there.

What Reference Files Are Available for the PalmPilot?

Imagine a piece of information you want to find out about. Chances are, it's available to be downloaded into your PalmPilot. Don't believe me? Okay, here are just a few of the things I found in about two and a half minutes of looking: wine databases, zip code lookups, maps, nutritional information, sports schedules, legal and financial information, episode guides to *Star Trek*, Grateful Dead lyrics, novels—well, you get the idea. A whole lot of stuff.

So how do you read all of it? You might think that you use Memo Pad. If you thought that, though, you would be wrong. Memo Pad can read only itty-bitty files of 4 kilobytes, and these reference files are a lot larger than that. Anyway, Memo Pad doesn't have a whole lot of built-in features that make for easy reading.

Most files are in what's called *doc format*. The only way you can read them is with a special piece of software called a *doc reader* that you put on your PalmPilot. You can find this type of reader on the Internet at sites such as `www.palmpilotsoftware.com`. You should check out the CD at the back of this book for doc readers as well. Some of the doc readers are free. Others let you try them for free but ask that you pay for them if you decide to keep using them.

Other kinds of reference files need a different kind of reader: a database reader. You'll find fewer of these files around than doc files. Typically, they're purely reference information, such as a database of restaurants.

What is shareware?

Some doc readers, such as TealDoc, are a kind of software called *shareware*. Shareware is software that you can try for free, but if you decide you want to use it after you try it, you're supposed to pay for it. The payments are usually not very large; for example, TealDoc cost $16.95. Look in the shareware file itself for information on how to pay. You can download shareware from the Internet at many sites, including `www.palmpilotsoftware.com`.

So How Do You Get and Use the Reference Files?

So how do you go about finding and using all these files? You take these steps:

- **First, download the reference files from the Internet.** These files have many sources. I list them for you later in this chapter. For information on how to download files, turn to Chapter 20, "Installing New Software on Your PalmPilot."
- **After you have the reference files on your computer, install them as you would any normal PalmPilot file, and do a HotSync.** The files look like normal PalmPilot programs with names ending in either .prc or .pdb. You install them as you do any other PalmPilot file. For information on how to install files, turn to Chapter 20, "Installing New Software on Your PalmPilot." For information on how to do a HotSync, turn to Chapter 5, "Keeping Your Life in Sync: HotSyncing Your PC and PalmPilot."
- **When the reference files are sent to your PalmPilot using HotSync, use a doc reader or database reader to read them.** Just tap on the name of the reader you're going to use, and it shows you a list of reference files. Tap on the one you want to read, and you're ready to roll. By the way, when you install a reference file, it doesn't show up as its own application; you can only read it using a special reader. So, for example, if you download a legal or medical journal, you don't see an icon for that journal in your PalmPilot. To read the journal, tap on the name of your doc reader.

What's Up, Doc? What Doc Readers Can You Use?

You can use several different doc readers on your PalmPilot. If you're looking to save some money, you should get AportisDoc; it's free (yes, as in nada, zero, zippo, no money). The only problem is that it's missing a few features, such as the capability to search for text and to use *bookmarks;* it can't do some other nifty things either. Still, if you can't stand the thought of parting with your hard-earned shekels, and you don't mind not being able to search and perform similar tasks, it's a great deal.

If you're willing to fork over about $30, try the AportisDoc Mobile Edition. It is a bulked-up AportisDoc reader—essentially a reader on steroids. With it, you can do searches, copy text, jump to specific spots called bookmarks in the doc, and create your own bookmarks, and you get a choice of typefaces in which you can display text. It also has a great "teleprompter" mode in which the doc scrolls automatically while you read so that you don't have to tap any buttons to have the text scroll by. It's a great feature.

You can create your own doc files.

Believe it or not, making your own doc files that you can read on your PalmPilot is not very difficult. You just need a word processor and special software that can convert PC or Mac files to the PalmPilot's doc format. The AportisDoc Professional Edition, which sells for around $40, includes a special converter that converts Microsoft Word files, text files, and HTML files into doc format.

Another excellent doc reader is TealDoc. It sells for about $17, which is less than AportisDoc Mobile Edition (though, of course, it costs more than the free AportisDoc reader). You can download and try TealDoc and the AportisDoc readers at various sites on the Internet, such as `www.palmpilotsoftware.com`.

How to Use Doc Readers

Using a doc reader is pretty straightforward. You run a doc reader just as you do any other PalmPilot program, by tapping on its button after you've tapped on the **Applications** button. When you open the doc reader, the first thing you see is a list of all the doc files you can read. Again, install these doc files as you do any PalmPilot program, and they automatically show up in your doc reader. The following figure shows the AportisDoc Mobile Edition in action.

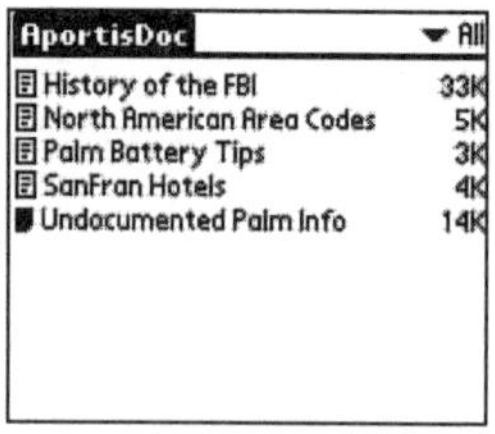

From the FBI to San Francisco hotels and more, AportisDoc shows you all the docs you've loaded into your PalmPilot.

To read any of the docs, just tap on one. AportisDoc then opens it, as you can see in the figure that follows.

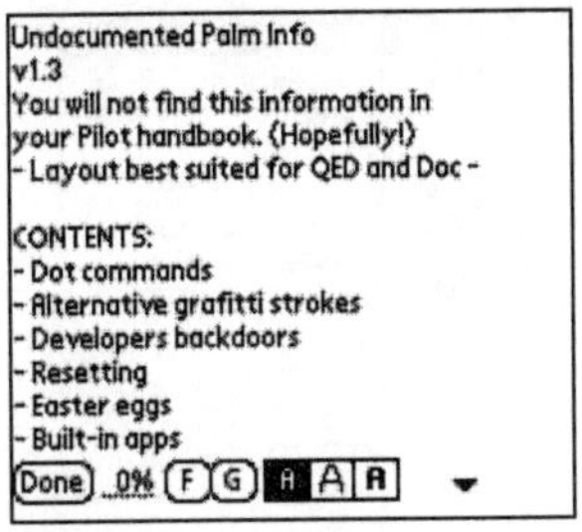

You can read a doc file with the AportisDoc reader.

Notice the few buttons across the bottom of the screen. They let you change the size of the font and search for text, for example. (Changing the font size is particularly welcome for people with aging eyes who can't always read page after page of the itty-bitty type on a PalmPilot.) The number and percent sign you see next to the Done button tell you what percent of the document you've read.

One of the most useful features of a doc reader is its capability to use bookmarks. To use a bookmark, tap on the triangle in the lower-right portion of the screen, and a set of bookmarks pops up, as you can see in the following figure.

Bookmarks make it easy to jump to specific parts of a doc.

Tap on any bookmark, and you can jump to a specific section of the doc. Whoever created the document created these bookmarks. But you can create them as well.

First, go to the portion of the document where you want to create a bookmark. Then tap on the triangle in the lower-right portion of the screen, and choose **Add a Bookmark**. A screen pops up, asking you to name the bookmark. Type the name, tap on **OK**, and you're done. From now on, whenever you tap in the bookmark triangle, your bookmark is listed. When you choose it, you jump to the spot where you created it.

You can customize the way you view text, the way you scroll through text, and generally how your doc reader works. To do so in AportisDoc, tap on the **Menu** button, and then choose **Preferences**. (Alternatively, you can use the Command stroke shortcut **/Z**.) You then see the Preferences screen in the following figure.

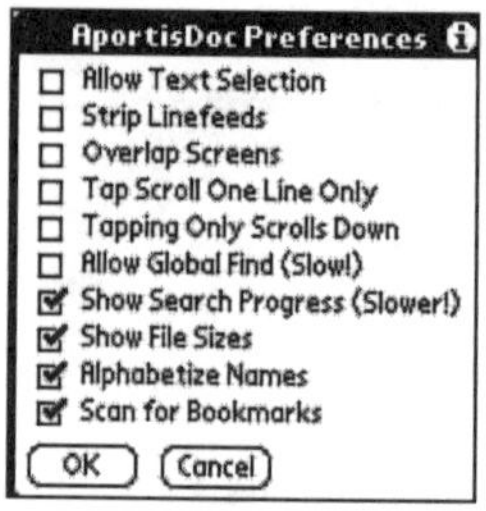

On this screen, you can control many of the ways that AportisDoc displays text and works.

You can copy text from docs using AportisDoc.

Many times you might like to be able to copy text from a doc and paste it into another PalmPilot program. For example, you might want to paste the address and phone number of a hotel into your To-Do List or Address Book. At first, you might think there's no way to do that. But, in fact, there is. With the text you want to copy displayed on the screen, go to the AportisDoc Preferences screen, as I explained previously. Tap on **Allow Text Selection** so a check mark appears next to it. Then tap on **OK**. Now highlight the text you want to copy, tap on the **Menu** button, and choose **Copy** from the **Options** menu. (You can instead use the Command stroke shortcut **/C**.) Now switch to the program and item where you want to copy the text. Tap on the **Menu** button, and choose **Paste** from the **Edit** menu (or use the Command stroke shortcut **/P**). Your text is then pasted in.

After you've copied your text, make sure, by the way, to go back into the AportisDoc Preferences screen and uncheck the **Allow Text Selection** box. As long as that box is checked, you can't scroll through the doc; AportisDoc assumes that whenever you tap, you're planning to copy text.

When you're done reading a doc, tap on the **Done** button. You then return to the doc reader screen where you can choose another doc to read.

Using Database Readers

Although most reference files you find are in doc format, a number of them instead require a database reader. Several database readers are available, but my favorite is J-File. To get a database reader, check out the CD at the back of this book, or go to a site such as `www.palmpilotsoftware.com` and download and install one from there. You can try database readers free of charge.

You download and install database files in the same way as you do files in the doc format. After you install them, they show up in whatever database reader you've installed on your PalmPilot. To read them, first tap on the name of your database reader, such as J-File. When your reader opens, you see a list of all the databases you can read. Tap on the one you want to read, and then get reading. The following figure shows a database that contains records about the complete episodes of *Star Trek*.

You can read a database of the complete episodes of Star Trek, *for example, using J-File.*

Database files differ from doc files; in essence, they're little databases, right on your PalmPilot. That means you can search through them, add records to them, and manipulate them in all kinds of ways. In fact, if you ever get geeky enough, you can even use a reader such as J-File to create databases of your own. But I can think of one big problem with many database files: Often, they've been created for a specific database reader and can't be read by any other database reader. So before you download a database file, make sure that you have the proper database reader for it.

Techno Talk

You need an image viewer to view image files on your PalmPilot.

You can find graphics and images on the Internet that you can download to your PalmPilot. For example, you can find maps, diagrams, and other useful (and not-so-useful) pictures. Here's the problem: Your PalmPilot can't view them—that is, not unless you get a special image viewer. Several of them are available. An especially good one is called, appropriately enough, Image Viewer. It's shareware, which means you can try it before buying it. If you do buy it, it'll run you $18. You can get it and other image viewers at download sites on the Internet such as `www.palmpilotsoftware.com`.

Where to Get Reference Files on the Internet

You can go to all kinds of great places if you want to get reference files. The following are some of my favorites:

- **Memoware** (`www.memoware.com`) Huge collection of reference material. You name it, and it's probably here. Travel information, medical and legal references, historical documents, business facts, almanacs and yearbooks, entertainment trivia, area code lookups—all that and more.
- **Macduff.net** (`www.macduff.net`) Big collection of fiction, drama, and world literature. You can find works by Shakespeare, Dumas, Dickens, Lawrence, and other literary heavy-hitters. And it even includes a Pocket Ink area where you can buy new, contemporary novels published specifically for the PalmPilot.
- **The PalmPilot Library** (`www.palmpilot.org`) Literature, children's books, mysteries, non-fiction books, historical documents, and similar "e-texts" are what you'll find here.
- **PalmPilotSoftware.com** (`www.palmpilotsoftware.com`) You'll find very few reference files here. Instead, you can download all the doc readers, database viewers, and image viewers you need to use reference files. This site also includes an excellent area giving recommendations on the best readers and viewers.

The Least You Need to Know

- To read reference files, you need special doc or database readers, which you can often try for free from the Internet.
- After you download a reference file, you install it as you would any PalmPilot program, and then HotSync to transfer it into your PalmPilot.
- To read a reference file, you open a doc or database reader; the file already appears in there.
- Check the CD in back of the book for doc readers and database readers.

Chapter 23

Traveling with Your PalmPilot

In This Chapter

- How the PalmPilot can help you prepare for your trip
- What add-on software can help you when you travel
- Tips, strategies, and techniques for using your PalmPilot when traveling

Your PalmPilot: It's the perfect traveling companion. It never complains, it always does exactly what you want, it never blocks the airplane aisles, and it costs nothing to house and feed it (apart from a few batteries every now and then).

You'll find that your PalmPilot can help you in many ways when you travel. In fact, in many ways, it's been designed specifically for travel; after all, an Expense program was built directly into it, and the PalmPilot's diminutive size makes it perfectly suited to traveling.

In this chapter, you find out how the PalmPilot can help you make your travel easier and more productive. You also learn tips, tricks, techniques, and strategies for how to use the PalmPilot when you're on the road.

Preparing for Your Trip with Your PalmPilot

Getting ready for a business trip is never very much fun. You have to plan. You have to pack. (In my pre-PalmPilot days, my packing looked a whole lot like a scene out of the *Three Stooges*: emptying my dresser drawers into a suitcase and sitting on top of the suitcase to try to ram everything in.) You have to check and recheck your schedule, your tickets, and then obsess about it all again.

The PalmPilot can make it easier to head off into the great unknown, or known, whichever the case may be. Before you head off on your next business trip, you should do the following:

- **Create a Travel category in your To-Do List, and list all the to-dos that need to be done before leaving.** It's amazing how a few simple notes help focus the mind. This way, when you leave, you'll never leave behind your tickets or worry that you left your stove on.
- **Make sure to input all your business contacts, schedules, and plans before you go.** Sure, at the moment you're absolutely *positive* that you couldn't possibly forget the name of the account manager who's going to meet you at your hotel tonight for a business meeting. But believe me, after several dreadful hours on a cramped plane, and after eating the meat matter that passes for airplane food, you'll forget your *own* name, much less the name of a stranger.
- **Do a HotSync before leaving.** Your PalmPilot will be no good for you if all the business contacts you put into your PC as you prepared to leave are left back on your PC and you don't have them with you on the road.

Create a single master packing list for all your trips, and then customize it each time you go.

Mostly, when you pack to travel, you bring along the same items: underwear, shaving kit, cosmetics bag, shirts, blue power suit, your favorite rubber ducky. You don't want to have to re-create that list every time you travel, but on the other hand, you might need to change the list each time you go. To solve the problem, create a single master packing list in the Memo Pad. Then, when you're going to leave on a trip, open the memo, highlight everything in the list by dragging your stylus across it, and then use the Copy command by tapping on the **Menu** button and choosing **Copy** from the **Edit** menu. Now create a new memo in the Memo Pad, and paste your master list into it by tapping on the **Menu** button and choosing **Paste** from the **Edit** menu. Your master packing list then appears in the new memo, and you can add to it or take away from it in any way you want.

- **Create a new Expense category for your trip.** You should have a separate Expense category for every one of your business trips; otherwise, tracking your expenses is too difficult. Before you leave, create a new Expense category, and make sure to include any business expenses related to the trip that you've paid for already, such as plane tickets, dry cleaning, and psychiatric consultation to get you over your all-too-understandable fear of flying. (Disclaimer: I am not a certified public account, so before claiming your shrink as a business expense, please check with your CPA.)
- **Don't install any new software or make major changes to your PalmPilot in any way before you go.** New software has the nasty potential for crashing, locking up, and in general wreaking havoc on your PalmPilot. That could mean that you'll have to do a hard reset on your PalmPilot when you're in a hotel room in Pago Pago, and your contact information, schedule, and everything else will be lost to you. Play it safe: Wait until you return home to install new software.
- **If you plan to do a remote HotSync, turn on your PC and modem, run the HotSync Manager, and test it before you go.** HotSyncing via modem when you're on the road is a great way to make sure that you have a backup of all your data should your PalmPilot lock up. So before you go, prepare your PC for a HotSync, and test it to make sure that it works. For more information on doing a HotSync and using the PalmPilot modem, turn to Chapter 5, "Keeping Your Life in Sync: HotSyncing Your PC and PalmPilot," and Chapter 17, "How to Use a Modem with Your PalmPilot."

Your modem needs batteries, too.

If you plan to use a modem when you travel, keep in mind that it needs power as well. Make sure to pack extra batteries for it, or else buy an AC adapter so that you can plug it in to your hotel outlet.

- **Bring along fresh batteries.** The PalmPilot is a battery addict; it sucks up the juice big-time. You don't want to be caught on the road with a dead PalmPilot. Bring along fresh batteries.
- **Print your travel itinerary before you go.** I love my PalmPilot as much as (or probably more than) the next person. Some things, though, you just like to have in print—such as your travel itinerary and schedule. So print your itinerary before you go. To print it, open your Palm Desktop, and then open the Address Book (and any other program in which you have your itinerary) and print from there. For more information about using the Palm Desktop, turn to Chapter 6, "Oh, Yeah...You Have a Computer, Too. Using the Palm Desktop."

- **Reset your PalmPilot's time before you go.** If you're traveling to another time zone, reset the PalmPilot's time to that time zone before you leave on your trip. You can easily forget to reset your time when you get there. If you don't, your schedule will be off, and you could miss important appointments if you set alarms to remind you of them.
- **Pack a paper clip or toothpick in case of emergency.** Sad but true: Sometimes you need to reset your PalmPilot. If you have a Palm III, you can reset it by screwing off the top of the stylus and using the little wire in the top. If you don't have a Palm III, bring along a paper clip or toothpick, which you can use to reset your PalmPilot. For more information about resetting, turn to Chapter 24, "Cures for the PalmPilot's Most Common Problems."

Software to Help Make Your Trip Easier and More Productive

The PalmPilot's basic programs, such as the Address Book, Date Book, and To-Do List, are well-suited for traveling. But you can find a lot more software designed for travel that'll make your next trip easier and more productive. You can download many of these kinds of programs from `www.palmpilotsoftware.com`, and you can find some of them on the CD in the back of this book. For more information about finding, installing, and using add-on software for your PalmPilot, turn to Chapter 20, "Installing New Software on Your PalmPilot."

Fax Software

Was there ever a time when we lived without faxes? Hard to believe that there was. It's become such a business necessity, though, that even when you're on the road, you need to be able to send faxes.

Luckily, you can send faxes from your PalmPilot, although, unfortunately, you can't receive them. To send faxes, get the program HandFax from Smartcode Software. It sells for $49.95, but you can try demos of it for free. It sends faxes but doesn't receive them. You need a modem, of course. This program works with any kind of modem, though. It also includes graphics tools so that you can create your own logos and graphics for cover sheets. (To be perfectly honest, though, unless you're a real pro, they look like a cross between a Jackson Pollock painting and a mud puddle.) The following figure shows a fax being created in the program.

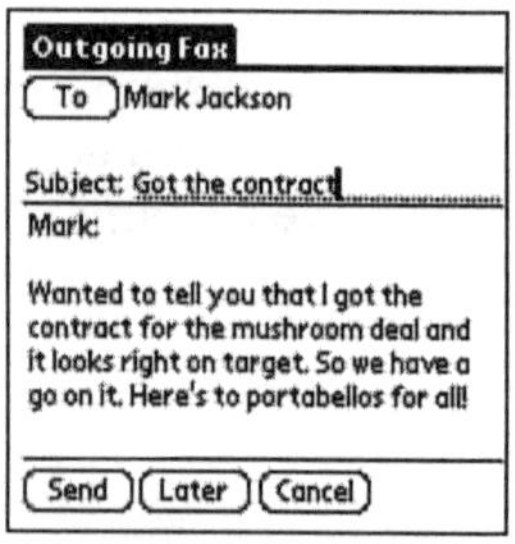

A fax in the hand...You can send faxes when you travel by using HandFax.

Use this trick for printing from your PalmPilot when you're traveling.

Sometimes you like to print something such as a memo or a proposal when you're traveling. If you're carrying only your PalmPilot, you might think that you can't print anything. Let me tell you a trick to get around the problem. You need a modem and HandFax software. Simply use HandFax to fax the memo you want printed, but send it to yourself at your hotel room. That way, the hotel receives the fax and delivers it to you in your room (and some rooms even have faxes in them these days). Using this trick, you have a printout of what you needed printed.

Email Software

If you're like me, going for more than half a day or so without email will have you suffering withdrawal symptoms. How can you spend several days on the road without being able to read and send email? The Mail program built into your PalmPilot doesn't let you send or receive email over the Internet. It's designed, instead, to work with your desktop email software. So what to do?

You can use email software that sends and receives email directly from your PalmPilot. HandMail (from the makers of HandFax), MultiMail, and One-Touch Communicator are all excellent mail programs. You can download trial versions of all of them. The one I prefer is One-Touch Communicator, shown in the following figure.

Keep in touch via email even when you're on the road, with One-Touch Communicator.

One problem with these programs is that they don't do a good job of syncing with your email program. When I use them, I therefore use options that let me preview mail before reading it, and then I read only the mail I absolutely have to. I also use an option that lets me leave mail on my mail server, even after I've read it. That way, the mail I get still shows up in my desktop computer's email program when I log into the mail server.

Doc Readers and Database Readers

An enormous amount of free, travel-related information is available for the PalmPilot, such as travel guides, maps, lists of hotel rooms, tourist information, and more. To read any of it, though, you need special software called *readers* or *viewers*. TealDoc and the various versions of AportisDoc are excellent readers, as is the J-File database and the viewer called Image Viewer.

For more information about readers, viewers, and reference files, turn to Chapter 22, "Using Reference Files with Your PalmPilot."

Map Software

Imagine this: You're in Manhattan and you're lost. No map is near at hand, and you're due at an important appointment in 20 minutes. You haven't a clue how to get there. What to do?

Head to MemoWare at `www.memoware.com` for a great selection of travel-related files.

A great place for a big selection of travel-related files is the Internet site MemoWare at `www.memoware.com`. You can find a great selection of free travel-related files.

If you had map software for your PalmPilot, you would know exactly where you are and exactly where you're going. A good deal of map software is out there. An excellent one is StreetSigns, which you can try in a demo version.

Even more amazing is the Earthmate GPS Receiver, which lets you use satellite navigation and mapping software together. A piece of Global Positioning Satellite (GPS) hardware hooks up to your PalmPilot, where you install Street Atlas USA mapping software. Then, not only can you get a map of where you want to go, but the satellite also beams to you exactly where you are so that you can see your position right on a map on your PalmPilot. It's available from DeLorme, but it doesn't come in a try-before-you-buy version.

Other Travel Software

You can get all kinds of other travel software for your PalmPilot. For example, you can find currency converters that help you convert from one country's money to another's. A program called AirMiles from Hands High Software tracks your air mileage for you. You can even find expense trackers. For many travel programs, head to `www.palmpilotsoftware.com`, and go to the Travel section.

Using a Web-Based Calendar with Your Date Book

What if you're traveling and your PalmPilot crashes or is stolen? How can you re-create your travel schedule?

Amazingly enough, you can HotSync your Date Book with a Web-based calendar, so all you need to do is find an Internet connection somewhere, and you can check your schedule, even if your PalmPilot is gone.

HotSync your Date Book with a Web-based calendar so that you can always get to your travel schedule, even if your PalmPilot crashes or is stolen. The Yahoo Web calendar at `http://calendar.yahoo.com/` and the PlanetAll calendar at `www.planetall.com` both let you do it. I prefer the Yahoo calendar, but you can use the one at PlanetAll as well.

You can HotSync in two ways using Yahoo! The first way doesn't require you to download any special software, and that's the way I describe here. Later in the chapter, I tell you how to use this technique if you want to download special software. (Head to PlanetAll for information on how to HotSync your Date Book there.) By the way, folks, this section might get a bit techie, so put on your propeller beanie, put on a pocket protector, and let's talk tech.

Start by signing up for the calendar at `http://calendar.yahoo.com/`. (There, that wasn't so hard, was it? Maybe it's not as difficult as I told you it would be.)

So, now you have a Date Book full of your appointments and a blank Yahoo! calendar. You have to get your Date Book into your Web calendar. To do so, you're going to export a special kind of database file called a .dba from your PalmPilot into the Web. Sounds like magic, but it can be done.

First, HotSync your PalmPilot to your PC. Your most current Date Book information is now on your Palm Desktop. Next, open the Palm Desktop and run the Date Book. Choose **Export** from the **File** menu, and choose a name and location where you want to store the file, such as **mycalendar.dba**, as shown in the following figure.

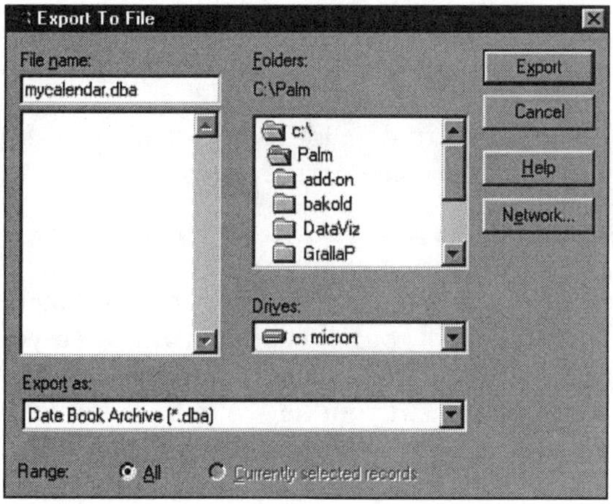

To sync your Date Book with the Yahoo! Web calendar, start by exporting this special file from the Palm Desktop Date Book.

It's time to get that file into your Yahoo! Web calendar. Head to your calendar at `http://calendar.yahoo.com/`. Click **Options**, and then look toward the bottom of the screen to where you see the Import from Palm Desktop section. Click **Browse**, and then choose the location and name of the .dba file you created. After you do that, click **Import Now**. You then get a message telling you the file has been imported. Now go back to your Yahoo! calendar, and amazingly enough, your entire Date Book is there.

Now you can get to your Date Book merely by heading to the Web, whether or not you have your PalmPilot with you. Whenever you make changes to your Date Book, you have to go through all these steps if you want to keep the Yahoo! calendar up-to-date.

Using Downloadable Software to Sync with Yahoo's Web-Based Calendar

The other way to use your PalmPilot with Yahoo's Web-based calendar is to download a special piece of software that does your synchronization for you automatically. Not only does it synchronize with your PalmPilot, but if you use the Outlook Personal Information Manager, it also synchronizes with it.

To use this technique, when you get to your Yahoo! calendar, click **Synchronization**. You then are led to a page detailing how to download and use a piece of software called TrueSync for Yahoo! Download and install it to your PC. Note that the software runs on your PC, not on your PalmPilot. (And, of course, it's not available for the Mac—but what else is new?)

After you download the software, follow the instructions for determining what and how you want to sync. Then, whenever you want to synchronize your calendar (and even your contacts and To-Do List) with Yahoo!, just follow the instructions for running the software and you're done.

Tips and Strategies for Traveling with Your PalmPilot

When you're on the road, your PalmPilot can do a lot to help make your trip easier. Follow this advice for using your PalmPilot when on the road:

- **Your PalmPilot sets off alarms when you head through the security gates, so be prepared.** Your PalmPilot contains so much metal that when you walk through the security gates at airports, you're going to set off alarms. To avoid this problem, hand the PalmPilot to the security guard when you hand over your keys and change. Also, make sure you have batteries in your PalmPilot because the guard might want you to run your device to make sure it works—and determine that you're really not a terrorist in disguise.

Use Expense to keep track of your frequent flier miles.

The PalmPilot doesn't contain a built-in program to keep track of your frequent flier miles. However, you can use the Expense program to do it for you. For each frequent flier program to which you belong, create a separate category in Expense. Then, whenever you rack up miles in any program, create a new expense item for it. Create each as a mileage item. In this way, you have a record of all your mileage. You can even tabulate the miles when you HotSync your PalmPilot with your PC, and the mileage is sent into an Excel spreadsheet.

- **When you put in the dates you'll be away traveling in your Date Book, use the No Time option.** You certainly want to note in your Date Book the days you'll be traveling. Make sure to use the No Time option when doing so. When you use the No Time option, you see in your Date Book that you're scheduled to be away for those days, but it doesn't take up every hour of the day. Using this option leaves your Date Book free for all the appointments you need to make when traveling.
- **If you travel with a laptop and a PalmPilot, bring along a special cable for HotSyncing.** You would probably rather not have to lug along your cradle for HotSyncing; it's just too awkward to pack and carry along. However, a special cable from 3COM attaches your PalmPilot directly to your computer. It's part #10104U for PC or #10112U for Macintosh. Get information on it from the `www.palm.com` site.
- **If you HotSync via modem when you travel, turn off some of the conduits to save time.** Doing a HotSync via modem can take a very long time if you have a lot of data to update. Save yourself time: HotSync only those programs you really need. You can easily turn off individual conduits. Each conduit handles a HotSync for a specific application, so when you turn off a conduit, you don't HotSync that application. To turn off conduits, first tap on **Applications** and then on the **HotSync** icon. Then choose **Conduit Setup** from the **Options** menu, or use the Command stroke shortcut **/D**. When you see the following screen, you can turn off certain conduits during your modem HotSync. When you uncheck any conduit, that application isn't HotSynced. Turn to Chapter 5, "Keeping Your Life in Sync: HotSyncing Your PC and PalmPilot," for more information about HotSyncs and conduits.

To save time when you're doing a HotSync from the road, turn off some conduits.

- **Get products to connect your modem to telephone systems anywhere in the world from Road Warrior International at** `www.warrior.com`. You can find adapters that can connect your modem to any kind of phone system, wherever you travel, from Abu Dhabi to Zimbabwe.

The Least You Need to Know

- Create a standing travel packing list in your Memo Pad that you can customize for each of your trips.
- HotSync before you go on a trip. If you plan to HotSync via modem, make sure to turn on your PC and modem before you go.
- Bring along fresh batteries so that you don't run out when you're on the road.
- Print your travel itinerary with your Palm Desktop software, and take it with you when you travel.
- Use add-on travel software such as faxing, email, and maps.
- Track your frequent flier mileage using the Expense application.

Part 5

Troubleshooting and Maintenance for Your Digital Companion

Sad but true: Sometimes the PalmPilot isn't a perfect companion. It can get flaky on you. It can crash and lose all your data, and you'll see your life go up in flames because you'll feel as if everything is lost. It can refuse to HotSync, or the Graffiti handwriting recognition software can turn your nicely formed letters into what looks like the Sumerian alphabet. Your battery can run out when you're in the middle of writing an important memo.

This section teaches you how to troubleshoot any problems you might come across. You see how to restore all your data, even if your PalmPilot crashes. You learn tips for fixing all of PalmPilot's major problems. You learn how to put together a maintenance program that will make it not at all likely you'll even run into troubles. You also find tips for getting around one of the PalmPilot's major drawbacks—its short battery life.

Chapter 24

Cures for the PalmPilot's Most Common Problems

In This Chapter

- How to restart your PalmPilot when it freezes
- How to do a soft reset
- How to do a warm reset
- How to do a hard reset
- How to fix the PalmPilot's most common problems

Sooner or later, it's going to happen. Just when you need to find the name and address of that important contact, your PalmPilot is going to freeze on you and refuse to respond to your taps and refuse to even turn off. Or you'll need to check your daily schedule, and when you press on the power button, the ungrateful thing won't bother to turn on. Or HotSync won't work. Or you'll get incomprehensible error messages. Or some other awful, nasty thing is going to happen.

Luckily for you, the PalmPilot is a relatively simple device; it's not nearly as problem-prone as a PC. When you do have problems, you often can use simple fixes.

In this chapter, you learn all you need to know about fixing the most common problems that might happen to your PalmPilot. This chapter is the place to turn when bad things happen to good organizers.

How to Recover from a Frozen PalmPilot by Doing a Reset

Take it from one who's suffered many times through the experience: Your PalmPilot one day will simply refuse to work, no matter what you do. The screen will freeze. You'll tap and tap away, but it won't respond. You'll press on the power button to turn it off—but no luck. It'll still be frozen.

It's not that your little friend doesn't like you anymore. It's just in the nature of the device to freeze at times. You might have installed some oddball software, or you might have done some weirdo combination of button pushes and stylus strokes. Who knows, the problem might be cosmic rays or the alignment of the stars. For whatever reason, the thing just doesn't budge. (At those times, it reminds me of when my children were two years old, and the only words out of their mouths were "No, No, No!")

This experience is thoroughly disturbing. Has the thing up and died on you?

If all else fails, your PalmPilot has a warranty.

Your PalmPilot carries a warranty with it, so if something happens to your little friend in the first year you own it, in most cases 3COM will repair it for you, free of charge. If it doesn't work, and the problem isn't the result of something you did (such as dropping it or throwing it against a wall), 3COM will fix it. 3COM will send you a shipping box, you'll send back your PalmPilot, and a few days later, it'll be sent back to you, as good as new. You won't even have to pay for the shipping costs. 3COM will also repair the device for you if something goes wrong after the warranty period, but you'll be charged $100 to fix it.

Not to worry. You can easily unfreeze your PalmPilot and get it working again. You do so by resetting it. When you reset your PalmPilot, in essence you turn it off and then back on again, and all will be well. You can perform the following three different levels of resets. You use them depending on the severity of the problem you face. Always start with the simplest reset and work your way to the most difficult.

- **Soft reset** This type of reset allows you to manually turn on your PalmPilot after it's been frozen. It doesn't do anything else. It's the equivalent of pressing on the power button to turn it off and then pressing on the power button to turn it back on again.

- **Semi-soft reset or warm reset** You have to use this kind of reset if you try a soft reset, but your PalmPilot still doesn't unfreeze. When you do this kind of reset, any special add-ons and patches you've added to the operating system vanish.
- **Hard reset** Here's the Big Kahuna of resets and your absolutely last resort. When a soft reset and a warm reset still don't unfreeze your PalmPilot, you have to do a hard reset. When you do a hard reset, you lose all your data and information, all the software you've installed, and any special add-ons and patches you've added to the Palm's operating system. Your PalmPilot is reset to work exactly the way it was when you first took it out of the box. You can, however, restore most of your data by doing a HotSync, as you find out later in this chapter.

To do any reset, you use the reset button on the back of your PalmPilot. It's not actually a button. Instead, it's a tiny, recessed hole, labeled with the word *Reset.* To reset your PalmPilot, push inside the hole. If you own a Palm III, screw off the top of your stylus. Inside you'll find a little wire-like thing you can use to push into the hole. If you don't have a Palm III, straighten out a paper clip and use it instead. Push until you hear a click. If you push too hard, you might damage the PalmPilot. Some people worry that using a paper clip could cause damage to the PalmPilot, so they instead prefer to use a toothpick.

Pack a paper clip wherever you go.

You never know when disaster might strike and you'll need to reset your PalmPilot. If you have a Palm III, all you need to do is unscrew your stylus and use the wire there. If you don't have a Palm III, what to do? The battery compartment is the perfect place to keep a paper clip or toothpick. Tape the paper clip or toothpick into the space between the two batteries, and it'll always be there when you need it.

In the following sections, I teach you how to do each of the resets and how you can recuperate from each.

How to Do a Soft Reset

When your PalmPilot freezes, the first thing to do is try a *soft reset.* Press into the reset hole. Your PalmPilot should now unfreeze, and the Welcome screen should appear for a moment, followed by the General Preferences screen. Your PalmPilot settings aren't affected in any way, you don't lose any data, and your software is left alone. Doing a soft reset is the same thing as turning your PalmPilot off and then on again.

How to Do a Semi-Soft or Warm Reset

Maybe you're not so lucky, and when you do a soft reset, nothing happens. Oh well. It's happened to more than a few of us. Now you have to do what's called a *semi-soft* or *warm reset.* If a soft reset doesn't work, the problem may have been caused by some kind of system patch or add-on to your operating system. A warm reset gets around that problem.

To do a warm reset, hold down the up scroll button, and while you're holding it down, press into the reset hole. If all goes well, this action starts your PalmPilot again.

Your PalmPilot isn't quite in the exact same shape it was in before you did the warm reset. The various operating system patches and similar add-ons are now turned off. You probably want to get those patches back in again, though. You can do so easily enough. Just do a soft reset, and they are put back in.

How to Do a Hard Reset

Sometimes neither a soft reset nor a warm reset works. Then the only thing you can to do is perform a hard reset. This action is the most drastic thing you can do, but at least it'll unfreeze your PalmPilot.

To do a hard reset, press the power button on your PalmPilot. With the button held down, press into the Reset hole. A message then appears on the screen that says "Erase All data? YES = 'up' button. NO = any other button."

Okay. Take a breath. It's time to bite the bullet. Press the up scroll button. When you do so, the PalmPilot unfreezes and you get the Welcome screen. That's the good news. The bad news is that all your data has been deleted, and all the programs and add-ons you've installed have been deleted; in short, everything's gone. Your PalmPilot is exactly the way it was when you first unpacked it. (If you press any other button, nothing happens, and your PalmPilot stays frozen.) You're going to have to set up your PalmPilot from scratch now, including using the digitizing alignment screen.

But what about all your data? Has it all been lost? Not if you HotSync regularly with the Palm Desktop. You can restore all your data by doing a special kind of HotSync.

Turn to Chapter 5, "Keeping Your Life in Sync: HotSyncing Your PC and PalmPilot," for details on how to do a HotSync. Before you actually do the HotSync, however, open each conduit, and choose the option **Desktop Overwrites PalmPilot** for each. (You get detailed instructions in Chapter 5 on how to do that.) When you choose this option, you're telling HotSync to take the information on your Palm Desktop and put it into your PalmPilot. All the information that's stored on your

Palm Desktop is put back into your PalmPilot when you do the HotSync, and all is well with the world. Well, not quite. All the add-on programs you've installed, such as games, faxing software, and other software, are gone. You have to reinstall them all.

By the way, heed a very big warning here: Make sure to change the direction of the HotSync so that the Desktop overwrites the PalmPilot. If you don't, you can end up deleting all the data on your Palm Desktop, and then everything you've put in there truly will be lost.

After a hard reset, you can restore all the programs you've installed.

When you do a hard reset, all the programs you've installed on your PalmPilot, such as games, email software, and the like, are deleted. Because these programs aren't part of the Palm Desktop, a HotSync cannot put them back into your PalmPilot. You can do something, however: Use a program called Backup Buddy. When you use this program, you can restore everything back to your PalmPilot easily—all the programs, the system updates, the customizations, the whole nine yards. It works by making a backup of your system every time you do a HotSync. Then, if you have to do a hard reset, you can restore everything easily. You can try Backup Buddy for free, and similar backup software, by heading to `www.palmpilotsoftware.com`.

Fixes for Other PalmPilot Problems

Freezes aren't the only problem you might encounter when using a PalmPilot. Other nasty things might happen as well, from it simply refusing to turn on to your being unable to do a HotSync. Next, I describe the most common PalmPilot problems and what you can do about them. Let's hope that this is one part of the book you never have to use.

Your PalmPilot Doesn't Turn On

One of the nastiest PalmPilot problems you might come across is if it simply refuses to turn on when you press the power button. If that happens, don't despair; all is not lost. You can do the following:

➤ **Put in a fresh set of batteries.** A common reason that a PalmPilot doesn't start is that it has simply run out of battery power without your realizing it. Put in a new set of AAA alkaline batteries, and make sure they're installed correctly (the plus and minus signs on the batteries should match with those printed on the PalmPilot). Then wait three minutes, and turn on the PalmPilot. In many cases, this solution is all it takes.

Try a double soft reset if a soft reset fails.

If you've done a soft reset and you haven't been able to unfreeze your PalmPilot, try a *double soft reset*. To do one, do a reset as you normally would, except press twice, quickly, in succession.

➤ **Adjust the contrast wheel.** Your contrast wheel may have been inadvertently moved to a setting that makes it impossible for you to read anything; in other words, your PalmPilot might, in fact, be on when you press the power button, but you just can't see anything because of the poor contrast. See whether adjusting the contrast fixes the problem.

➤ **Try doing resets, as outlined earlier in the chapter.** Start by trying a soft reset, then a warm reset, and finally a hard reset.

If you've tried all these tricks and nothing works, it's time to call the PalmPilot support line and hope the tech support people can help you.

HotSync Doesn't Work

One of the most common headaches with a PalmPilot is that HotSync simply doesn't sync; for some reason or another, it refuses to work. Hope this one doesn't hit you because this kind of problem can be maddeningly difficult to track down. Still, you can do a lot to fix it and get your PalmPilot and computer back into sync with HotSync. Here's what to try:

Contact 3COM for technical support.

3COM, the makers of the PalmPilot, is the first place to turn for technical support. You can get technical support information on the Web at `www.palm.com`, or you can send email to `support@palm.com`. You can also call the technical support line at 876-676-1441.

➤ **Check to see that the HotSync Manager is running on your computer.** If it's not running, you can't HotSync. If it is running, close it and then start it up again. Surprisingly enough, this trick sometimes solves the problem. It has for me several times.

➤ **Make sure that no software is interfering with the communications (COM) port that your cradle is plugged into.** Software you run on your computer can interfere with the COM port. Fax software, for example, often interferes with the COM port. So can communications software such as America Online or CompuServe, or dial-up networking into the Internet. Close any of that software, close the HotSync Manager, and then run the HotSync Manager and try again.

➤ **Turn off your computer and PalmPilot, restart them, and then try to HotSync again.** Computers are mysterious devices with mysterious ailments. Sometimes doing something as simple as turning them off and then back on again makes them better. Try this tip. It can't hurt—and it's worked for me at times.

➤ **Make sure that the cable is connected properly to your serial port and that the PalmPilot is seated in the cradle snugly.** If any of the connections are off, HotSync doesn't work. Check to make sure that all the connections are in place and secure.

➤ **Make sure that you've selected the correct serial port on your PC for the cradle.** If you've chosen the wrong serial port, HotSync doesn't work. Double-check to make sure that you've chosen the right one in the HotSync setup, from the HotSync setup screen on your Palm Desktop, shown in the following figure. Turn to Chapter 5, "Keeping Your Life in Sync: HotSyncing Your PC and PalmPilot," for more information.

Do a HotSync before you install software that uses your HotSync port.

Software that uses the HotSync port can cause HotSync problems. You therefore should do a HotSync before installing such software. That way, you have a complete backup of your data on your desktop PC should anything go wrong.

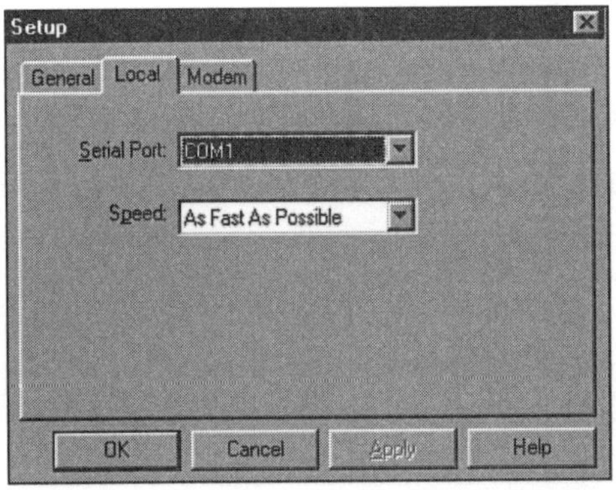

On this screen, you can check that you've chosen the right COM port for your cradle.

➤ **Check your HotSync log.** Little-known fact: Your PalmPilot keeps a log detailing what's happened to your last HotSync. To view your log, tap on **Applications** and then on **HotSync**. When you see the HotSync screen, tap on **Log**. You then see a message describing what's happened to your last

HotSync. The log might hold a clue for you. A more comprehensive log is kept on the Palm Desktop. To get to the log on the Palm Desktop, choose **View Log** from the **HotSync** menu. You then see a log like the one shown in the following figure—although you should hope that your log doesn't have as many problems as this one. By the way, unfortunately, the log is often written in programmer-speak, so you might not be able to understand it. But it'll help when you call the tech support people and can read off your log to them.

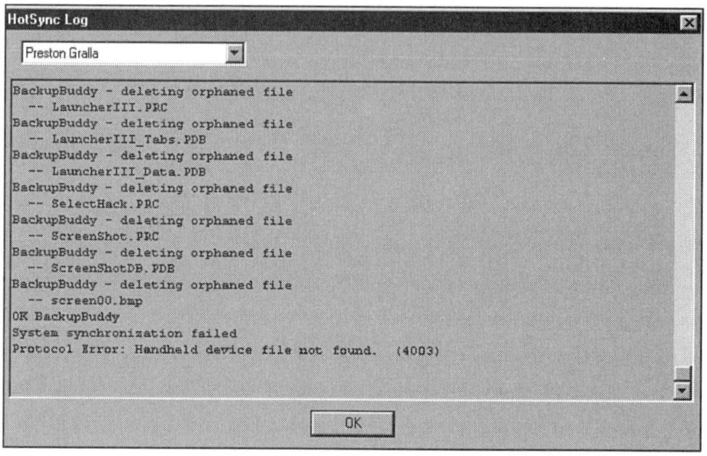

Uh, oh, there's trouble here. The HotSync log in the Palm Desktop shows HotSync woes.

- **Set your connection to a lower speed in the HotSync setup.** From the HotSync setup screen, shown earlier in the chapter, you can change the speed of your HotSync connection. Sometimes setting a slower speed solves your HotSync woes.
- **Re-install your Palm Desktop software.** Some kind of problem might have developed with the Palm Desktop software. Reinstall it and see whether that trick solves your HotSync problems.

FATAL ERROR FONT C, LINE 120, INVALID FONT

Ain't engineers grand? Wouldn't it be nice if they spoke a language that at least resembles English in some vague fashion? Well, they don't, so get used to it. The message "FATAL ERROR FONT C, LINE 120, INVALID FONT" is a not-uncommon one on the PalmPilot. If you get it, do a reset—first a soft, then a warm if that doesn't work, and finally a hard reset if all else fails. One of those resets should solve the problem.

Remove HackMaster files if you're having PalmPilot problems.

HackMaster is a program that lets you add other little programs that can customize your PalmPilot in all kinds of neat ways. Sometimes, though, those little programs—called hacks—can cause big trouble. If you often have PalmPilot problems, turn off the hacks. To do so, tap on the **Applications** button, and then choose **HackMaster**. Now uncheck the hacks listed there to turn them off.

The Touch Screen Doesn't Work Properly

Sometimes the touch screen seems off: You tap on it, and it doesn't respond, or you have to tap it a little to the right or left or above or below where you should be tapping. If that's the case, first clean the touch screen. Turn to the next chapter, Chapter 25, "Care and Maintenance of Your Digital Companion," to see how. Also, recalibrate the screen by digitizer by tapping on **Applications**, choosing **Prefs**, and then choosing **Digitizer** from the drop-down menu.

Low Battery Message After Installing New Batteries

Getting a low battery message is a fairly common occurrence. Right after you put in new batteries, you get a message saying that your batteries are low, and your battery gauge indicates that they're low as well. Not to worry: The PalmPilot sometimes takes a little while to recognize that you've put new batteries in. After a few minutes, the gauge will appear full and the message will disappear.

Your PalmPilot Starts Making Humming Noises

Feel free to hum along. Your PalmPilot making humming noises isn't a problem. As engineers like to say, "It's not a bug; it's a feature." Your PalmPilot may hum when its power supply makes noise through its speaker circuit. Then again, maybe it's not humming; maybe it's purring because it's content. In either case, it's perfectly normal behavior—for a PalmPilot, that is.

Don't change your laptop's or computer's regional time zone settings.

On a PC, you can change your time zone settings in the Windows Regional Settings. You might do so on your laptop when traveling from one time zone to another. Here's a big tip for you: Don't change those settings. If you do, you're going to screw up your Date Book in a big way. Times and dates of some events will mysteriously change, some repeating events will be deleted, and the events in the Date Book on your PalmPilot may not match the events in the Date Book on your Palm Desktop. All this happens because you changed the time zone settings on your PC. Instead of changing the time zone settings on your PC, change the time zone in your PalmPilot.

A Message Tells You the PalmPilot's Memory Is Full

It can happen to the best of PalmPilot users: You've installed too many programs and put too much data into your PalmPilot. And now you're being told that you have no memory left. What to do?

The first thing to do is delete any programs that you don't really need. To do so, tap on the **Applications** button; then tap on the **Menu** button, and choose **Delete** from the **App** menu. (Alternatively, you can use the Command stroke shortcut **/D**.) You then see a screen like the one shown in the following figure. Tap on the name of the program you want to delete, and then tap on the **Delete** button. This way, you delete the program you highlighted. Keep deleting programs in this way until you've deleted all the programs you want.

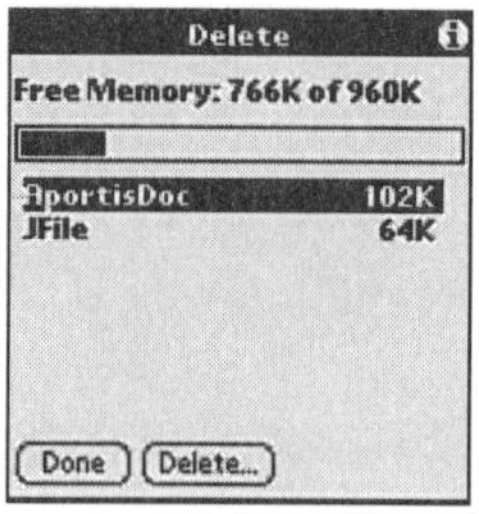

On this screen, you can delete applications to free memory on your PalmPilot.

To free memory, you can also purge the Date Book and the To-Do List. In those applications, when you finish events and to-dos, you have the option of marking them done instead of completely deleting them. When you do that, they still take up memory. To recover memory, purge them by choosing the **Purge** option in each program.

Another solution—although one that will cost you some money—is to add more memory to your PalmPilot. For information on how to add memory, turn to Chapter 25, "Care and Maintenance of Your Digital Companion."

The Least You Need to Know

- If your PalmPilot freezes, the first thing to try is a soft reset by pressing into the reset button. If that approach fails, try a warm reset and then finally a hard reset.
- If you want to be able to recover the programs you've installed after you've done a hard reset, use the program Backup Buddy.
- If your PalmPilot doesn't turn on, try installing new batteries, then adjusting the contrast wheel, and finally trying to do resets.
- If HotSync doesn't work, check to make sure HotSync Manager is running and that no software is interfering with your desktop computer's COM port.
- Don't worry if your PalmPilot makes humming noises; they're perfectly normal and don't mean that anything is wrong.
- If you get memory full messages, delete unneeded applications, and purge the Address Book and To-Do List.

Chapter 25

Care and Maintenance of Your Digital Companion

In This Chapter

- How to extend the life of the batteries in your PalmPilot
- How to take care of your PalmPilot's screen
- How to care for your PalmPilot
- How to upgrade your PalmPilot's operating system and desktop software
- How to upgrade your PalmPilot with a new memory card

Battery Watch: Advice for Using Batteries in Your PalmPilot

Batteries: Can't live with 'em, can't live without 'em. Few things inspire so much talk among PalmPilot aficionados than discussions over how to extend battery life and subjects such as the best batteries to use in your little device.

This topic is so popular because PalmPilots drink battery juice at such an alarming rate. Now, if you've read your Palm III manual (not a chore I would wish even on my enemies), you probably came across this startling statement, "Under normal conditions, your Palm III organizer batteries should provide several months of use." Sure, and if you believe *that*, I've got a bridge I'd like to sell you. Maybe 3COM thinks that "normal conditions" means turning on your PalmPilot less than four times a week and never using a backlight. As the saying goes, your mileage may vary, but many people I know don't get more than a month or so's worth out of their batteries.

Still, you can do a great deal to extend the battery life on your PalmPilot. You should know the following tips about PalmPilot battery usage:

➤ **Check how much power is remaining by looking at the fuel gauge on the Applications screen.** Tap on the **Applications** button. At the top of the screen that appears, you see a battery gauge, as shown here. This gauge shows you how much juice is left in your batteries.

This battery gauge shows a rare site: a fairly full battery.

➤ **Change your batteries as soon as you get a low power warning.** When your batteries get low, you get a warning message. Depending on how you use your PalmPilot, you may have a few days of use left on your batteries, or you may have hardly any time at all. Be safe rather than sorry: HotSync and then change your batteries as soon as you get a warning. When the charge gets low, your PalmPilot starts to act sluggish (kind of like I feel after a big meal), and you might even need to press the power button a few times to get it started. Don't let the power get that low, though: Change batteries when you get a warning.

Let me explain what happens to your batteries as they run down.

When you put in a new pair of AAA batteries, they have a charge of 3 volts of power. As you use them, that voltage runs down. When only 2.1 volts of juice are left, you get a low power warning on your screen. You would be wise to do a HotSync at that point. Depending on how you use your PalmPilot, you may have a few days of minimal use left on your batteries. However, you should be safe rather than sorry: HotSync and then change your batteries when you get a warning.

- **HotSync before you change your batteries.** When you change your batteries, you should put in your new ones quickly after taking out your old ones. If the PalmPilot is left too long without working batteries in it, all your data could be lost. 3COM says the data will be lost if the batteries are out for a minute, but most people report that you have several minutes. In any event, play it safe so that you won't be sorry: HotSync before you change your batteries. That way, if you experience a problem when you change them, you have a backup of all your data on your Palm Desktop, and you can easily restore everything.
- **Turn off your PalmPilot before changing the batteries.** It shouldn't be running when you take out the old and put in the new.
- **Use alkaline batteries instead of NiCads.** Alkaline batteries are better than NiCads for several reasons. One big reason is that they last longer, so you don't have to keep changing them so often. Alkalines offer another benefit as well. They're used up at a more even rate than NiCads, so the PalmPilot can accurately and more easily gauge when you need to change them.

Be careful if you use rechargeable batteries.

Rechargeable batteries aren't necessarily the best choice for your PalmPilot. Most rechargeables are NiCads, and these rechargeable NiCads are unreliable when discharging their voltage. When they start to get low, they can suddenly lose their charges very quickly, giving your PalmPilot no time to warn you that you need new batteries, thus endangering your data. Rechargeable alkalines are a better bet, but they are usually good for only about 25 charges or so.

- **Don't leave the PalmPilot in its cradle—it drains your batteries.** The cradle draws power from your PalmPilot; it has no way to get electricity on its own. That means every time you do a HotSync, you draw extra power. But here's something worse: The cradle sucks battery juice from your PalmPilot even when you're not doing a HotSync. So, if you make a habit of keeping your PalmPilot in its cradle, you're running your batteries down unnecessarily.
- **To save on battery life, use the backlight as little as possible.** Probably nothing you do with your PalmPilot drains its battery as much as using its backlight. Use it as little as possible. Instead, try adjusting the contrast wheel so that you can read your PalmPilot without using the backlight.

- **Change the auto shutoff feature to one minute to extend your battery life.** Your PalmPilot has a feature that will shut it off after a specified amount of time if you don't tap it or use it. By default, it shuts off after two minutes. If you change the shutoff time to one minute, you can save battery life because it will shut off automatically more quickly. To set the auto shutoff time, tap on **Applications**, and then tap on **Prefs**. Tap on the little triangle in the upper-right portion of the screen, and choose **General** from the drop-down list that appears. In the resulting screen, tap on the triangle next to **Auto-Off After**, and choose **1 minute**. You can see this option in the following figure.

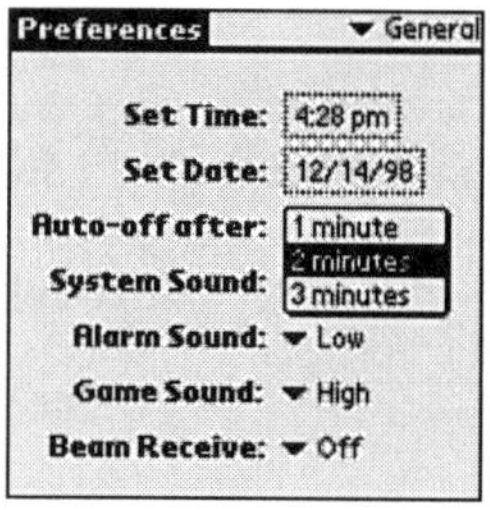

Save on battery life by changing the auto shutoff to one minute.

- **If you use a Palm III, upgrade to version 3.0.2 of the operating system, and change your preferences to turn off the Beam Receive feature.** This patch to the operating system (and later patches) cuts down battery consumption when you turn off the Beam Receive feature. For details on how to upgrade your operating system, turn to "How to Upgrade the Operating System," later in this chapter. For information on how to turn off Beam Receive, turn to Chapter 19, "Beam Me Up, Scotty! Using the Palm III's Infrared Port."
- **Duracell Ultra batteries and Energizer Advance Formula batteries last longer than other alkaline batteries.** Both Duracell and Energizer have come out with batteries designed for electronic devices such as the PalmPilot. People who have used these kinds of batteries (including yours truly) report that they last longer than normal alkaline batteries.

Screen Scenes: Taking Care of Your Pilot Screen

To a great extent, your PalmPilot is your screen. It's what you look at all the time, and it's what you tap on to be able to work the thing. You should keep your screen in tip-top shape. Here's what you need to know:

- **Don't use a normal pen, pencil, or other kind of sharp object on your PalmPilot screen.** They all scratch your screen, which makes it hard to read the screen and can make it difficult for the PalmPilot to correctly interpret your taps. Use the stylus instead, or use another plastic-tipped pen specifically designed to be used on a touch screen. Some people claim that Teflon-tipped styli are the safest.

- **Don't carry your PalmPilot in your back pocket.** The next time you sit down, you could easily crack the screen. (No, that's no comment on how much you weigh; no matter how svelte or pleasantly plump you are, your weight could crack the screen.) Also, take care not to drop your PalmPilot because its screen might break.

Consider using WriteRight on your PalmPilot screen.

One popular way to protect your PalmPilot screen is to use a product called WriteRight, which is a clear, plastic overlay that you put on your screen. These overlays also cut down on screen glare and offer a bit of friction to your stylus, which makes it more like writing on paper and less like writing on glass. You'll go through about one of these overlays a month. A package of 12 costs $27.99. I use them all the time, by the way. Get them at `www.conceptkitchen.com`. And if you want to protect just the Graffiti area, you can use a piece of #811 Scotch tape from 3M. It can be easily removed and replaced.

- **Clean your screen regularly with a diluted glass cleaner such as Windex and a soft cloth.** Cleaning the screen keeps it free from grime and makes it easier to read. It's better not to to spray the solution directly onto the PalmPilot, but to spray on the cloth and then wipe the screen. You might also consider buying a product specifically designed to clean the screen, such as Brain Wash from `www.conceptkitchen.com`.
- **If you don't have a Palm III, consider buying a hard case to protect the screen.** The Palm III's flip-up cover protects its screen. Unfortunately, earlier models of the PalmPilot have no such protection. You can buy many kinds of protection, such as the $9.95 hard case. Check the `www.palm.com` site for information on where to order cases.

General Tips on Caring for Your PalmPilot

Your PalmPilot doesn't ask much of you—just that you protect it from the elements, don't throw it around, and keep it dry and safe. Follow these general tips for caring for your PalmPilot, and it should be your friend for a long time:

- **Protect your PalmPilot from rain, snow, and other moisture.** The PalmPilot isn't waterproof. If it gets wet, water could seep into its innards, wreaking havoc with its circuitry. So keep it dry and away from rain, snow, sleet, and any other kind of precipitation. Don't jump into a pool with it, either.
- **Don't subject your PalmPilot to extreme temperatures, particularly high heat.** In other words, don't keep it near a heater or similar heat source. You also shouldn't leave it on a car dashboard exposed to the sun on a hot day.
- **Don't keep your PalmPilot in places that are very dusty, wet, or damp.** Moisture and dust can harm your PalmPilot, so keep it free from them.

Getting Better All the Time: Upgrading Your PalmPilot

One of the neatest features of the PalmPilot is how easy it is to upgrade. If you have a desktop computer and want to upgrade, you're going to spend some very serious money and some very serious time, and probably end up with little more than aggravation. However, upgrading your PalmPilot is a breeze. Whatever model you have, you can upgrade it to a better version. You can do the following kinds of upgrades:

- **You can replace the memory/ROM card and upgrade to a more powerful PalmPilot.** For example, you can upgrade from a PalmPilot Professional to a Palm III, saving yourself money because you don't have to buy a whole new device. You can even replace the memory/ROM card with other kinds of devices, such as one that lets the Palm work like a pager as well.
- **You can upgrade the operating system (called the Palm OS).** This upgrade doesn't cost you a penny; you can do it for free. Just make sure you get the right version for the PalmPilot that you have. (More on this shortly.)
- **You can upgrade the desktop software, such as the Palm Desktop.** Again, you can upgrade for free. No matter what version of the PalmPilot you have, you can upgrade to the most recent version of the Palm Desktop.

In the rest of the chapter, I cover how to perform each of these upgrades.

How to Upgrade the Operating System

Operating systems always need a little bit of tweaking. Sometimes minor bugs need to be squashed. Sometimes minor new features are added. For example, the Palm OS 3.0.2 that I installed literally three minutes before writing this chapter offers a way to extend battery life when you shut off the Beam Receive option on your PalmPilot.

You can easily upgrade your operating system. Operating system updates, often called *patches*, are made available on the 3COM Web site at `www.palm.com`. You can download the patches from there. After you download the patch, you install it just like any other piece of software. For more information on downloading and installing software, turn to Chapter 20, "Installing New Software on Your PalmPilot." You also can find information on how to install the patches on the `www.palm.com` site.

What's an operating system?

The PalmPilot, like any other computer, needs an *operating system* to be able to work. The operating system in the PalmPilot handles the most basic tasks, such as accepting input from a tap on the screen, displaying letters on your screen, running the various PalmPilot applications, and performing similar tasks. It's commonly called the *Palm OS*. Each new version of an operating system is identified by a number, such as the Palm OS 1.0, the Palm OS 2.0, and the Palm OS 3.0. Often, minor updates are made to the operating system. In that case, the update is called something like 3.0.1.

By the way, not every PalmPilot can use every version of the operating system. Older PalmPilots use earlier versions of the operating system, and newer PalmPilots use newer versions. So a Pilot 1000, for example, uses the Palm OS 1.0 and its patches, such as 1.0.1, 1.0.2, and so on. The PalmPilot Personal or PalmPilot Professional uses Palm OS 2.0 and its patches, such as 2.0.1, 2.0.2, and so on. And the Palm III uses the Palm OS 3.0 and its patches. So you can't install Palm OS 3.0 onto a PalmPilot earlier than the Palm III. However, if you install a memory/ROM card to upgrade an earlier PalmPilot to the Palm III—such as putting a card into a PalmPilot Professional—then that PalmPilot with the new card can use the newer operating system.

How to Upgrade the Palm Desktop

How's this for confusing: No matter which version of the PalmPilot you have, you can use the latest version of the Palm Desktop, which as I write this chapter is version 3.0. That's right. Even if you own a PalmPilot Personal, for example, you can use version 3.0 of the Palm Desktop. (Unless you own a Mac, that is. In that case, as I write this, you can use only Pilot Desktop 1.0—although upgrades are on the way.) So although the version of the PalmPilot you own ties you to a specific version of the operating system, you can always use the latest and greatest version of the Palm Desktop.

All this talk of operating systems and desktops may well confuse a lot of people. If you're a Windows 95 or 98 user, you often think that an operating system and a desktop are one and the same thing. In the PalmPilot world, though, things are different.

The Palm Desktop is the software that you run on your PC (or Mac) that you sync with your PalmPilot. The operating system is the software that runs on your PalmPilot to make the whole thing operate.

You can also upgrade HotSync Manager and individual conduits.

Not only can you upgrade the Palm Desktop and your operating system, but you can also upgrade individual components of your software. For example, 3COM sometimes offers upgrades for the HotSync Manager and individual conduits. You download and install them as you do any other piece of software. They're all available at the `www.palm.com` site.

So how do you know what version of the Palm Desktop you use? Simple. First, run the Palm Desktop. Then choose **About Palm Desktop** from the **Help** menu. You then are told what version of the Palm Desktop you're running. You see the following screen if you're running Palm Desktop 3.0.

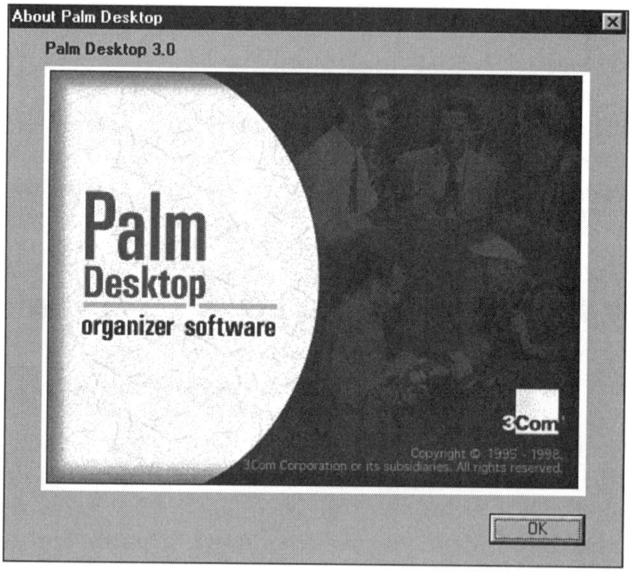

You have the latest and greatest: This screen identifies your version of the Palm Desktop as 3.0.

You can get the latest version of the Palm Desktop at `www.palm.com`. Download and install it as you do any other kind of software. For more information on downloading and installing software, turn to Chapter 20, "Installing New Software on Your PalmPilot." You also can find information on how to install the patches on the `www.palm.com` site.

How to Upgrade Your PalmPilot with a New Memory/ROM Card

One of the more amazing things about PalmPilots is how easily you can upgrade them. To turn your PalmPilot Professional into a full-blown Palm III, for example, all you need to do is open the case, slip out your old memory/ROM card, and slip a new one in. When you do that, you turn that PalmPilot Professional into a Palm III, with features including infrared beaming. And instead of paying the $370 or so that you would have had to pay for a new Palm III, you'll spend only $130. Not a bad savings for about five minutes of your time.

In fact, you can upgrade *any* model of your PalmPilot to a Palm III. If you have an early version of the PalmPilot, you don't get backlighting, and you don't get the flip-up case. Apart from those factors, though, in every other way, you get a fully functional Palm III.

Palm IIIs can be upgraded as well. For example, the Technology Resource Group sells an 8MB SuperPilot Memory Board that you can put into your PalmPilot. That's a whole lotta memory.

Before doing an upgrade, HotSync your data, just to be safe. Now turn off your PalmPilot, and lay it face down on a flat surface. Next, it's time to open the memory card door. On a Palm III, you do so by unscrewing four tiny Phillips-head screws. Make sure that you have a screwdriver small enough to remove them; you don't want to strip the heads. If you have an earlier PalmPilot model, press a straightened paper clip into the tiny pinhole in the center of the memory card door. You then can release a latch and slide off the door.

You've now exposed the memory card that you're going to replace. Push the small tabs on either side of the memory card outward. Pushing these tabs releases the card enough so that you can lift it out. Put that card in a safe place should you need to use it again. Now push the new card into the place where the old card was. Put the memory door back on. That's it! You're done, and you're now the proud owner of an upgraded PalmPilot.

The Least You Need to Know

- ➤ To extend battery life, don't leave your PalmPilot in its cradle, use backlighting as little as possible, and set the auto shutoff time to one minute.
- ➤ Use alkaline batteries. Duracell Ultras and Energizer Advance Formula last the longest.
- ➤ Don't use a normal pen, pencil, or other kind of sharp object on your PalmPilot screen because it will scratch.
- ➤ Protect your PalmPilot against rain, moisture, and dust because they can damage it.
- ➤ You can download the latest operating system patches and desktop software updates for free from `www.palm.com`. You install them as you would any other software.
- ➤ You can upgrade any PalmPilot to work like a Palm III by installing a new memory card.

Appendix A

Easter Eggs and Stupid Digital Tricks

Sure, the PalmPilot is great at organizing your life and helping get it under control, as you've seen throughout this book. But is that all there is to life and computers? Of course not. You also want to be able to spend useless time tracking down senseless but entertaining diversions on it. Why else own a piece of electronics, after all?

Well, let me share the good news, PalmPilot owners, because when it comes to senseless but entertaining diversions, the PalmPilot is second to none. Believe me, if you're in search of creative, entertaining time-wasters, you can find a lot on your digital companion.

The PalmPilot is rife with hidden secrets and with what are called *Easter Eggs*—hidden little messages, pictures, secrets, surprises, and animations buried by programmers in odd little nooks and crannies of the device. These Easter Eggs can be called up only when you perform a very specific set of taps, presses, strokes, and button pushes in certain applications and in a very specific order. Even then, they might not always work. Why are they called Easter Eggs? Because to find them, you have to hunt around, and you never know where they're hidden.

You can find bunches of Easter Eggs on your PalmPilot; just follow the directions that follow, and you can go on an Easter Egg hunt of your own.

Why do programmers put in Easter Eggs?

Imagine this: You're a programmer, and you live on Jolt cola and greasy pepperoni pizza. Most nights you stay up until 2 or 3 a.m. writing lines of code incomprehensible to all but a few people in the world. So you're appreciated and recognized by no one. Your social skills are...well, let's just say that grunts, head nods, and hand motions would be a step up from the way that you usually communicate with others. Wouldn't you like to make your mark in the world in some way and be recognized? (Of course, all these negatives are mitigated by the fact that, as a programmer, your skills are in such demand that you've got stock options on the order of $2 or $3 million.) So you get recognition where you can: You put an Easter Egg or two or three into whatever you're programming.

The Waving Palm Tree Easter Egg

If you've ever played the Giraffe game that teaches you how to write Graffiti, you may have noticed a waving palm tree pop up. It normally pops up only when you get a perfect score, and even then it doesn't appear all the time. But let's say you like that cute, animated tree and want to see it even if you stink at the game. No problem. You can use a hidden Easter Egg to call it up whenever you want.

First, you have to install Giraffe. It's on the CD that accompanies your PalmPilot, or you can download it from the `www.palm.com` site. Turn to Chapter 20, "Installing New Software on Your PalmPilot," for information on how to install software.

To make the infamous waving palm tree appear, first tap on the **Applications** button, and then run Giraffe by tapping on its icon. When Giraffe starts, tap on the **Help** button. Now write the Graffiti stroke for the # symbol by tapping once in the Graffiti area and then drawing a backward capital *N*. When you do that, an animated palm tree appears, waves around for a while, and then disappears. You can see it in the following figure.

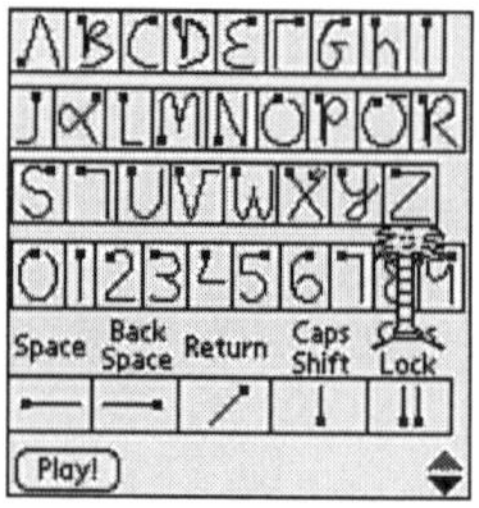

Here, you can see the infamous waving palm tree Easter Egg.

The DOS Error Message Easter Egg

One of the nicest things about using the PalmPilot is never having to see an error message written by Microsoft—especially the much feared "Not ready reading Drive C. Abort, Retry, Fail?" that means your system has been hosed (*hosed:* the technical term for crashed), and you can't get onto your hard drive.

Ah, but let's say that you're nostalgic and actually *like* seeing that message. No problem. Whenever you want, you can display it right on your PalmPilot.

To display this message, run Giraffe as outlined in the preceding section. Now hold the stylus point down anywhere on the top part of the screen where it says *Giraffe,* and press the down scroll button. You then see the infamous DOS error message, as shown in the following figure. Just tap anywhere on the screen to make the message disappear.

Oh, no, it's a DOS flashback! Luckily, it's a fake message.

The Two Fancy Guys Easter Egg

You want pointless entertainment? Good. Because it doesn't get more pointless than this one. You can call up an Easter Egg that's a picture of two guys dressed in tuxedos. Who are these guys? I haven't a clue. Who cares, anyway?

To call up the Two Fancy Guys Easter Egg, start Giraffe as I described in the first section of this chapter. Then place the stylus by the lower-right corner of the Graffiti screen, and press the up scroll button. Here they are, as you can see in the following figure: two guys who appear to be dressed in tuxedos, holding drinks in their hands, and smiling to beat the band.

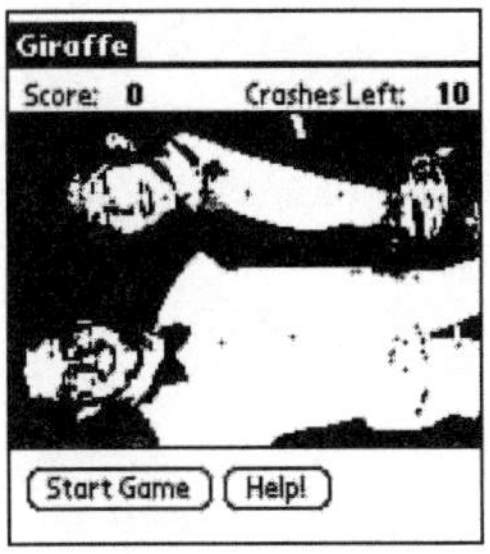

Who are these guys? Got me. But you can visit with them whenever you want by calling up this Easter Egg.

The Easter Egg Easter Egg

You knew it had to be hidden there somewhere: An Easter Egg Easter Egg. Do the right things, and you see a picture of an Easter Egg on your PalmPilot.

This one's hidden in the General Preferences area. To get there, tap on **Applications**, then tap on **Prefs** and choose **General** after you tap on the triangle in the upper-right corner of the screen. Now draw a small counterclockwise circle on the lower-right corner of the screen. When you draw the circle, you see a picture of an Easter Egg, as shown in the following figure. To make the Easter Egg vanish, tap on it.

Mary Hartman Mary Hartman would be pleased to see this Easter Egg Easter Egg.

The Taxi Easter Egg

One of the most famous and elusive of all Easter Eggs is the Taxi. A cartoonish-looking car that looks a whole lot like an old VW Beetle drives across your screen from right to left and vanishes.

You can find this one in several ways. The easiest, though, is to first get the Easter Egg Easter Egg onto your screen, as I described in the preceding section. Then, with it still on your screen, hold the down scroll button, and draw a long stroke with your stylus, starting from the center of the Graffiti area and continuing through the space between the Applications and Menu silkscreened buttons. When you do that, a taxi should appear. (Unfortunately, I can't show you this one because I can't capture the animation and show it in a book. But it's there, believe me.)

The Developer Team Credits Easter Egg

The final Easter Egg is one that lists all the people who worked on developing the PalmPilot. It's an animated display in which the top of the screen lists the version of the operating system you're running and then includes the word *By* (as in, brought to you by...). Scrambled letters appear, fly across the screen, and then combine together to spell out people's names, one after the other, for about two minutes. At the very end, thanks go to "All the beta testers & Sheldon, too!!" Sheldon, by the way, is not a person. He's a Palm tree...the same one that is hidden in an Easter Egg detailed earlier in this chapter.

To find this Easter Egg, tap on the **Applications** button. Then tap on the **Menu** button, and choose **Info** from the **App** menu. A screen that gives you information about your PalmPilot's memory then appears. Put your stylus on the top of the screen, and then press on the PalmPilot's down scroll button. The Easter Egg then appears, as shown in the following figure.

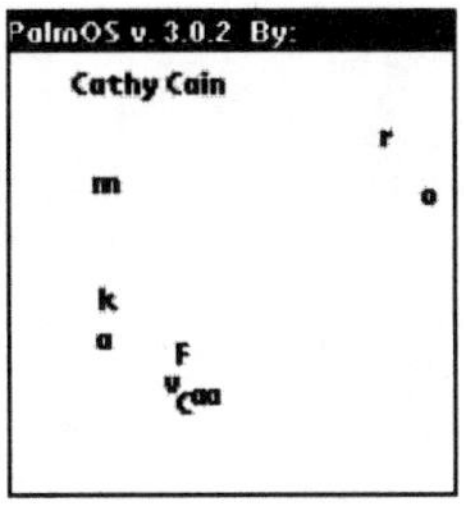

Roll 'em. Here, you can see part of the credits for the developers who created the PalmPilot.

Other Undocumented Secrets of the PalmPilot

Easter Eggs aren't the only undocumented secrets you can find in the PalmPilot. There are others as well, most notably what are called *dot commands*. These dot commands let you burrow deep into your PalmPilot and order it to do things that it normally can't do. They're really for programmers only, so if you're not a programmer, you probably shouldn't be using them.

What the heck, though. You probably at least want to know what they do. To enter a dot command, you draw the shortcut command with your stylus in the Graffiti area (it looks like a lowercase cursive *l*), then draw a period by tapping twice, and finally enter a number. The following is a list of the seven undocumented dot commands. Again, if you're not a programmer, don't use any of them.

- **1** This command puts your PalmPilot into a special programming mode called *debug mode*. It might also freeze your PalmPilot and drain your batteries. To escape from a freeze, you have to do a soft reset.
- **2** This command puts your PalmPilot into another kind of programming debug mode. Sheesh! Why do programmers need so many of these modes?
- **3** This command disables the auto power-shutoff feature; in other words, your PalmPilot shuts off only if you tell it to. The words *No Auto-Off* appear when you use this command. To get back to auto power-shutoff, you have to do a soft reset.
- **4** This command displays the username on the PalmPilot and weirdo numbers that make no apparent sense. The weirdo numbers are used by Windows when new applications are installed.
- **5** This command deletes your HotSync log as well as your username and causes you to get duplicates of every one of your records next time you do a HotSync. What fun! You have to do a hard reset to get out of this one.

- **6** This command shows you the day your PalmPilot's ROM chips were created. You can sing *Happy Birthday* to it if you'd like.
- ***7*** This command lets you adjust your battery gauge if you use NiCad batteries instead of alkalines. The word *NiCad* appears, and your battery gauge more accurately reflects NiCad use. NiCad batteries, though, are not recommended for the PalmPilot. To restore it to reflect alkaline use, use the dot command again. The word *Alkaline* then appears.

Appendix B

Glossary: Speak Like a Geek

Address Book The application in your PalmPilot that lets you keep track of names and addresses.

application buttons The four large buttons across the bottom of the PalmPilot that, when pushed, run the Date Book, Address Book, To-Do List, and Memo Pad.

archive A set of backups of items you've deleted from the PalmPilot that is kept on your desktop computer.

backlight A light in the PalmPilot Personal, PalmPilot Professional, Palm III, and Palm VII that lights the screen and makes it more legible.

battery cover A cover on the back of the PalmPilot that holds in the batteries.

beam To send information from one Palm III to another via the infrared port.

business card A record in the Address Book that you designate as your contact information and that you can beam to other Palm III owners from your Palm III.

Calc The PalmPilot's built-in calculator.

check box A box that you check by tapping on it; it lets you enable or disable an option.

Command stroke A Graffiti stroke that lets you quickly enter PalmPilot commands without having to use menus.

COM port A connection on a desktop computer that allows the computer to communicate with other devices. You plug the PalmPilot's cradle into the desktop computer's COM port. COM ports are commonly referred to as COM Port 1, COM Port 2, and so on.

conduit A software link that synchronizes data between your PalmPilot and your desktop computer for a specific application, such as the Date Book. Each PalmPilot application has its own conduit.

contrast wheel The wheel you turn to change the PalmPilot's screen contrast.

cradle The device that lets you HotSync your PalmPilot to your PC. You plug it into your desktop computer's serial port, and you place your PalmPilot into it.

Date Book The application in the PalmPilot that lets you keep track of your schedule.

Day view The view in the Date Book that shows you the day's appointments.

Doc file A reference file that you can read on your PalmPilot.

Doc reader A special program you use for reading Doc reference files.

Drop-down list A list that drops down when you tap on a triangle. You can choose an item from the list by tapping on it.

Easter Egg A small picture, animation, or other message hidden in the PalmPilot that can be called up only by a specific series of taps, strokes, and button pushes.

Expense The application in your PalmPilot that lets you track your expenses.

Extended Shift stroke A stroke used in Graffiti that lets you enter special characters, such as the copyright symbol.

Giraffe A game included on the PalmPilot CD that teaches you how to use Graffiti.

Graffiti The PalmPilot's handwriting-recognition system.

Graffiti area The area on the PalmPilot where you write with your stylus to input text.

HackMaster A program that lets you customize the PalmPilot's operating system and the way that it works.

hard buttons Another term for the application buttons. See also *application buttons*.

hard reset A reset in which you restart your PalmPilot, and all data and add-in programs are deleted.

HotSync To synchronize information between your PalmPilot and your desktop computer.

HotSync Manager The software you need to run to do a HotSync between your PalmPilot and your desktop computer.

IBM WorkPad A device sold by IBM that looks, works, and functions exactly like the PalmPilot.

infrared port The port on top of the Palm III, covered by a piece of plastic, through which you can beam information to other Palm IIIs via infrared beams.

Internet Service Provider (ISP) A company that provides you with Internet access by letting you dial into it for a monthly fee.

IrDA A standard for sending data between computers and other hardware via infrared light. The PalmPilot's IR port doesn't work with the IrDA standard.

IR port See *infrared port.*

kilobyte A measurement of storage capacity on a computer such as the PalmPilot, typically abbreviated as K or KB.

MacPac A cable adapter and software that you need to plug your PalmPilot into a Macintosh.

Mail The application in your PalmPilot that lets you use your desktop computer's email program to send and receive email.

megabyte A measurement of storage capacity on a computer such as the PalmPilot, typically abbreviated as MB. A megabyte is made up of approximately 1,000 kilobytes. See also *kilobyte.*

Memo Pad The application in your PalmPilot that lets you write notes and memos.

memory cover A cover on the back of the PalmPilot that holds in the memory card.

Month view The view in the Date Book that shows you a month at a glance.

operating system The software built into a computer such as the PalmPilot that performs all its basic functions, including accepting input from the stylus and displaying information on the screen.

Palm Desktop The PalmPilot desktop software that runs on a Windows-based PC.

Palm OS The PalmPilot's operating system. See also *operating system.*

PalmPilot Personal The second-generation PalmPilot, which has 512KB of memory and backlighting.

PalmPilot Professional The second-generation PalmPilot, which has 1MB of memory, backlighting, and additional features such as Mail.

Palm III The third-generation PalmPilot, which has 2MB of memory and has features such as the capability to beam information to other Palm IIIs.

Palm VII The fourth-generation PalmPilot, which allows you to send and receive messages and get information from the Web via wireless communications.

PDA Short for *personal digital assistant*, a term first coined for Apple computer's Newton, and sometimes used to refer to a device like the PalmPilot or Palm.

personal information manager Software such as Outlook and ACT on a desktop computer that lets you track names, addresses, appointments, and other similar information; in other words, it performs the same tasks the PalmPilot does.

pick list A list from which you pick an option by tapping on it.

Pilot Desktop for the Macintosh The PalmPilot desktop software that runs on a Macintosh.

Pilot 1000 The first-generation PalmPilot, with 128KB of memory.

Pilot 5000 The first-generation PalmPilot, with 512KB of memory.

PIM See *personal information manager.*

POP 3 server A computer used by an Internet Service Provider (ISP) that lets you receive email.

purge To delete archived items.

repeating events Events that occur on regular basis, such as on the first day of every month or on every Tuesday.

reset To restart the PalmPilot after it freezes.

reset button A tiny pinhole in the back of the PalmPilot that lets you reset the PalmPilot if it freezes.

scroll arrow An onscreen arrow that, when tapped, shows a new screen of information.

scrollbar An onscreen bar that lets you scroll through a screen by tapping on it or dragging it.

scroll buttons The plastic buttons in the middle of the front of the PalmPilot that let you scroll through screens.

semi-soft reset A reset in which you restart your PalmPilot, and any operating system patches or add-ins are deleted.

serial port The connection on the bottom of the PalmPilot that slips onto the cradle to allow the PalmPilot to communicate with a desktop computer. You can also connect the serial port to a modem. A *serial port* is also another term for a *COM port* on a desktop computer.

ShortCut A Graffiti stroke that lets you enter abbreviations that are automatically expanded into words or phrases.

silkscreened buttons Buttons that have been silkscreened onto the bottom of the PalmPilot and that, when tapped, let you run programs or functions.

SMTP server A computer used by an Internet Service Provider (ISP) that lets you send email.

soft reset A reset in which you restart your PalmPilot but in which no data or programs are lost.

spreadsheet A piece of software that is like an electronic ledger that lets you perform many different kinds of calculations, especially having to do with budgets.

stylus The plastic-tipped pen included with the PalmPilot that you use to write in the Graffiti area and to tap on the screen.

TCP/IP The underlying technology that allows computers to communicate with each other on the Internet.

To-Do List The application in your PalmPilot that lets you keep track of your to-dos.

warm reset Same as *semi-soft reset.*

Week view The view in the Date Book that shows you the week's appointments.

What's on the CD?

As you've no doubt noticed by now, there's a CD at the back of this book. What you might not have noticed, however, is that the CD is full of great PalmPilot software—all kinds of programs that can make your little digital companion jump through hoops. Included on the CD are programs to organize your life, to help you when you travel, and to help you manage your finances. There are games, Internet programs, readers that enable you to read documents, and informational files you can download from the Internet. In fact, you'll find a whole lot of programs there...count 'em—more than 40 of them.

You can try out all the programs for free. Some are free to use forever, whereas others ask that if you continue using them, you pay the people who developed them. You'll be able to find information on how to pay inside the programs themselves.

For details on how to install any program on your PalmPilot, turn to Chapter 20, "Installing New Software on Your PalmPilot." For details on how to use the CD, turn to the end of this appendix.

Here's a list of all the programs on the CD, organized by category. So, pop the CD in your PC and start installing. Your life is about to get easier.

Communications and Internet

BeamLink

JP Systems

Combine the power of your PalmPilot with the convenience of a pager. You'll be able to send and receive email using your pager with BeamLink, as well as send messages to two-way and one-way pagers. There's a whole lot more here as well for anyone who wants to use their PalmPilot and their pager for communications.

OneTouch Mail

JP Systems

This is the email software I use all the time on my PalmPilot. It has all the power you'd expect in a full-featured, PC email program—but puts it into the palm of your hand. Send and receive mail from multiple email accounts, check message headers without downloading full messages, and much more.

PageNOW!

Space Softworks

Send a message to any paging device with this program. Hook up your PalmPilot to a modem, run this program, and it sends out the page for you.

Online

Space Softworks

Amazingly enough, you can turn your PalmPilot into a VT100 terminal emulator with this program. Dial into the Internet, and then run this program. You can also use Telnet or other terminal emulators.

Documents and Readers

J-File

Land-J Technologies

This has a whole lot of reference information for the PalmPilot—everything from travel information to business data, and more. To read much of it, you need a special database reader, and J-File is a great one. In addition to reading reference files, you can create databases of your own and can even import PC files and create PalmPilot database files out of them.

MobileDB

MobileGeneration

Read a variety of informational databases with this database reader. In addition to reading existing databases, it lets you create databases of your own from PC files.

TealDoc

TealPoint Technologies

If you're looking for a way to read many of the informational files available for the PalmPilot, here's where to go. It includes all the features you'll need to read documents, and it can even view embedded images.

Games

Code Cracker

Jeff Brown

Come on, you're smarter than your PalmPilot, aren't you? Well, aren't you? Not so sure? Then try a game of Code Cracker. It's a logic/puzzle game much like the classic MasterMind brain teaser game. You have to correctly identify a sequence of digits, and then you are scored on how well you do. You can configure the level of difficulty, the number of guesses allowed, and more.

J-Stones

Land-J Technologies

Here's an addictive game for puzzle fanatics. You play on a 12×8 board and get 72 stones. Your goal: Score the highest number of points by placing stones on the grid in accordance with a set of rules that govern scoring and allowable locations.

Jookerie

Land-J Technologies

Jookerie is a Scottish word meaning trickery—and that's your objective in this game. Similar to the classic game of Dictionary, it tests your word knowledge. Play it alone or with up to three other people. The PalmPilot chooses an obscure word from a word list, and players enter definitions that they believe other players will think is the right one. The game is won by the person who collects the most points by picking the correct definitions, or fooling others the most.

Organizing Your Life

MemoPlus

Hands High Software

Get a more powerful Memo Pad with Memo PLUS. With it, you can add drawings to memos, set alarms, and create templates for new memos. You can even set passwords to protect individual memos.

DATEBK3

Pimlico

Replace your Date Book with this powerful program. It includes five new views that aren't in the normal Date Book, and has a host of other features as well, including snooze alarms, a daily journal, and more.

Weekview

Pimlico

What needs to be done this week? Find out with WeekView. It shows you, at a glance, all the appointments and To-Dos for the week in a single place.

ListMaker

Synergy Solutions, Inc.

Anyone who makes lists for any reason will want to give this program a try. You can make single lists, master lists, lists within lists, lists of lists...well, you get the idea. I use this one every day.

PhoneLog

Hands High Software

Having a hard time keeping track of your phone calls? Give PhoneLog a try. You can track the date and time of each call you make; PhoneLog includes a timer to track the length of the phone call. You can also attach notes to each entry to detail the call. It ties into the PalmPilot Address Book, so when you need to make a call, tap on the name of the person you'll be calling, for easy tracking. You can sort calls by many different ways, as well.

ThoughtMill

Hands High Software

One thing missing from the PalmPilot is a good outliner—which is where ThoughtMill comes in. You can create outlines to organize your life and thoughts. You can use collapsible arrows and bullets to add text and reorganize your ideas.

Mobile Account Manager

MobileGeneration

Keep track of all your passwords, Personal Information Numbers (PINs), account numbers, URLs, phone numbers, credit cards, checking and savings accounts, and similar information.

ToDo PLUS

Hands High Software

Power up your To-Do List with this replacement program. You can add drawings, set alarms, create repeating tasks, and see all your categories at a glance. Those who have infrared capabilities on their Palm can easily use it to beam items and categories to others.

DateMate

Common Sense Software

Never forget a birthday, anniversary, or other special occasion. Put your important events into a single list, and those events are automatically synchronized with the Date Book.

Today

Synergy Solutions, Inc.

What do you need to do today? Find out at-a-glance with Today. It enables you to see all your Date Book and To-Do items that you need to do today. You can also customize it in many ways.

J-Shopper

Land-J Technologies

Make shopping easier with this simple program. It does what it says—makes it easy to create shopping lists. You can keep track of coupons as well.

TealGlance

TealPoint Technologies

If you want to see everything of importance in your PalmPilot at a single glance, you'll want to try this one out. It shows you important information such as your To-Dos, the date, the time, your appointments, and more.

Personal Finance

Stockhand

Finpoint, Inc.

This portfolio program manages your stocks, mutual funds, options, and currency. Enter information about your holdings in the Windows portion of this program, get the latest prices over the Internet, and then have the program sum up your portfolio. Do a HotSync, and you'll be able to carry your entire portfolio in your pocket.

Personal Money Tracker (PMT)

Charles Morris

Track all your finances with this easy-to-use personal finance program. You can track various checking, savings, and credit card accounts. You can also record expenses such as gasoline and grocery bills. It will show all your transactions for each account, give you a summary balance sheet, and even do income and expense reports. You can also export data to a PC, and import data from programs such as Excel. Great for tracking your money.

Travel

AirMiles

Hands High Software

Keep track of all your frequent-flyer miles. You'll be able to track up to 14 airline programs, and tracks miles from flights, as well as hotels, rental cars, and other ways you earn mileage. You can easily create reports for your current balances for each program.

TravelTracker

SilverWARE

Keep track of all your travel plans when you're on the road. It tracks plane flights, hotel reservations, car rental reservations, dinner reservations, and transportation.

WorldMate

Common Sense Software

Prepare for travel anywhere in the world. It shows you the time in four different cities of your choosing anywhere in the world, is a great currency converter, and even includes a clothing size converter so you can figure out what shoe or suit size fits you in Europe or the UK.

City Time

CodeCity

Want to know the time anywhere in the world? Then check out this program. It lets you put four world-time clocks on the bottom of the screen so that you can see the time in four cities across the world. It also shows a plot of the day and night areas of the world, with the night areas shown dark and the day areas bright.

Trip

Hands High Software

Trip will track your automobile mileage so that you can track business expenses and tax deductions having to do with car expenses. To make it easier to use, pull-down screens are available for things such as Trip Category, Who, Where, and Why—and you can customize pretty much anything you want. If you're lucky enough to own more than one automobile, Trip can track expenses for up to 16 cars simultaneously—although it's unlikely you'll ever need to track that many cars.

Miscellaneous

TrekSounds Hack

Glen Aspeslagh

Warp into the 24th century with TrekSounds. You can add futuristic sounds into your PalmPilot. Note that this program requires Hackmaster, which you can download from many sites on the Internet, including `www.palmpilotsoftware.com`.

J-Tutor

Land-J Technologies

If you need to learn something, check out this tutor program. Whether for business, school, or personal learning, it can help you study. Create your own study aids. J-Tutor features multiple choice, true/false, and flash card modes.

PalmQuotes

PalmQuotes

Need to find the perfect quote for a special occasion? That's what PalmQuotes will do for you. It includes hundreds of famous quotes that you can quickly search through.

Affinity Publishing's Software & Resource Guide

Palmtop Publishing

Find information about hardware and software for your PalmPilot. It's organized by category, includes hyperlinks, and the Find feature makes it easy to find what you need.

Private Pilot Pocket Review

Palmtop Publishing

If you're a would-be pilot, you can study for the FAA private pilot exam. If you're already a pilot, you can study just to stay sharp. This program is an interactive quiz that helps student pilots study for the FAA private pilot written exam and private pilots "stay sharp and safe."

Girls and Women in Sports Guide

Palmtop Publishing

Learn about women in sports with this informative, interactive pocket guide. You can learn about women's accomplishments in sports with a trivia quiz, and get a quick reference to foods and good health habits.

PenguinBackup

Rene Witte

If you're worried about a backup should your PalmPilot crash, this program's worth a try. It's a single, bootable 3.5-inch floppy disk that includes a complete operating system, utilities, and communication software for all kinds of Pilots (OS 1.x - 3.x).

Launch 'Em

Synergy Solutions, Inc.

Make it easy to find and launch your programs with Launch 'Em. You organize your applications into convenient folders that you name. You can also drag any application to the TrashCan, BeamMe, GitInfo, or BackMeUp icons to easily delete, beam, see detailed information, or change the backup status in any application.

SynCalc

Synergy Solutions, Inc.

If the PalmPilot Calculator isn't powerful enough for you, here's what you need. This powerful, scientific calculator has every kind of feature you can imagine, as well as a printer tape/calculation log of past calculations, and the capability to store up to 100 customized calculations covering business, medical, scientific, and other fields.

TealEcho

TealPoint Technologies

If you're looking to improve your Graffiti recognition, try this one. It shows you the letters as you draw them.

TealLock

TealPoint Technologies

This program protects your PalmPilot and all your vital data. It locks the device or individual items inside it and gives you many ways to customize security.

TealMagnify

TealPoint Technologies

Here's a simple program: You can magnify any portion of your PalmPilot screen by looking through a small, virtual magnifying glass.

TealMeal

TealPoint Technologies

Where to eat tonight? Find out with TealMeal. It's a database that lets you create and edit a list of your favorite restaurants, and lets you look by topics, category, and type of food.

TealPaint

TealPoint Technologies

Amazing, but true: You can draw on your PalmPilot. You'll be surprised at how sophisticated a drawing device your PalmPilot can be. Try it out, even if you can't draw a straight line.

TealScript

TealPoint Technologies

Tired of Graffiti constantly misreading what you write? Then try out TealScript, which makes it easy to teach Graffiti to better recognize your handwriting.

How to Use the CD

Using the CD is quite easy. Here's what you need to know.

System Requirements

To use the CD, you need a PC (sorry, Mac owners) with a 486 or better, 16MB of RAM, 265 colors, Windows 95, Windows 98, or Windows NT 4.0. And you'll need 90MB free hard disk space if you want to install every single piece of software on the CD.

Browsing the CD via the CD Interface

If you have AUTOPLAY turned on, then your computer will automatically run the CD after you put it into your CD drive. If AUTOPLAY is turned off, follow these directions:

1. Insert the CD-ROM into your CD-ROM drive.
2. From the Windows desktop, double-click the**My Computer** icon.
3. Double-click the icon representing your CD-ROM drive.
4. Double-click the icon titled**START.EXE** to run the CD.

Index

Symbols

A

B

C

D

E

F

G

H

I

J - K

L

M

N

O

P

R

S

T

U - V

W - Z

License Agreement

This package contains one CD-ROM that includes software described in this book. See Appendix C for a description of these programs.

By opening this package you are agreeing to be bound by the following:

This software is copyrighted and all rights are reserved by the publisher and its licensers. You are licensed to use this software on a single computer. You may copy the software for backup or archival purposes only. Making copies of the software for any other purpose is a violation of United States copyright laws. THIS SOFTWARE IS SOLD AS IS, WITHOUT WARRANTY OF ANY KIND, EITHER EXPRESSED OR IMPLIED, INCLUDING BUT NOT LIMITED TO THE IMPLIED WARRANTIES OF MERCHANTABILITY AND FITNESS FOR A PARTICULAR PURPOSE. Neither the publisher nor its licensers, dealers, or distributors assumes any liability for any alleged or actual damages arising from the use of this software. (Some states do not allow exclusion of implied warranties, so the exclusion may not apply to you.)

The entire contents of this disc and the compilation of the software are copyrighted and protected by United States copyright laws. The individual programs on this disc are copyrighted by the authors or owners of each program. Each program has its own use permissions and limitations. To use each program, you must follow the individual requirements and restrictions detailed for each. Do not use a program if you do not agree to follow its licensing agreement.